BEYOND

COUNTERFEIT

REFORMS

Forging an Authentic Future
for All Learners

William Spady

The Scarecrow Press, Inc.
A Scarecrow Education Book
Lanham, Maryland, and London
2001

SCARECROW PRESS, INC.
A Scarecrow Education Book

Published in the United States of America
by Scarecrow Press, Inc.
4720 Boston Way, Lanham, Maryland 20706
www.scarecroweducation.com

4 Pleydell Gardens, Folkestone
Kent CT20 2DN, England

British Library Cataloguing in Publication Information Available

Library of Congress Cataloging-in-Publication Data

Spady, William G.
  Beyond counterfeit reforms : forging an authentic future for all learners / William Spady.
    p. cm.—(A Scarecrow education book)
  Includes bibliographical references.
  ISBN 0-8108-4008-1 (alk. paper)—ISBN 0-8108-4009-X (pbk. : alk. paper)
  1. Educational change—United States. 2. Education—Aims and objectives—United
States. 3. Learning. I. Title. II. Series.

  LA217.2 .S69 2001
  370'.973—dc21

                                                        00-054752

∞™ The paper used in this publication meets the minimum requirements of
American National Standard for Information Sciences—Permanence of
Paper for Printed Library Materials, ANSI/NISO Z39.48-1992.
Manufactured in the United States of America.

CONTENTS

FOREWORD

The mind is a fire to be kindled, not a vessel to be filled.
—Plutarch

A little more than ten years ago, I reluctantly wandered into a theater in my hometown to listen to a day-long presentation about the need for school reform. At the time, I had other, far more pressing matters on my mind. Truthfully, I was there only out of a sense of loyalty and obligation to my district. Silently, I schemed that I would put in my time and then, at the appropriate moment, gracefully depart to attend to my other pressing professional matters.

More than six hours later, I remained glued to my chair, utterly transfixed and transformed by the powerful observations that Bill Spady was making about education. Many questions swirled in my head—questions that seemed to challenge my every assumption about schools and learning—questions that compelled me to step back from more than twenty years of professional experience and completely reconsider the Who, What, When, Where, Why, and How of what we do in the name of education.

Now a decade later, Bill has replicated the genuinely awesome character of that presentation in this book. But on a broad scale his critical questions remain unaddressed and unanswered by us. Be certain, we are living in dangerous times, and Bill's issues have become more important than ever. Why? Because we are facing an educational crisis of monumental proportions in virtually every part of this country. From coast to coast and border to border there appears to be a furious, top-down, heavy-handed, test-driven approach to schooling that is primarily being promoted by politicians, corporate officials, and others with mainly political agendas, not by educators.

For the most part, these "reform" advocates seem unaware of and uncon-
cerned about the research on how children learn best and on the most effective
approaches for helping all children become enthusiastic, competent, independent thinkers and life-long learners—which Bill addresses persuasively in
chapter 11. As a result, we are facing a situation where almost all of the important, relevant, and meaningful things we need to do with and for our children
are being abandoned in favor of oft-repeated, empty clichés and slogans such
as Accountability for All, Tougher Standards, Higher Achievement, Teacher
Performance, and Raising the Bar. Instead of helping children to become more
confident and competent learners, and teachers to become better teachers,
schools are increasingly being transformed into educational factories that reinforce the mentality of processing students as products through one-shot, high-
stakes, win-or-lose testing schemes.

As I travel throughout this country, visiting schools and classrooms, I am
overwhelmed by scenes such as the one I witnessed in October 2000 in a large
Southwestern state, where the students were brought to the gym to prepare for
their high-stakes exams and taught to chant "Three in a row—no, no, no!"
(three letters in a row that are the same means that one of them is wrong).

I grieve for teachers who tell me that they feel compelled to abandon sound
curriculum to teach to the test because their jobs as well as those of the ad-
ministration depend entirely on their students being successful on the test.

I mourn the fact that an increasingly large portion of valuable and limited educational dollars are being spent on test preparation materials and tests rather
than learning resources and staff development.

And I profoundly regret the diminished vision of learners and learning this
"official" neglect of Bill's "research realities" in chapter 2 is creating because
parents and educators know that these factors and qualities are critical to children's success in today's rapidly changing world.

Do I care how this all plays out? Yes, of course I do. Education is far more
than preparing children to do well on tests. In the United States, education is
the primary means through which people learn to take part in participating in
a democracy. Personally, I feel it would be tragic if politicians, administrators,
and communities were to ignore the powerful message contained in *Beyond
Counterfeit Reforms* and continue to "yes, but" into this new millennium.

FORGING AN AUTHENTIC FUTURE FOR ALL LEARNERS

I personally know that Bill shares my pain and frustration over these issues,
which is why he fervently calls for dramatic changes that portray how far we
have to go just to catch up with the realities of the world outside of school reform. In dealing with this enormous challenge I heed the advice of my wife
Anita, who reminds me never to mistake a clear view for a short distance. Can

we envision a different kind of schooling? Of course, and Bill emphatically does this again and again in this book. Can we change our institutions to reflect these changes? Of course—they are human inventions and therefore subject to adaptation by humans—and Bill offers us a clear and compelling pathway for getting there.

But will we have the courage to make the changes needed to bring educational practices in line with the needs of twenty-first-century learners? In my opinion, this is the essential question this book compels us individually and collectively to answer. How we answer it will decide the future of education, our children, and—directly—this nation.

I deeply hope that we will have the insight and courage to make the enlightened changes that Bill urges us to consider. But even if we don't, future generations will still be well served by this book—not by our current, outmoded educational mindset. Schools that fail to adapt to the needs of the society in which they exist will simply disappear, replaced by new educational institutions funded by individuals, the public, and the private sector. If this view appears far-fetched, one need only look back as far as Horace Mann to see how his model of the common school dovetailed with the needs of Massachusetts employers in the 1800s—a view so ingrained that it prevails yet today.

The book you hold contains some simple yet powerful ideas. Bill has provided a detailed map—the Strategic Design Process—to take us from where education is to where it needs to be. It's not the only existing map by any means, but it is a compelling, systemic set of steps for truly transforming an aging and increasingly irrelevant institution into something that will have real meaning and relevance to the lives of this and future generations.

But the challenge and opportunity of using the many insights in *Beyond Counterfeit Reforms* will be up to you. How will you use this map and process? What will you see and how will you respond when you confront the terrain and realities that stand in front of you? Most important, what concrete actions will you take as a result of reading this book and seeing what you see?

As you begin your journey across the territory called "school" in Bill's introduction, heed the words of Helen Keller:

> *The only thing worse than not being able to see,*
> *is being able to see and having no vision.*

In *Beyond Counterfeit Reforms*, Bill gives us both: clarity of sight and a penetrating vision of what we can do to forge an authentic future for all our learners—which is why every parent, educator, and policy maker in the country should read and act on it!

IAN JUKES
December 2000

PREFACE

I've spent over thirty years focused on what most of us would call "school reform." The first twenty years of it was devoted to helping teachers develop and
raise their standards and expectations so that more students would learn successfully in their classes.

Our approach was to ask teachers to identify the things that were really critical in what they were teaching and translate those into concrete statements of
what they would want every student in their classes to be able to do to be successful in that learning area. We pushed and pushed until they could identify
truly significant, high-level things. Then we showed them how to get that to
happen in their classes by consistently applying a short set of very powerful
principles to their teaching and testing.

A REALITY CHECK

I thought we were doing great. In place after place, students got better grades
and, became more motivated, and test scores went up—in some cases, very up!
But in 1987 I read an article in the *San Francisco Chronicle* that stopped me in
my tracks and made me realize just how narrow my vision of learners, learning,
education, and reform had been.

The article that shook my thinking to its core described a study of the career
status of a large sample of the nation's recent university valedictorians—"the
cream of the crop" of the best of our very best students. Unfortunately, I was

never able to track down the original study, but three things from the article stuck in my mind and changed my thinking and work forever:

1. As a group of university graduates, the career status of these valedictorians was lousy.
2. As a group of university valedictorians, it was dismal. Large numbers were unemployed, and even larger numbers were under-employed.
3. It was unclear about what to do next. They were unprepared for the new, fast-changing, high-tech world and global economy that lay beyond the walls of their universities.

The article's punch line: they were *great academic achievers* while in school, but they were *unprepared for their futures*! In short, their academic learning didn't "transfer" to the real world; and the real world, it turned out, was the proof of their educational pudding.

Wow! Or maybe Charlie Brown would say, "Argh!" One of the great myths of post–World War II America had just been dispelled. No longer was high academic achievement and university graduation the guaranteed route to somewhere special. Being a great student, getting to college, and graduating with top honors did not deliver the First Prize these outstanding students expected. In fact, "No Prize" was more like it. Their bubble had burst.

And so did mine because I had just spent those first twenty career years helping teachers (1) design rigorous standards/outcomes for the curriculum they were teaching, (2) focus themselves and all their students on achieving those standards, and (3) help all their students perform successfully on those standards (and the tests that measure them) so that they could go on to college to become even more successful students there. I was doing *exactly what today's standards-based reforms are doing* in the name of *improving achievement*!

I knew the minute I finished the article that this educational reform path was marked "Dead End," both for the teachers and students I was working with, and for me. The study clearly pointed out that the world of work was changing dramatically, and the very best of our very best students weren't equipped for it. They lacked the performance abilities and orientations to deal with what we now, fourteen years later, routinely call the Information Age. Their courses didn't give them, their textbooks didn't contain, and their tests didn't measure what they needed in order to succeed in the future they faced.

And neither do today's Standards-Based Reforms and "high stakes" testing programs!

My career took a dramatic turn after reading that article—a turn to the future! From that day forward those who've chosen to work with me and I have had one major starting point for everything we do in education: the future challenges and conditions our students will face once they walk out the door of our educational cocoon. Our logic is simple but compelling. If what we do in schools doesn't really prepare young people for the concrete realities they will be facing, then we should do something that does. Period.

Since 1987, our work has been focused on helping communities and educators discover, design, and implement what that something should be. The process we use is called Strategic Design, and it is the backbone of chapters 7 through 12 of this book.

FIVE NEW REALITY CHECKS

Strategic Design is profoundly different from what people call "strategic planning." The latter takes the existing programs and structures of schools and districts as given and looks at how they need to prioritize and adapt what they're doing to emerging needs in their communities. In the end, all those programs and structures generally remain in place, but they have new goals and action plans for proceeding.

Strategic Design starts with a giant blank sheet of paper, five compelling questions that have nothing to do with existing programs and structures, and five bodies of evolving research that should represent the bedrock of any future-focused, learner-centered system design. I call these new "research realities" human potential, human learning, domains of living, future conditions, and life performance.

Each is described and explained in chapter 2. That's the place to start if you want to decide whether this book is for you. But be careful. You might become convinced like I have that if you started with any one of these five new realities as the foundation of your Strategic Design—or any combination of the five—you'd never create the schools we have today. Never!

Instead, you'd create something I call a Total Learning Community (TLC). TLCs aren't schools with extra computers or nicer staff. They're places that operate around a culture of what I call "Total Professionalism" in chapter 8, and that culture provides the paradigm perspectives, core values, and operating principles for designing and implementing something incredibly more enlightened, future-focused, and empowering than the Industrial Age schools our children attend. You'll find the latter described in greater depth and with more insight than you're accustomed to in the introduction and in chapters 4 and 5. You'll find the counterfeit reforms that are forcing them into even more constraining boxes exposed for what they are in chapter 6.

Those three chapters summarize the bad news about the deep systemic flaws in our current system—flaws structured into our system over a century ago that we've simply institutionalized and reinforced over the decades; flaws that create and promote conditions of failure for countless learners; flaws that should be intolerable to every parent and educator in America; flaws that are glossed over in the seductive reform rhetoric of higher standards and greater accountability.

These are flaws that look even worse than normal when compared to the model developed in the last half of the book: a Total Learning Community shaped around five compelling research realities and embodying five sound and enlightened operating components, each developed systematically one at a time in chapters 8 through 12.

If the five new research realities in chapter 2 are a TLC's bedrock, then the Total Learning for Total Living framework in chapter 3 is its heart and soul. This is an approach to learners, learning, and living that speaks to both the deep humanity and common sense in all of us. It portrays a picture of the possible and desirable in American education and society that makes the current political obsession with curriculum standards, test scores, accountability, and reforms look superficial, sterile, extremely limiting, and profoundly misguided.

But you be the judge. This is truly an invitation for you to examine learning and education from a unique and compelling perspective. It's also an invitation to forge a different future for our learners and for learning itself, both of which are being reduced today to nothing more than scores and numbers that fit into tiny boxes on testing reports. If this fact unsettles you, then keep reading. You may discover that we share a very similar vision of what education should be in today's world of continuous discovery and constant change.

ACKNOWLEDGMENTS

Writing *Beyond Counterfeit Reforms* has been a true labor of love, largely because I've received so much love, encouragement, and support from so many people in writing it. What began as intense personal frustration with the mechanistic and counterproductive nature of what we call "school reform" in the United States transformed over time into an opportunity to share with the wider public ideas I had been developing and sharing with my closest friends and colleagues for years. Happily, those wonderful people have steadfastly supported my ongoing search for deep personal meaning and encouraged me to imbed my discoveries in my professional work.

I will start by thanking profoundly the four Spady "Valkyries" who, to me, have truly been sent by the gods to bring enlightenment and good to the world. They are my sisters Karen and Sha, my wife Pam, and my daughter Vanessa. Each is an incredible role model of intelligence and integrity, an astute sounding board, and an unwavering advocate of the message in this book. Each has given me ideas, inspiration, encouragement, and candid feedback when I've needed it most; and Vanessa again gets credit for generating all of the figures in one of her Dad's books.

Close behind are the special people who have been my closest colleagues and advocates over the years and who have supported the writing of this book in a variety of ways. They include Ron Brandt in Virginia, Helen Burz in Michigan, Des Collier in South Africa, Richarde Donelan in Michigan, Sharon Hill in Arizona, Roy Killen in Australia, Vickie Phelps in South Carolina, Chuck Schwahn in South Dakota, Mona Snodgrass in Arkansas, Steve Waddell in Texas, and Bruce Wenger in Virginia. Each of them has expanded my horizons as a professional, contributed to my growth as a human being, and shored up my commitment to conveying this message. Without their encouragement and feedback, this book never would have been written.

Three others have contributed directly and substantively to this book, and I am honored that they have joined me in sharing their insights and convictions. Ian Jukes touches thousands each week with his visionary perspectives on educational change and has shared his wisdom in the foreword. Ursula Ahern is a parent and school board member in Grayslake, Illinois who lives the message of this book and compellingly shares it in her "invitation to action." And Arnold Fege, recently honored with the Nelson Mandela Prize for his public advocacy for children, honors us with his advocacy of this work as well.

Finally, two other individuals have my deepest thanks and respect for their roles in bringing this book to fruition. One is Bill Hamilton of Skaneateles, New York, whose perceptive, candid, and constructive feedback on initial draft chapters allowed me to redirect and frame the book in an altogether more productive way. The other is my editor, Tom Koerner, of Scarecrow Press. His openness to my initial ideas gave me the confidence to proceed to write, his support and encouragement for this endeavor never wavered, and his steadfast advocacy for my cause was quietly heroic and appreciated more than he knows.

INTRODUCTION

KNOWING THE TERRITORY CALLED "SCHOOL"

Say the word "school" and everyone knows what it's all about—all the labels, all the features, all the practices, and all the expectations. Consequently, anyone who wants to change the fundamental and familiar features and practices of "schools" in any way is up against massive inertia.

At the beginning of *The Music Man*, a group of traveling salesmen are on a train headed for River City discussing in a staccato interchange the fact that, to be successful, "you have to know the territory."

Indeed we must. To those of us deeply concerned with creating the kind of education that truly empowers and equips our children to live and thrive in tomorrow's fast-paced, complex world, there are two aspects of this challenge. First, knowing the territory *of* school—the many entrenched and hidden features of schooling that define it as an institution and that give it its unique character. This requires that we look deeply and critically at familiar aspects of schooling that we often take for granted to see what is really there and what purpose they serve. We'll do that in chapters 4 and 5.

Second, knowing the territory *around* school—the world in which it is situated and for which it is preparing our young people. There are two major aspects of this issue, and we'll do our best to keep them separate. The first is that the current context that surrounds our educational system is one of mounting frustration. This frustration is manifest in repeated efforts across the United States to give parents "choice" about where their children attend school—in some cases through voucher systems that would encourage them to pull their children out of public schools to attend private ones, in others through the establishment of alternative/charter schools in their local districts that are funded with district dollars, and in yet others by keeping their children at home and educating them there. While home schooling is an alternative that many families cannot consider, it is, nonetheless, the fastest-growing sector of American education.

This frustration is also manifested in the widespread attempts to reform public schools by making them more accountable to their taxpaying publics, usually embodied in their state governments. The single most prominent expression of these accountability demands involves the standardized testing of pupils in various learning areas and grade levels as proof that schools are doing their jobs. The essence and consequences of these pervasive and intrusive reforms are described in chapter 6. Whether one agrees with them or not, they are dramatically affecting what goes on in classrooms from coast to coast; and they are dramatically impacting the territory both of and around school.

The other aspect of the territory around school has to do with the realities that exist in our world apart from educational policies and pressures. These realities relate to the accumulating knowledge and practice in many different arenas of contemporary life and living. As we address these new realities in chapters 1 and 2, we'll see they are fundamentally incompatible with the foundations of our current educational system, which were poured well over a century ago. Think of the radical contrast: Americans went to the moon and back thirty years ago and walk around today with hand-held microcomputers that enable them to instantaneously communicate across the globe via networks of satellites. But their children attend schools whose form and functions were established in the days of the horse, buggy, and kerosene lamp—long before the technologies, conveniences, transportation tools, standards of living, and scientific breakthroughs we now take for granted were even imagined.

So as we get to truly "know" the territory of and around school, we need to keep in mind that our current system was created at the turn of the past century to serve the needs of a slower-paced, far less developed world—an era called the Industrial Age. Even though we all recognize that the Industrial Age is over, schools still embody its structural forms and legacy. Why? Because during the course of the twentieth century:

- Educators institutionalized that structure
- Policy makers legalized that structure
- We parents and citizens psychologically internalized that structure because we all went there for years and years
- The media continuously reinforce that structure because it was the only alternative we had

The result:

> Say the word "school" and everyone knows what it's all about—all the labels, all the features, all the practices, and all the expectations.

Consequently, anyone who wants to change the fundamental and familiar features and practices of "schools" in any way is up against *massive inertia*. Despite all the frustration and clamor, do people really want to change schools? No! Well, do they want to "improve" them? Definitely! They want to improve what's there, but they don't want to change what's familiar. It's the paradoxical challenge of making education better while keeping it the same.

That's the dilemma that concerned parents, citizens, policy makers, and educators now face. Here we are in the middle of the Information Age with an institutionalized, legalized, internalized, and culturally reinforced icon in our midst that was created from the understandings, needs, priorities, and biases of a century ago. And that cultural icon is supposed to get our children to a future that is transforming with every new breakthrough in every field of endeavor.

What is it about the territory called "school" that we continue to embrace? Let's take a candid look from a more systemic and penetrating perspective than is common.

SCHOOL AS UNIQUE TERRITORY

The territory called school is very familiar. We were there for the greater part of our youth, and the longer we stayed the more familiar it became. But the territory wasn't always so familiar to us because school is really an entity unto itself. Nothing else in "real life" is quite like it, so we've had to learn what it's all about through personal experience. Educators, however, know the territory extremely well because they've been in school since they were five, and most of them have no major work experience beyond it. For them, school is a way of life.

When we first got to school we didn't know anything about the territory unless an older brother, sister, or friend told us. But we soon learned that the territory of elementary school was very different from our homes. Almost everything we did there happened in a big rectangular room. We had to learn about our teachers, who they were, what they were like, and what they controlled. Almost immediately we learned about the long list of ways we could get into trouble. The list seemed to go on and on.

Boy, did we learn about "classes"! They were the large group of kids we spent just about all day with in our specific room, and all of them, we discovered, were just as old as we were. Most of us had never been with so many kids at the same time for so long before, and that was hard to get used to. It was clear that they and the room and the class "belonged" to our particular teacher.

We also learned about "grades." That's what level you and your teacher were in the "curriculum." And oh, that very big word was a very big part of the new territory because it determined which books you got to read and work with, and which ones you didn't. After a number of years we figured out that the number on our books almost always matched the number of our grade, and that somehow, each of our numbered books took exactly a year to "cover."

As time went on, we had to learn about "report cards" and the "grades" or marks teachers put on them. Obviously some of the marks and numbers the teachers put on them were good and some were bad, because they got very different kinds of reactions from our parents when they saw them. Some made them happy, and some made them sad or angry, so we had to learn which were which and why they were there. To get good marks on our card we had to do what our teacher asked right away, keep quiet, not get into trouble with other kids, and not make any mistakes on our papers. It was hard not to make mistakes, but it was the only way to avoid getting bad marks.

Reading as Intelligence

We also learned how smart we were. That was determined by our first-grade reading group. We had three groups: the Robins, the Blue Birds, and the Parakeets. The readers of this book were in the Robin group. We read faster and better than most of the other kids, partly because we had a big head start at reading before we even got to school. It never dawned on us until much later that it was really our moms and dads that made us good readers because they could give us so much individual attention. Our teacher had to divide that attention among all the kids in the Blue Bird and Parakeet groups who mostly depended on her to help them learn to read.

After a few years we learned that good reading skills were the key to school success because you couldn't really do much of the other assigned work if you couldn't read well.

Eight years later we Robins ended up in the same high school classes, too, but our teachers changed our name to "College Prep" or "Honors." We rarely saw our Parakeet friends from elementary school after that because we took different classes and had different teachers than they did. Their classes got renamed "Remedial" or "Basic." They didn't go to college like we did, but that was already certain when they got to high school. The "track" and classes they were put in prevented it because the course didn't have the right names or the right content to let them enter college.

Then there were the "special tests" we took, which were printed nicely in big pamphlets. We'd get them once or twice a year. We were told to take them seriously because they determined everything about us: whether we were smart, were good students, had good teachers, would get "promoted" to the next grade and set of books with our class in June, could graduate, and could go to college or not. Our teacher seemed really concerned on those big test days. And something seemed strange because our teacher had to send our score sheets away for someone else—probably in Iowa—to figure out if we got the right answers. This confused us because we thought our teacher was smart and already knew the right answers. But maybe these tests were so special that regular teachers just didn't understand them.

THE NUMBERS GAME

The older we got the more important "points" became as a critical part of the territory. At first, school was fun because we just did a lot of interesting things and our teacher helped us learn and improve. But after a few years things changed. Suddenly everything we did was "worth" points. In every assignment, test, paper, or project, we either gained points or lost points. Nothing was overlooked because *points were our achievement.* If we wanted perfect achievement, we had to get 100 points the first (and only) time we were required to do something. But once in a while we could be even better than perfect by doing something called "extra credit." Extra credit gave you points you could add to your 100 if you wanted to.

But the scales weren't balanced. There were many more ways to lose points than to gain them—be late, talk without permission, chew gum, behave rudely, and, most of all, *make mistakes.* Mistakes meant "points off," and the only way to get some of those points back was good old Extra Credit, but it didn't come along that often. We had to be perfect the first time around on the right day—usually Friday—or some points would simply be taken away and *be gone forever,* even if we learned it and could do it perfectly later.

Naturally, the teachers controlled all the points, and each had his or her own method of doling them out. Some gave you lots for how you wrote, but little for homework. Others gave more for tests and assignments. Some had very elaborate point systems, and others had simple ones. But the basic dynamic was clear: they were *their points* and it was our job to "earn" them however each teacher set the rules. The rule: "Do what I want when I want it and you get points; don't and you don't." It was usually pretty clear and consistent, except when it wasn't.

Yes, when you think about it, everything we ever learned or "achieved" in school came down to getting points, and the more points the better! Why? Because, even though those points stood for very different things and got calculated in totally different ways, eventually they all got added and averaged and added and averaged by every teacher again and again until our ultimate set of points was determined. They gave it a code name: GPA. All we had to do was look at our report cards to see that GPA had replaced those other categories and marks on our earlier cards as the real indicator of how good and smart we were. We all knew kids who were so desperate for points that would improve their GPA that they manipulated and bribed their teachers—and they were good at it, too. Some didn't bother with bribery; they just cheated. Others took the easiest courses they could during their senior year to "protect" their GPA.

GPA was critical because the colleges wouldn't know whether to admit us or not unless we had one, and our teachers made it very clear that the colleges would be very particular about how high our GPA was. *The higher the number the better*, of course, because the colleges also wanted to know if our GPA was higher or lower than that of our classmates. To cooperate, our high school counselors ranked all of our GPAs and assigned us a "class rank." The higher our class rank, the better a student and "candidate for admission" we were, they said. Colleges clearly held kids with very high class ranks in very high esteem, even paying some of them to come there. Whether we liked it or not, we were all compared and ranked against each other based on our points.

That's probably why all that our parents saw on our high school report cards were the names of the "subject" we were "taking," the average number of points we got during a given block of time, and the ultimate average of all the points we had ever "earned." Alas, if we did something special or outstanding that didn't translate into points, it was never calculated in our GPA, shown on our report card, or included in our "permanent record." Only a specific set of abilities and performances related to our course work got points. Our other abilities were pretty much ignored—except in sports.

So eventually, the real territory of school revealed itself to those of us who figured it out as a "numbers game." Some of us took the game very seriously, but many didn't. In this game, the only learning that really "mattered" had points attached to it. The territory called school encouraged us to do assignments on time and study for tests so that we would get enough points to pass our courses, make our parents happy, and get into a "good" college. The controlling factor seemed to be something called "deadlines." You were given a certain amount of time to learn or do something, and if you couldn't or didn't, you lost the points for that time block, no excuses and no exceptions. Points were clearly about doing things *on time*.

Interestingly, once the points were safely entered in the teachers' record books, we really didn't have to pay more attention to whatever it was that earned us the points because the record was "permanent." In fact, we often couldn't remember things on Monday that had earned us points on Friday, but we were safe because the points for that week were safely recorded in ink.

Anything we learned or did with more depth and integrity than this "points minimum" was the result of our parents' expectations, our own motivation, and the dedication and extra effort of our highly professional teachers. Otherwise, our points were our achievement, and our achievement—our GPA—was who we were in the system's eyes, for better or for worse.

THE FIVE AGENDAS CALLED LEARNING AND ACHIEVEMENT

A key part of knowing the territory of school is recognizing that just about anything and everything that moves in schools is called, or is treated in some way or other as, learning and achievement. Why? Because those things get mixed into your points and grades, and grades are—you guessed it—the alleged "measures" of learning and achievement! Researchers have used terms like Official Curriculum, Real Curriculum, Ideal Curriculum, and Hidden Curriculum to ferret out the mishmash of what's real learning and what are "other agendas" that distort any true measure of learning.

Keeping these various factors straight isn't easy, but you'll find that the contest over points and how many you get ultimately comes down to five very different things which all happen to start with the letter "C": Custody, Compliance, Competition, Competence, and Content. Let's start at the end of the list and work forward.

Custody as Achievement

Custody is the school's ultimate agenda because, at the turn of the past century, schools were made a safe haven for young people who were being exploited in the streets and workplaces of the day. Great efforts were made to see that children were protected from physical, financial, and social harm until they were deemed mature enough to deal with life responsibly on their own. Today we know the vehicle for assuring their safety as "compulsory attendance"— young people up to a given age are legally required to be in school, and parents and employers are obligated to honor that mandate.

As you explore the territory, note how much of the school's resources and attention are given to this Custodial function. Virtually every school has personnel assigned to monitor and enforce attendance. Why? In part because school funding is based on average daily attendance. The more students there are in seats each day, the more the district receives from its state in operating revenue. Absent students are lost dollars!

Grades, credits, and diplomas are students' official tickets out the door and their passports to the future. In a credential-dominated society such as ours, the more official documents you can accumulate showing what you've "achieved" educationally, the better. How do you get a diploma? By accumulating enough credits in the right subjects. How do you get a credit? Two ways: first, by getting a "passing" grade—enough points—from the teacher of the subject. Second, *by being in attendance the right amount of time*. No attendance, no credit—no matter how good your learning is.

Why is this? Because credits are based on "seat time": 120 hours of sitting there gets you a full "Carnegie unit" of credit. Sixty hours of sitting gets you a half credit. Credits only come in multiples of sixty hours, and they are not based on your learning. If they were, you could get them at any time. They're based on your seat time—being "in custody" the right amount of time. Just try getting a credit because you can do the stuff without being there. It's rarely allowed. Furthermore, in many districts if you're absent or tardy so many times in a grading period, your grade automatically gets lowered by so many points. That's about Custody and control, not about learning.

Compliance as Achievement

The school's Custodial mission is, in turn, the key driver of its second most important agenda: *compliance* and control. Because they *have to* attend school for a specific amount of time, students' participation is inherently involuntary. Like it or not, they have to put up with the school, and the school has to put up with them. Clearly, most schools do the best they can to interest and motivate their students, but when all else fails, schools control the ultimate carrot/reward/stick that assures Compliance: credit. No credit, no diploma.

As we explore the territory, keep your eyes peeled for how often and in how many ways points and grading, the key elements of credit, are used to gain student Compliance and maintain control. Bad attitude? Five points off. Throw a spit-wad? Ten points off. Mouth off to the teacher? A zero for the day. And remember, these points are tallied up as your overall grade.

Is social control in some form or other necessary? Yes, definitely. Are Compliance and control learning and achievement? No. But you'll be hard pressed to find grading systems that don't have Compliance and control factors mixed right in with everything else. It's often what researchers call the school's "hidden curriculum," and it's a potential element in all classroom interactions.

Competition as Achievement

Competition is the third factor that distorts the meaning of learning and achievement in schools. It is both the philosophical cause of the school's numbers game and the psychological result of it. As we'll explore in more depth in chapters 4 and 5, our educational institutions, from graduate schools on down, have decided—based on a worldview of privilege and scarcity—that there are only so many goods and valued objects (e.g., 100s, As, 4.0s, places in elite colleges) of any kind to go around. Valued resources are simply scarce, so if you want them, you'll have to outdo your peers in some way or other to get them. This, in short, is the essence of the contest over points described earlier.

So if a teacher only has so many high marks to distribute, and they get distributed week after week based on assignments and tests, who will be the students who get them? The most motivated, you might guess. Or the most diligent. Perhaps. But also consider these two likelihoods: (1) those who already *knew a lot* about it before they started; and (2) those who *learn faster* than others—often because they already knew a lot about it too. The worst thing you can be in a competitive situation is *behind*—behind in learning level, behind in rate of learning, or behind in points. Is being a fast learner the same as successful learning? Not at all. But it *is* in school when there aren't enough points to go around, and they're distributed on a tight schedule.

Competence as Achievement

Competence is one of the "official" components of learning and achievement. That's the good news. The bad news is that the official curriculum that really counts in schools isn't organized around Competence development, it's organized around Content. To develop Competence, students need to do things: plan, design, organize, write, produce, perform, and so forth, and on a continuous basis. These words are what Language Arts teachers call "action verbs"—you actually carry out a process and do something to execute them, and doing requires Competence.

But as you explore the territory of school, look at the verbs that describe the school's curriculum and course goals, and you'll be hard pressed to find verbs other than "know," "interpret," and "understand." Even worse is the current emphasis on test taking. What are the dominant verbs there? "Remember" and "recognize." So be aware of how much lip service schools pay to developing Competence, but then compare it to the extremely narrow range of performance abilities that they actually develop and evaluate. Why?

Content as Achievement

Because Content is king! For centuries educators have equated education with acquiring, remembering, and mentally processing Content. That's good and necessary, but "knowing" Content doesn't make you Competent. Nor does "understanding" Content. Competence is the ability to apply Content in some useful way.

With that in mind, examine the course offerings in your schools. You're likely to find two things: (1) the courses are almost all labeled according to the kind of Content they contain (e.g., social studies, biology, etc.), not the kind of Competence they develop (e.g., Systematic Planning, Effective Communicating, etc.); and (2) the courses are almost all divided into two categories: academic and applied. Look closer and you'll find that "academic" is about "rigorous Content for smart kids." "Applied" is about having "dumb kids do practical things." This profoundly false, counterproductive, and misleading myth has been driving education forever; and, as we'll see in chapters 4 and 6, it is limiting our vision of education, ignoring the talents and shortchanging the opportunities of countless learners, and jeopardizing our future as a nation. It's a dominant feature of the territory, so watch for it:

Academic = Rigorous = Smart

Applied = Practical = Dumb

It's everywhere, today's reforms embrace it, and it's hogwash!

Other Cautions

As you continue your explorations of the territory, you'd be well advised to keep your eyes peeled for three other things. First, the standardized, assembly-line nature of curriculum delivery that has all children of a given age in the same grade level working on the same page of the same textbook on the same day. It's a sure sign that the learner is not the focal point of instruction, the curriculum is.

Second, a heavy emphasis on children performing on state-mandated standardized tests that have serious consequences attached to them—at the expense of other kinds of learning and development. It's a sure sign that the learner is not the focal point of instruction, the state mandates are.

Third, report cards that only have tiny boxes next to the name of subjects for fixed blocks of time. It's a sure sign that the learner is not the focal point of instruction, the numbers game is.

The big question, of course, is what should you do if you come across all of these things in your explorations? Ask "Why do we do this?"—and don't stop asking because the explanations are hidden in our long-forgotten past. Then suggest that everyone in the school read and discuss chapters 1 and 2 and what they mean to them personally and collectively.

The chances are that they'll begin to understand that the familiar territory of Industrial Age schooling must change, not just improve, because the gap between what we know as a people and a profession and what we continue to do in the name of education has never been wider.

How wide must it be before the entire foundation shatters? And if it does, what should replace it? The answer to the first question is that it's intolerably too wide already, and today's counterfeit reforms are widening it even more!

The answer to the second lies in chapters 1 through 3 and 7 through 12. They offer a vision of a learning system that focuses on the future, empowers all learners, and elevates the meaning of education far beyond its traditional constraints. May this vision inspire and motivate all of us to move *beyond counterfeit reforms to forge an authentic future for all learners.*

I

MOVING BEYOND
EDUCATION'S DEAD END CHOICE

The world today's high school seniors face is profoundly different from the 1983 world that (Theodore) Sizer's seniors faced, and it is completely unlike the world of 1893 when the Committee of Ten did its work. The basic question we now face is: For which world are today's schools designed to prepare them?

In 1983, Theodore Sizer, one of the most notable school reformers of our era, likened the American high school to a Model T Ford. Both were products of the same early twentieth-century era, he argued, and both are hopelessly out of date. What we need, he stated, is an entire "re-engineering" of the high school, not yet another coat of paint on the Model T in the name of school "reform."

Think about it: the design template of the high schools we all attended, know so well, and just revisited with some penetrating new perspectives in the introduction was developed in 1893 by an elite group of university presidents called the Committee of Ten. Actually their work shaped our schools years before Henry Ford ever constructed his first horseless carriage, let alone produced the Model T; and it's been our model for educating young people ever since. If you remember: "Four years of English, three years of math, four years of social studies, and three years of science . . . ," we got it from them.

What's significant about this period is that the turn of the past century was a time when the "modern" assembly line factory was viewed as the most advanced form of organizational productivity possible, so the policy makers of the era created schools to match it. Based on the thinking of the day, which is documented in a riveting book by Raymond Callahan called *Education and the*

Cult of Efficiency (1964), both factories and schools strove for standardized products, standardized procedures, mass production, technical efficiency, and an assembly line process that required all work to proceed at a uniform pace.

In such a system there is a premium on regulation, compliance, and uniformity, and this seemed like the perfect approach to schooling for a society flooded with immigrants from abroad, most of whom spoke no English and had never experienced life in a political democracy. Just think: Industrial Age/Model T schools for an Industrial Age/Model T economy and work force. Wow!

1983: EDUCATION'S FATEFUL CROSSROADS

Well, here we are in the twenty-first century facing the same dilemma that Sizer described, only worse: nearly two more decades have passed without any significant change in our educational model! Children born the year Sizer's insightful article was published have already graduated from high school, and during their lifetime the world changed dramatically.

As we look back, 1983 was the dawn of what we all now recognize as the Information Age, an era of incredible discoveries, technological advances, and rapid, complex change that we've all experienced. The world today's high school seniors face is profoundly different from the 1983 world that Sizer's seniors faced, and it is completely unlike the world of 1893 when the Committee of Ten did its work. The basic question we now face is: For which world are today's schools designed to prepare them?

The Year of the Reports

But Sizer was just one of a cast of thousands speaking out on education in 1983. It was, by all accounts, the year that America's frustration with its schools really took concrete form, and it set the course of reform that we are still encountering. In fact, the deluge of major reports and books that were issued in 1983 by various agencies, experts, commissions, and foundations on the status of education and what to do about it easily numbered in the twenties (see Spady and Marx 1984).

Hence, 1983 was called "The Year of the Reports," and the most visible and politically leveraged of them was issued by the U.S. Department of Education. It was called *A Nation at Risk*, and it was given enormous visibility, legitimacy, and political endorsement by both the policy makers and leading educators of the day.

For all its good intentions, however, *A Nation at Risk* has left us a nation at even greater risk than before. Why? Because in the name of "reform," it took all of the structural and operational features of our existing Industrial Age/Model T schools as fixed and given. Its five sets of recommendations focused on how to make schools function more effectively with all their inflexible, outmoded structural features intact. The centerpiece of its recommendations was called "The New Basics." What were they? "Four years of English, three years of math, four years of social studies, and three years of science . . ."—a direct repetition of the Committee of Ten's work in 1893. Amazing. Or better yet, shocking!

Ninety years later America was still being offered the same vision of education that heralded the twentieth century: subjects with "academically correct" names being "covered" in a traditional agrarian calendar year by teachers in isolated classrooms working out of prescribed textbooks. The only differences: *A Nation at Risk* recommended a ten-month year instead of nine, and thicker books that would compel teachers to cover more material within the scheduled time. The critics among us called it the "Longer, Harder, Better" model of reform because there were no other signs of genuine change in it.

There we were, the United States of America—a country that prided itself as being the "most advanced" on the planet, having already successfully sent several crews of astronauts to the moon and back—recommending in the name of "excellence" that it continue to entrust its young people into the foreseeable future to schools modeled on the thinking, tools, and knowledge base of nearly a century before—a time of no automobiles, no airplanes, no rockets, no satellites, no radios, no television, no tape recorders, no home freezers, no computers, no Internet, no brain research, no laser surgery, no digital anything, no Palm Pilots, no cell phones, no deeper understanding of human learning or potential. Note: this model worked for a minority of students a century ago, and it's still working for a minority of them today!

Such, says futurist Joel Barker (1988), is the power of "paradigms" to blind us to new realities. In 1983 we lost sight of the forest because of all the trees and took the wrong path to the future—a path that turned into a tragic dead end street.

Well, the future that *A Nation at Risk* charted has arrived, and here we are having moved along its path of reform experiencing the same frustrations, the same dilemmas, and the same kinds of reform proposals that motivated the policy makers of 1983—only worse. In the name of higher standards and greater effectiveness, improvement, and accountability, today's policy makers are forcing educators to adhere to an even narrower, more standardized, and much more heavily regulated approach to educating our children than ever. Their "reforms" feature

standardized standards, standardized content, standardized timelines, standardized expectations, standardized opportunities, and standardized tests, with a heavy price to pay for both students and educators if the results and scores on the tests don't "measure up."

And most citizens and politicians are eating it up like hotcakes when they should be storming the barricades instead.

Why? Because, as we'll see in more detail in chapters 4 through 6, there's no room in these impersonal reforms for originality, flexibility, innovation, change, learner needs, individuality, cutting-edge research, real life, or genuine professionalism. Today's reforms are simply about doing Model T assembly line things better, harder, and more precisely than in 1983. And if you don't, or can't, meet the predefined standard as measured on the one and only standardized test, you're simply bumped off the line and declared unfit.

At their core, the reforms are extremely system-focused rather than learner-focused and assume that, because learners are a given age, they all have the same learning readiness, learning rate, learning style, learning interests, language background, and aptitudes. In addition, they assume that there's only one date in an entire calendar year for formally assessing and advancing students through a program of study. The learners must bend to the system's requirements, rather than the system adapting to learner differences. The underlying thinking behind the reforms, if there is any, seems to be:

There is only one way to do "school": If it doesn't look like familiar Model T education, sound like familiar Model T education, operate like familiar Model T education, and give you familiar Model T results, it can't be a "school," and it can't be called "school reform." School only comes one way: Model T.

THE REAL PATH TO THE FUTURE

We didn't have to take this dead end Industrial Age path to the future in 1983, but we did. By the time *A Nation at Risk* was released in early May '83, Tom Peters and Robert Waterman's revolutionary book *In Search of Excellence* (1982) had already been on top of the *New York Times* Bestseller List for four months and remained there for almost the entire year. "Everyone" read it and almost instantly claimed to embrace its "new paradigm" message about totally reversing the old Industrial Age way of organizational functioning. Educational policy makers may have read it, but they certainly didn't figure out how to apply it.

A New Paradigm for a New Era

In today's terminology, *In Search of Excellence* was about visioning, future-focusing, organizational purpose, flexibility and adaptability, client-centered operations, employee empowerment, collaboration, shared decision making, and innovation, innovation, innovation—factors that underlie the transformation in how business has had to "do business" to compete successfully in today's constantly changing world. If *In Search of Excellence*'s essence could be boiled down to three essential elements, it would be (1) cultivate your clients, (2) empower your employees, and (3) continuously assess and improve everything that moves. None of these factors was addressed in *A Nation at Risk*, and only few of the other 1983 books and reports focused on any of them.

But the most important Peters and Waterman insight for education was imbedded in the seventh of their eight "themes" about what constituted "excellence" in this new (1983) era of continuous change. The theme was called "Simultaneous Loose-Tight Properties"—words that don't easily translate into a clear message. But their explanation offered a compelling way to contrast "bureaucratic" (i.e., Industrial Age/Model T) organizations from those that embodied an "excellence" way of doing business. And it gave education an entirely different path of change to follow.

First, in its very simplest form, Peters and Waterman explain that organizations need two different kinds of elements in order to function. One is the "ends" or purposes they are trying to accomplish, and the other is the "means" or procedures they are employing to achieve those ends. In education, learning, results, performance, outcomes, and achievement are ends, and curriculum, time, teaching, materials, opportunity, and programs are means. An ends-oriented educational model recognizes that what ultimately matters is student learning success. Programs, curricula, and teaching, for example, are simply means for getting there.

Second, they showed that organizations can deal with each of these two kinds of elements in two different ways. One is "tightly" by directly defining, focusing on, and structuring what they seek to accomplish. The other is "loosely," by more indirectly, flexibly, responsively, and variably doing so. By putting these two broad sets of factors together, we can see that an organization's ends can be either tight or loose, and its means can be either tight or loose as well. Therefore, how an organization or school operates will be a function of how these two sets of factors are defined and brought together (see figure 1.1)—tight or loose on ends, and tight or loose on means—leading to profoundly different patterns of organizational functioning.

Peters and Waterman's unique and powerful insight was that excellence organizations operate exactly opposite of bureaucratic ones. As figure 1.1 shows, Bureaucracies (Model T schools) are simultaneously loose on ends and results, and tight on means and procedures. In effect, they're procedure-driven, which often makes them inflexible and unresponsive. By contrast, excellence organizations are tight on ends and intended results, and loose on means and procedures, making them both purpose-driven and more client-responsive. Ironically, both kinds of organizations have Loose-Tight properties, but their patterns are reversed, as are the perspectives and dynamics that drive them and the ways they serve their clients.

When we translate this Peters and Waterman terminology into two key messages of this book, it says: Model T schools are tightly defined and organized around time, curriculum, and programs, but loosely organized around

ENDS FACTORS

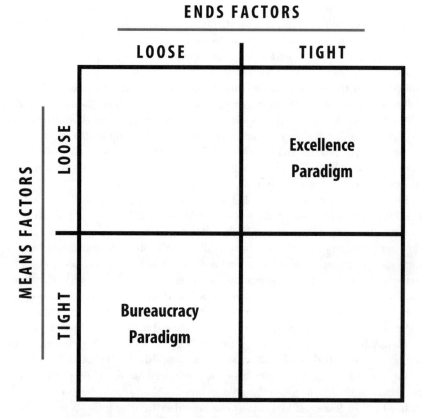

Figure 1.1   Paradigms of Organizational Functioning

intended learning outcomes and results. What do today's new paradigm realities demand? Just the opposite:

> A tight focus on life-performance learning results and a flexible, learner-responsive way of getting all learners to achieve them.

THE TRANSFORMING PARADIGM SHIFT

What the advocates of *A Nation at Risk* failed to do in 1983 was pay attention to the future and use the paradigm breaking insights provided by Peters and Waterman to imagine that they could define, focus, and operate schools around:

- Ends rather than Means
- Purposes rather than Procedures
- Results rather than Resources

- Outcomes rather than Programs
- Goals rather than Roles
- Learners rather than Time
- Learning rather than Teaching
- Challenges rather than Content
- Performance rather than Curriculum
- Competence rather than Credits
- Learner Potential rather than Grade Levels
- Possibilities rather than Precedents
- The Future rather than the Past
- Life rather than Schooling

It only takes a moment to read the elements on the left and see what an exciting set of "open system" options they provide. What if we really chose to organize education around virtually any cluster of ends elements from the left side, rather than retaining the current focus on their means counterparts on the right side? Answer: We'd create the kind of empowering learning system described in chapters 7 through 12.

More specifically, what if we really organized education around the unique potentials of our learners, the challenges they'll face once they finish their schooling, and the competences and performance abilities they'll require in life? Answer: We'd create the kind of empowering learning system described in chapters 7 through 12.

Or, what if we considered the wide range of possibilities for organizing the time and talents of all those involved in the learning process to maximize our intended learning results? What would such a learning system look like? Chapter 11 in particular gives us some exciting options to consider.

Let's stop for a moment and consider what's happening here. As we carefully consider the tremendous differences in approach these two sets of elements embody, the paradigms they reflect, and the implications they have for our children's learning and development, we're both expanding our horizons about education and engaging in a process that cultural anthropologist Jennifer James describes as "wide-band thinking"—thinking that extends beyond the often "narrow band" of past experience and fixed beliefs. This is also widely known as "open system"—as distinct from "closed system"—thinking.

When we expand our imaginative horizons and look at education from this new perspective, one compelling insight jumps out at us again and again:

If we would imagine organizing education around these ends-based, wide-band, open-system possibilities, we would never recreate the Industrial Age/Model T schools we've inherited from past generations. Nor would we accept as "authentic" any reforms that reinforce them.

OVERCOMING "EDUCENTRISM"

However, by using the means elements on the right side of this framework as the fixed and non-negotiable factors in their reform thinking, the National Commission that authored *A Nation at Risk* fell into the trap that has plagued educators for the past century: using existing features of schools (their means) to define the ends they're trying to accomplish. For example, when people write "outcomes" (ends) for seventh-grade social studies (means), they are taking the curriculum category called social studies and grade level called seventh as fixed, given, constant, and unchangeable—they're just how the system is.

Then they proceed to define the ends they desire for that particular set of means. Or worse yet, they define ends in means language, as in: "All learners will take four years of English before graduating." This is very much like having the tail wag the dog, or the tail be the dog. But it happens literally everywhere in education all the time. Goals, outcomes, and/or objectives are written for and about grade levels and curriculum areas rather than the way it should be: Starting with a clear picture of the learning results we ultimately want students to successfully demonstrate and designing "down" or "back" from there the learning experiences (i.e., curriculum) that will get students there.

This fixation on the system's programs, structures, and procedures is called "educentrism" (see Spady 1998a, 1998d, 1998e), and it is the twin brother of narrow-band/closed-system thinking. The only way to overcome it is to keep focused on the left-side words and concepts and insist that all questions be asked and answered in "non-educentric" left-side terminology. It takes lots and lots of practice to master this paradigm shift because educentric thinking and words are so deeply ingrained in educational policy and practice. But chapters 7 through 12 will show us how it's done.

Placing Function Ahead of Form

Focusing on the left-side elements and applying the Tight Ends/Loose Means combination of organizational properties is the fundamental nature of things in today's highly dynamic, wide-band Information Age. Our children see and live this reality every day. And as their imaginations, available knowledge, and the power and versatility of existing technologies continue to expand, our society becomes increasingly capable of discovering and implementing more and more ways of accomplishing the same fundamental ends. In effect, no one *has to* do things "the way they've always been done before." The new reality is that

This expansion of possibilities relates to the basic difference between what anthropologist James calls "form" and "function." Function is the purpose that something serves—its end, why it exists. Form is the means we employ for achieving that end or purpose. The fundamental message of wide-band, open-system, Information Age thinking is more and more people are seeing that inflexible patterns of organizational structuring, decision making, and action are the result of people choosing to operate that way. They're not inevitable; they're just old habits.

Tom Peters, the co-author of *In Search of Excellence* and noted change guru, illustrates this basic truth about form and function best in his more recent work with three simple examples. Peters points out that, in today's technology-driven world:

no one set of means, or procedures, or structures is sufficient for accomplishing a given function or end. Many possibilities are open to us. Similarly, no standardized model of schooling or reform is an end in itself. Many different approaches are possible, and some of them are far better equipped than others to getting our highly diverse population of young people to the future successfully.

1. *Groceries* (function) are necessary, but *grocery stores* (a specific form) are not. All kinds of alternative food distribution systems are available to consumers.
2. *Banking* (function) is necessary, but *banks* (a specific form) are not. Countless financial transactions are possible today without having to go to a bank.
3. *Education* (function) is necessary, but *schools* (a specific form) are not. Going to a specific physical place to acquire information or develop skills from a limited range of adults on a fixed schedule is outmoded.

Clearly, this last example causes us to pause and scares lots of educators to death because it confirms what reformer Lewis Perelman implied in his 1992 book *School's Out*. In the Information Age, he asserts *the paradigm has shifted from schooling to learning*! And that means that with the advanced technologies that are widely available today—especially personal computers and the Internet—if you want to *learn* something, anyone can learn anything at any time from anywhere from worldwide experts to advance their knowledge and lives. It's an open-access, unlimited-opportunity system!

Perelman's key message: In today's world of continuous discovery, learning is a critical end, and the means for attaining it—the forms that support it—are infinitely flexible. In short, he argues, today's world of learning is filled with unlimited opportunity and options. *School's Out!* No one has to go there anymore to learn what's important to them—which may help account for the tremendous growth in home schooling noted in the introduction.

If these distinctions between ends and means and function and form are true, as Peters, Perelman, and countless other futurists allege, then the new realities that accompany the Information Age compel us to rethink both the form and the function of education. In today's world, rather than the world of 1893 or even 1983, learners—children and adults alike—are no longer bound by the formal constraints of Industrial Age/Model T/educentric/closed-system schooling and reforms where

specific students must learn specific content on a specific schedule in a specific classroom from a specific teacher out of a specific textbook to pass a specific exam on a specific date with a specific score that qualifies them to go on to the next specific grade, classroom, teacher, and book the next year to repeat this pattern over and over for a specific number of years in order to collect a specific credential that allows them to attend "higher" education.

This is a picture of inflexible boxes within boxes driven by boxes within boxes . . . without end. And every time we see the word "specific," we're boxed in by some artificially constraining factor. Take a moment to re-read this description and compare it with the essence of Perelman's message. He's describing a reality in which access to learning is open and available, and opportunities for learning what is important are unconstrained and unlimited. But this description represents just the opposite: A system with extremely restricted conditions of access to learning/teaching, and a severely constrained and limited structuring of opportunities for learning what is prescribed.

Let's be clear: Today's extremely educentric Standards-Based Reform movement, which we'll examine in more detail in chapter 6, simply reinforces all of these "specific" constraining boxes. In doing so, it's also:

- Primitively narrow in its conceptions of learning, standards, performance, and assessment
- Rigid in its curriculum and organizational structures
- Insensitive to the characteristics or needs of individual students
- Hierarchical in its control structures
- Punitive in its orientations
- Archaic in its endorsed instructional methods
- Intimidating and de-professionalizing to educators
- Committed to sorting and selecting students
- Severely constraining in its opportunities for learning and success

The desire to escape the standardization and impersonality of these dead end boxes and conditions may account for some of the phenomenal increase in home schooling in the United States in the last decade, partly, at least, because it embodies the more learner-empowering "Anyone Can Learn Anything from Anywhere at Anytime" paradigm that Perelman so ardently advances.

OUR LEARNER-EMPOWERING EDUCATIONAL GOALS

But this is not a book about alternatives to education per se. Instead, it's about creating open-access, unlimited-opportunity learning systems that embody the very best of what we know about learners, learning, life, the future, effective instruction, authentic life performance, organizational cultures, opportunity structures, systemic change, and effective leadership—knowledge that is fully in our grasp if we choose to use it to our children's and society's advantage.

When we apply this enlightened knowledge to creating learning systems that genuinely prepare *all* our children for the lives and challenges they face, we'll want a model of learning that consistently and creatively achieves the following paradigm-shifting goals:

1. Equip them for a future of continuous discovery and constant change—not for an Industrial Age past that is now behind us.
2. Prepare them to lead totally fulfilling lives—not just qualify for more advanced schooling.
3. Foster the kinds of complex abilities needed to succeed in and shape tomorrow's dynamic and complex world—not to master curriculum and standards that one only encounters in schools and on tests.
4. Encourage students to be producers of their own knowledge and products—not passive consumers of content from teachers and texts.
5. Develop the kinds of orientations and abilities needed to remain a self-directed learner throughout one's life—not to limit one's learning to what is taught in school subjects or formally tested and scored.
6. Nurture the many dimensions of learning and talent that reside within all human beings—not just the verbal and mathematical skills needed to pass paper-and-pencil tests in academic subjects.
7. Respond sensitively to differences in student learning rates and the unique challenges many learners face when confronted with abstract, lecture-type instruction—don't assume that a uniform rate of "covering the material" is the same as "teaching."
8. Focus on achieving the ultimate level of competence possible for each learner—not on the time blocks in which courses are typically offered.
9. Respond positively to the emerging possibilities that the new research on learning, human development, and the future are continuously revealing—don't lock students into routine grade-level/assembly-line content, instructional methods, and learning opportunities.

10. Welcome and implement promising innovations that advance future-focused learning—don't stick to old habits and time-honored practices.
11. Create a culture in which everyone learns from everyone, children and adults alike—not according to age-determined teaching-learning roles.
12. Establish ways of continuously assessing and improving everything education does—don't embrace familiar, routine practices for their own sake.

If we were to collectively internalize, openly embrace, and publicly advocate these new paradigm goals, we could divert public education in the United States from its current dead-end/old-paradigm course. The new course educators chart for us is fundamentally about learners and their future, not about maintaining existing system structures; and it reflects the enormous advances in research, thinking, and practice that characterize the world outside of education. These research advances form the rationale for choosing this more enlightened path and the bedrock on which we'll want to construct our new learner-empowering model. We'll examine five of the most relevant and compelling of these new research realities in the following chapter.

CONCLUDING PERSPECTIVE

This book is absolutely about all of us being "at choice." That means using the most enlightening ideas we can find as the basis for choosing our paradigm perspective, choosing our goals and priorities, choosing the rationale and foundation on which we would construct a model of education, and choosing how we would work together to do this. There is nothing in what follows that reflects the "we've always done it this way before" orientation of Industrial Age thinking and practice. And there's nothing that legitimates the prevalent meaning of "choice" in today's policy debates. Choosing to take children out of Model T public schools so that they can attend Model T private schools is a symbolic/political choice, not a substantive one. And choosing to impose "reforms" on schools that reinforce everything about them that doesn't work for most learners is, to be polite, a "counterfeit" choice at best.

Real choice involves moving from narrow-band to wide-band thinking, from closed-system to open-system planning, and from means-based to ends-based operations. When we choose to make these paradigm shifts, we'll be choosing to create an educational future for our children and our country that is not encumbered with the archaic thinking and outmoded practices of a century ago. That's when choice and change will become synonyms and all learners can rightly assume their deserved status as the focal point and "bottom line" of why and how we educate.

2

EMBRACING THE NEW
RESEARCH REALITIES

If we designed a learning system around any one of these new research realities, let alone all of them, we'd never create the Model T schools we've inherited from 1893.

If we are going to move education off of its means-driven, educentric, Industrial Age, closed-system, narrow-band dead center and take it down a more enlightened and empowering path, we're going to need to use some powerful and persuasive resources. As we noted previously, this constellation of boxed-in systemic features has been legalized, institutionalized, internalized, and reinforced for nearly a century. Consequently, the cultural and institutional inertia that surrounds and supports it is massive and deeply entrenched.

Given these conditions, is there any hope of our moving down the new paradigm path described in the second half of chapter 1? If there were no hope then students across the country wouldn't be boycotting their mandated state tests, their parents wouldn't be organizing anti-reform action committees, the educational media wouldn't be filled with articles exposing the serious negatives of recent reforms, and you wouldn't be reading this book.

Frustration and resistance to the worst aspects of the reforms have been building, particularly in states like California and Virginia where the reforms have gone beyond rhyme and reason. And they will continue to generate more resistance as they alienate more and more parents and committed educators. In addition, three particularly noteworthy books—Susan Ohanian's *One Size Fits Few* (1999), Peter Sacks's *Standardized Minds* (1999), and Alfie Kohn's *The Case against Standardized Testing* (2000)—are exposing their costly and counterproductive nature and consequences.

THE POWER OF WORDS

We're all familiar with the adage that, to be effective, leaders need to "walk the walk." Well, in this case we need to reverse the message. Decades of experience suggest that the change we're advocating won't happen unless we and thousands like us focus our attention on, embrace, and advocate the more enlightened and empowering alternatives to our Model T schools that now exist or can be created. And that means "talking our walk" in a different way, using a different vocabulary, asking different questions, and citing different examples from those commonly used in school reform discussions.

Things stay the same in education because we keep reinforcing the status quo by using its old-paradigm vocabulary and concepts to describe the changes we desire. By using these familiar educentric terms over and over—such as *grade levels*, *subjects*, *grades*, and *credits*—we continue to give legitimacy to the very things that most need changing. Hence, we end up merely relabeling things or tinkering around their edges without really addressing and changing their fundamental nature.

So here are four concrete things we can do to initiate and reinforce the kind of change we're seeking:

1. *Never Say "School"!* The word *school* is synonymous with all the educentric/closed-system boxes described in chapter 1. If we try to change or improve schools, we'll still end up with "school" when we're finished because our focus and frame of reference won't have changed. Lewis Perelman has it right: The paradigm has shifted from schooling to learning. So we need to keep the entire purpose and focus of our discussions and questions on learning, not on schooling. For example, what's really critical for our young people to be able to do successfully after their schooling is finished? Better yet, we should focus them on "learners" because that personalizes the discussion and *brings human beings into the picture*—not courses, standards, and test scores. What matters more than learners? Nothing—especially school!

2. *Embrace and Advocate New-Paradigm Words.* This will require that we return to the side-by-side comparisons of ends and means terms shown in the middle of chapter 1 and deliberately keep our thinking and comments focused on the list's left side. We must be careful not to get drawn over to the right side, which is incredibly easy to do because of all the inertia that surrounds it. For example, we shouldn't talk about procedure until purpose is clearly established and agreed upon; we shouldn't talk about programs until ultimate learner outcomes are clearly defined and agreed upon; and we shouldn't talk about curriculum until expectations about learner performance are clearly defined and agreed upon. When we get the hang of it, we'll find ourselves saying over and over: "I'm sorry, but I can't really discuss ____ until we have its larger purpose clear and have examined a range of alternatives that might give us a more desirable result."

3. *Embrace and Advocate the Twelve Learner-Empowering Educational Goals*. This will require us to study and reflect on the meaning and implications of the twelve goals stated at the end of chapter 1 and consistently use them as the basis of our questions and discussions about educational change. As we study each goal, we'll see both its new-paradigm and old-paradigm forms side by side. We should call attention to those differences and use them to keep conversations and planning on track. Clearly these goals are intended to serve as criteria for assessing a learning system's progress toward real change, and we should encourage our colleagues and constituents to use them that way.

For example, take Goal 1 and ask: "Are we really equipping all our children for a future of continuous discovery and constant change? What evidence do we have for that?" Continually asking questions around these goals can encourage a profound change of perspective among those who've simply never thought about education this way.

4. *Embrace and Advocate the Five New Research Realities*. This will require that we thoroughly acquaint ourselves with the five following bedrock knowledge bases for creating and operating a learner-empowering learning system. These powerful and growing knowledge bases (1) underlie and reinforce many of the elements in the new paradigm framework and the learner-empowering goals just mentioned, (2) offer us a set of compelling resources for expanding people's thinking about the larger purposes and character of a genuinely non-educentric learning system, and (3) serve as the research bedrock for taking education down the path to the future that it ignored in 1983. Paradoxically, these research realities are not "new" to those who think about learners, learning, life, competence, and the future. But they may be new to those wholly immersed in an educentric/narrow-band approach to schooling and reform.

FIVE REALITIES THAT GROUND NEW PARADIGM CHANGE

Achieving paradigm change requires at a minimum that we have an unassailable rationale for the models we wish to create. Described below are five compelling research "realities" for which solid bodies of research and experience now exist and continue to accumulate. These five realities cover a range of critical factors underlying learning for life-success and fulfillment, and they offer us an enlightening view of:

1. The enormity of *human potential*—the many kinds of talents and capacities our learners possess as unique human beings.
2. The dynamic nature of *human learning*—the unfolding picture of how the brain works and the complexity of how and why we learn.
3. Our highly interrelated *domains of living*—the key aspects of life that make living joyous, productive, and fulfilling.

4. Emerging *future conditions*—the key problems, challenges, and opportunities that our children will likely face in the years ahead.
5. Effective *life performance*—the complex abilities and attributes that lead to success and fulfillment, both on the job and off.

Designing a new-paradigm learning system on these five realities enables us to move beyond the past century's educentric definitions of learning, achievement, performance, and success to ones that reflect the true nature of learners, learning, life, and living—the place beyond Model T schools and counterfeit reforms where learners and living mean more than points and scores.

Human Potential

The irony surrounding the human potential research base is that it involves both the most elusive and most controversial, yet most fundamental, aspect of human nature: the inherent make-up of the human being. To deal honestly and openly with human potential is to ask the following two questions:

1. What is the inherent state of a human being's nature and capabilities before families, cultures, nation-states, and schools begin to impose their agendas, expectations, fears, and constraints on the individual?
2. Who is the individual as a unique being and identity, apart from all of these expectations and agendas, that we must honor and nurture?

In his 1998 book *Awakening Genius in the Classroom*, Thomas Armstrong summarizes an enormous amount of work on brain and early childhood development and concludes that as humans we are inherently curious, playful, imaginative, creative, full of wonder, wise, inventive, vital, sensitive, flexible, humorous, and joyful. That's an impressive list of inherent attributes. Yet, according to John Kehoe's 1997 book *Mind Power*, Armstrong should also add spiritual, intuitive, trusting, teachable, and powerful to the list. Clearly, this set of seventeen attributes provides us with a rich and challenging foundation from which to begin to think about human potential and its development.

But a rather different approach to this issue is taken by the noted psychologist Howard Gardner. His 1983 explanation of the concept of "multiple intelligences" in his book *Frames of Mind* has been one of the most widely discussed bodies of work during the past decade. Gardner's key idea is that skill, ability, intelligence, "smarts," potential, talent, and genius come in many forms, even though our formal educational system typically only honors two of them. Gardner's initial research documented seven "intelligences," which he called linguistic, logical-mathematical, spatial, musical, bodily-kinesthetic, interpersonal, and intrapersonal, but he has recently added an eighth and ninth to his framework which he calls naturalist and esoteric, respectively.

In his earlier book *Seven Kinds of Smart* (1993), Armstrong fully describes and illustrates each of Gardner's original seven intelligences and provides a rich bibliography of research and practices that support each. These resources provide a wealth of information for expanding our vision of learning and achievement far beyond the two intelligences that schools stress: linguistic and logical-mathematical.

By discussing the talents of accomplished and successful people that we admire, we could probably identify other intelligences besides Gardner's nine and add them to the list of twenty-five we'll be seeing in chapter 3. We could then integrate the things on this larger list with the seventeen attributes identified by Armstrong and Kehoe, generating an impressive master list with which we can then work. Think of the eyes that will open when we have our colleagues and constituents take time to reflect on this master list of at least thirty capacities that children bring with them to school, hoping that they will be recognized and strengthened by those who "educate" them.

Armed with our individual master lists, we should each take some time to personally address and answer the following questions for ourselves: What are the key attributes and domains of human potential that our learning system needs to cultivate and strengthen, and what kinds of learning experiences will best foster their continued growth and application? Once we have answers that satisfy us, we should share all of the above with others, reminding them that the purpose of an empowering education system is to enhance, rather than ignore or diminish, this wide range of gifts, talents, and capacities that lie within our learners. Guaranteed, after getting our peers to address these findings and answer these questions for themselves, they're highly likely to describe Model T schools and reforms as sterile, shallow, and limiting.

Human Learning

Numerous scholars and writers have characterized the era we've been calling the Industrial Age as being mechanistic and "hyper-rational," where the world was seen through a lens that required everything to be precise, orderly, and predictable. This worldview was projected onto human learning as well, and it accounts for a lot of what Raymond Callahan explains in *Education and the Cult of Efficiency* (1964) about the dawn of mass public education in the United States. We tried to make students into regimented "learning machines" so that they would be equipped to play efficient roles on the assembly lines of the day, doing precisely defined tasks over and over as accurately and rapidly as possible.

Much of that legacy remains in education's obsession with "right answers," and changing this culturally entrenched mindset is likely to be extremely difficult. Nonetheless, there is a large and growing body of work on brain development, mental functioning, and early childhood development that profoundly challenges this mechanistic model. For an outstanding synthesis of much of this work, read Ronald Kotulak's *Inside the Brain* (1996). This new research reality is wholly consistent with the following definition of *learning*: A change in understanding and behavior that results from encountering new experience. If we look carefully at this definition, three key things jump out.

First, learning is about understanding or making sense of new experience. It assumes that some frame of reference or "meaning structure" already exists in learners which gives them a basis for assessing the relevance/importance/meaning of new things they encounter. In other words, the brain is inherently and continuously trying to build connections between what it already has stored and "understands" and what each new experience represents.

This is why brain researchers and learning psychologists overwhelmingly endorse the notion that the brain is an active, dynamic, and continuously evolving "meaning-making" device that automatically seeks to make connections, expand meaning, and enlarge its own capacity to function. That is, the brain is always in "creation mode." Because learners are constantly constructing their own meaning from the things they encounter, this approach to learning is called "constructivism."

This readily leads to the conclusion that we're born curious and seek stimulation and challenge in order to grow and function. When we don't get the necessary stimulation from our environment, this capacity atrophies and we become less capable of building new pathways for operating. The antidote: Stimulate, stimulate, stimulate!

Second, learning is about doing, and doing leads to learning. Learning is a change not only in understanding/meaning, it is a change in our capacity to do something with that enlarged understanding. This ability to "do" is called competence and "performance." Performance and understanding are intimately interconnected in a chicken-and-egg relationship. Doing and exploring expand the range of stimuli we encounter, and they also compel our brains to process what we're experiencing. The more active we are and the more we change the sensory patterns that the brain must process, the more it builds new connections and pathways, not only expanding our understanding but expanding our psycho-motor performance as well (see figure 2.1).

Just think about playing a musical instrument and you have the picture. There's a complex interrelationship among the notes on the page, the movement of the hands and fingers (and mouth and lips), and the sound that is the outcome. There's a constant assessment and feedback process going on that leads to changes in behavior and in understanding why those changes are necessary. Then put that instrumentalist in an ensemble in a performance hall or in a marching band doing maneuvers on a field where interaction with others intensifies the experience, and the complexity of the doing/assessing/understanding process gets enormous. The bottom line: thinking (i.e., abstract mental processing) is a very narrow slice of what learning is and a limited way of promoting it. Doing, on the other hand, is a tremendous catalyst for learning.

The Human Learning Process

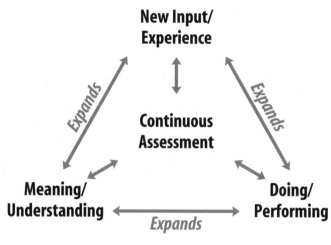

Figure 2.1

Third, new experience is the catalyst for developing both understanding and performance (as shown in figure 2.1). If the issue is *expanding* the brain's capacity to process and manage learning and performance—that is, "improving learning"—then the more new and stimulating experiences learners can have (in the most diverse ways of encountering them), and the earlier in life they can have them, the better. Brains/learners want stimulation, challenge, activity, and diversity of experiences, and enlightened learning systems must acknowledge and foster this inherent orientation. Having learners sitting in straight rows by themselves absorbing prescribed content for a narrow performance task is a severely constraining approach to human learning, and it's why so many learners instinctively resist or avoid it.

We need to bring this new research reality to our educational discussions by showing our colleagues and constituents figure 2.1 and developing strategies for ensuring that our learning system embodies a strong exploration/action/ performance orientation to instruction—which we'll more fully elaborate in chapter 11. And we'll need to continually remind them that right answers aren't the right answer to the human learning challenge.

Domains of Living

Although it is a truism that the main purpose of education is to prepare young people for "life," we'll be hard pressed to find a cogent framework about life and living underlying the curriculum designs or learning standards of very many U.S. districts. Philosophy statements, yes. Design frameworks, no. An applied life-performance curriculum, definitely not.

This reality struck us over a decade ago when pioneers in what was then called the Outcome-Based Education movement realized that education had neither any explicit outcomes about student competence *after* completing their studies nor a "bedrock" rationale for defining such abilities. "Outcomes" were simply "content objectives" about the curriculum that teachers were already addressing in their classes. But wait, we argued: If we want our young people to lead productive and fulfilling lives, wouldn't it be good for us to be clear about what life is all about so that they can better understand it and prepare for it?

That question eventually led us to develop an explicit design process for looking at life and the future. Over the years this comprehensive, systemic, future-focused process came to be called "Strategic Design," and it has been successfully employed in school districts of all kinds and sizes across the United States and Canada (see Schwahn and Spady 1998). The bedrock element in this process we called "Spheres of Living" (see Spady 1998d, 1998e). And we quickly found that with a little prompting the very large and diverse constituencies that were involved in these Strategic Design efforts could easily grasp and address this concept by answering minor variations on the following question: In what spheres of life and living do you want your children/students to be successful after finishing school?

The results of their answers in districts large and small from coast to coast formed quite consistent pictures of the spheres/areas/dimensions/domains of life that people felt were key to successful and fulfilling living. Over and over people came up with similar frameworks containing either seven or eight major spheres. So in the mid-nineties we consolidated all these local frameworks into a "composite example" that reflected almost every dimension that had surfaced in any particular setting. That composite was described in my book *Paradigm Lost* (Spady 1998d) and is shown in figure 2.2.

The figure portrays a set of eight intersecting circles intended to reflect the totally integrated nature of life, one for each sphere/domain. The diagram shows three key domains associated directly with the primarily inner functioning of the individual, and five other domains (resembling the petals of a flower) depicting her/his connections with others and the external environment. These eight widely endorsed domains are:

- Personal Potential and Wellness—Your inner essence, mind, and physical body are ever-present and define who you really are.
- Learning Challenges and Resources—Life is a continuous new experience that requires us to constantly assess, learn, and adapt.
- Life and Resource Management—Every day requires managing your food, shelter, time, finances, and relationships.
- Close and Significant Relationships—Nothing in life is more fulfilling than deep, caring connections with others.

Major Spheres/Domains of Living

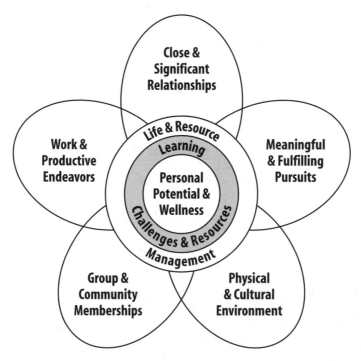

Figure 2.2

- Meaningful and Fulfilling Pursuits—People work for inspiration, satisfaction, self-expression, and self-actualization.
- Physical and Cultural Environment—Water, air, climate, scenery, food supply, congestion, media, people, and politics surround us.
- Group and Community Memberships—We're fundamentally members of social entities: families, organizations, communities, and so forth
- Work and Productive Endeavors—A key definer of our status is self-esteem, financial welfare, life-style, and capacity to contribute.

Once we develop a framework like this with our particular communities, we'll be equipped to ask the following challenging questions about the legalized and institutionalized curriculum structure we've had for a century:

- If these are the major domains of life and living in which we conduct our lives, why isn't our curriculum designed to extensively teach all our young people about them?

- How can we expect our learners to live fulfilling lives without a deep grasp of what life in these domains is really all about?
- How much better prepared for life would our young people be if these domains were the explicit substantive focus of the curriculum they regularly encountered?
- How much better would our learners understand and deal with themselves, others, and the world around them if our curriculum were structured around these domains of living?

With these four provocative questions as a backdrop, don't be surprised if your colleagues and constituents undertake a thorough examination of these major domains of living and begin raising enormous doubts about continuing to offer a curriculum consisting of four years of English, three years of math, and so on, complete with standardized tests to reinforce them.

Future Conditions

Another very key component of our Strategic Design Process for local districts is the concept of "future conditions." We define them as the problems, challenges, situations, and opportunities that lie on our horizons and with which we'll all need to engage and cope in order to flourish. The 1980s were filled with insightful books telling us that the future we faced wasn't going to be like "the good old days" we had experienced in our youth. The technological genie was out of the bottle, literally transforming the world of work and global economy, and there was no way to get him back in.

For us, these stark realities made four years of English, three years of math, etc., look like a pathetic approach to educational change, as do standardized test scores. We realized that any educational change effort that cares about the future success of its young people must explicitly be designed around *the future they face*, simply because the future is the *context* in which they must eventually apply their learning. The content they learn, the competences they develop, and the attributes and qualities they acquire will be useful to them to the extent that they directly apply to two key things: (1) the domains of living in which they'll be engaged; and (2) the challenges and circumstances they will likely encounter in those domains.

So from 1988 onward, our Strategic Design work has been generated off of one overriding question: *What will they face?* Some very compelling answers to this question are provided in *The Future Is Now* (Schwahn and Spady 2000). It is a thorough synthesis of dozens of major futurist books and reports over the past decade, and it suggests that we and our learners face:

- A *high-quality, global marketplace*, where, quality is an entrance, requirement, customers are king, quality and success are transitory, the world economy is seamless and doesn't rest, an "electronic herd" has unlimited Internet access and influence, even small "Mom and Pop" enterprises are directly affected by these global forces, China and the rest of Asia are coming full steam ahead, and enterprises do well by contributing to the greater good.

- *Transformational technologies* that are affecting and redefining every aspect of life and living—through almost universal access to the Internet, by making almost everything "e," by continuously refining interactive machines and tools that do increasingly sophisticated tasks at less and less cost, through on-demand interactive communications that make miles meaningless and paper disappear but that simultaneously render high-level thinking mandatory and ultimately leave us "e"-dependent.

- Adept *empowered employees in nimble organizations* will be the only long-term economic winners in a world where change is the only constant, mass customization is the key to survival, small is powerful because it enables you to adapt quickly . . . and the quick get richer faster, competence is capital, and knowledge is power, expert independent contractors will replace full-time employees as reliable sources of production, the economy runs on a twenty-four-hour-per-day cycle, seven days a week, and "value added" is the only criterion that fuels employment opportunities.

- The *virtual workplace* becomes the milieu of choice for those with the abilities and technological tools to create a work environment which operates anywhere at anytime on a schedule that suits them, enables the "techno-able" to "cocoon" their work and themselves in ideal life-style settings, encourages the creation of virtual organizations that exist and produce only through Internet connections, as well as short-term strategic alliances which form only to accomplish specific projects, and utilizes the power of transformational technologies to create "virtual everything," everywhere.

- *Transformational leadership* is at a premium—leadership that shapes purpose-, value-, and vision-driven change in continuously transforming organizations, where imagination and new possibilities are the gateway to the future, information is openly and widely shared, the "feminine factor" shapes more open and personal avenues of management and decision making, internal cooperation rather than competition characterizes organizational culture, genuinely empowered employees willingly and consistently produce to high levels, future-forecasting is a highly valued core competency across the organization, continuous personal and organizational learning is the norm—and the key to marketplace survival, and much more than formal training and technological expertise matters in work and living.

- A *stressed society* whose quality of life and stable fabric are being threatened by a population bomb placing excessive pressure on the planet's environment for improved standards of living, a maldistribution of wealth

and support as the rich get richer while the poor bear children in dispro-
portionate numbers, persistent class-based inequalities in education and
training that further widen the historical opportunity gap, paradigm paral-
ysis in education due to regressive accountability reforms that ignore
and/or disavow anything "new" or "progressive", intense pressure toward
individual responsibility by taxpayers tired of government "waste", a "gray-
ing of America" that shifts demands for public resources and services away
from the young toward the elderly, a diversification of America that will
shift the racial balance in U.S. schools to a non-Anglo majority by early in
the twenty-first century, and a political and cultural "center" disillusioned
by ideology-driven activists on the right, ethno-focused politics on the left,
and special interest campaign money flowing freely everywhere.

These conditions raise two profound questions that we'll continue to address
throughout the book:

1. What abilities will all our young people need for success as they face these
   incredibly challenging future conditions?
2. What must our learning system do to assure that all our learners are
   equipped to identify, face, and even shape these challenging realities successfully?

We'll be well advised to examine these future conditions in great depth and raise
these two questions repeatedly in our discussions about educational change.

Life Performance

Performance is about doing, and doing requires competence. Complex performances require complex competences, and "life performance" is about as
complex as it gets. Life performance requires more than specific skills for specific tasks. It requires complex combinations of skills and abilities called "role
performances"—being able to do the complex and open-ended things that real
people do in what are called "life roles," things like being an effective parent,
employee, entrepreneur, or citizen.

Role performers are people who can take a complex set of competences and
successfully apply them across a range of situations and settings—things we
called "performance contexts," like the domains of living and future conditions
just described. That, of course, takes lots of focused practice and experience,
something which requires years and years to develop, apply, and refine. This is
why our Strategic Design Process was ultimately focused on helping districts
derive a set of these role/life performance abilities.

Very simply, we recognized that if districts wanted their learners to be competent role performers equipped to meet the kinds of challenges described

above, both their teachers and their learners would need years and years to cultivate, practice, apply, and refine these complex abilities. And those abilities would need to be learned and practiced continuously across all kinds of learning areas, grade levels, and performance contexts. They weren't simple skills you could teach or learn from a textbook in a couple of weeks while sitting in a classroom seat.

Early in the nineties we developed a framework that began to capture the range of these role/life performance abilities needed in the various domains of living. That framework has evolved into the diagram shown in figure 2.3. We call it the Life Performance Wheel, and it's divided into two parts.

The upper part contains what Howard Gardner would call "interpersonal" role performers with a heavy dose of "intrapersonal" competence thrown in. Others might call them "right-brain" performers. They include listeners, communicators, leaders, organizers, mediators, negotiators, coaches, facilitators, advocates, and supporters. These are complex abilities you can't do by yourself or learn from a textbook or sitting at a computer console. Other people are required in both learning and carrying them out. And they can only be developed by having people interact on a continuing basis around what we call the "essential performance components" of each role.

The Life Performance Wheel

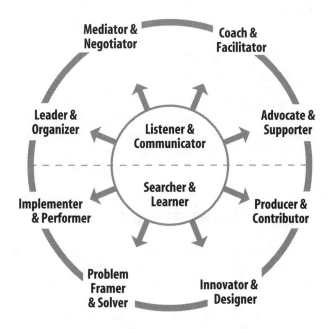

Figure 2.3

The lower part of the wheel contains what we call *technical/strategic role performers*. They are searchers, learners, implementers, performers, problem framers, problem solvers, innovators, designers, producers, and contributors. Developing those abilities requires that learners intensively engage with information, plans, tools, and tangible resources of all kinds. In real life they will sometimes be done solo and sometimes collaboratively. Notice that most of them have what psychologists would call a strong "left-brain" or rational character.

The wheel has enormous first-glance appeal to the thousands of parents, businesspeople, and educators who have seen it. Adults see themselves in its ten pairs of role performers and value its practicality and comprehensiveness for the real-world challenges they face every day. They can also see its enormous relevance to their children's lives. That's why people who've been involved in our Strategic Design Process and have seen some version or other of the wheel universally want learning outcomes for their schools that contain many of these same role performer abilities.

It's also significant that the wheel matches up extremely well with the findings in Daniel Goleman's blockbuster book *Working with Emotional Intelligence* (1998), mainly because his book summarizes the key findings in two hundred different studies on the factors that account for job and life success. These studies show that the kinds of IQ-related abilities in the bottom half of the wheel are key for getting people into their careers. But once there, the kinds of "emotional intelligence"-related abilities in the top of the wheel are critical for their advancement and ultimate success, both in their careers and in life. Clearly both halves of the wheel are necessary for developing what we'll call "total learners" and "total performers" in chapter 3, but Goleman shows that it's the top half that's really the key to life success.

With a framework and research base like this available to us, we're powerfully equipped to challenge the adequacy of test scores of any kind as indicators of a person's readiness for anything other than more schooling. In fact, we'll be able to easily convince our colleagues that no conventional paper-and-pencil test can adequately assess any of the life performance abilities in the wheel. So why are standardized tests driving today's reform policies?

EMBRACING THESE NEW RESEARCH REALITIES

From the beginning of chapter 1 to here, we've taken several huge steps in embracing the new research realities that surround but have yet to affect formal educational policies and change efforts. It's clear that 1983 was a pivotal year in our educational history and, in retrospect, an opportunity lost. The vast majority of educators and policy makers took the paved superhighway of traditional/educentric *Nation at Risk* thinking and practice that have become a dead-end road. State-driven accountability-based reforms are the destination reached by that road, and, as we'll see in chapter 6, we're truly "a nation at risk" for having taken that path.

But others of us were truly *in search of excellence* in 1983 and took the uncharted road with the inspiring and promising vistas. Along that road we discovered a host of new research realities—for example, that means are not ends; that the Industrial Age is over; that wide-band thinking opens up dramatically different possibilities for education; that many forms can serve the same function; that anyone can learn anything at anytime from anywhere if their paradigm is learning rather than schooling; that life and schooling are currently a universe apart; that the potential in our learners is diverse and enormous; that learning is synonymous with active creation; that the domains of living can become significant bases for designing and organizing curriculum; that the future offers both enormous challenges and the bedrock for redefining learner outcomes and curriculum; that life performance learning is our future and can't be taught or assessed by traditional methods; and, most of all, that if we designed a learning system around any one of these new research realities, let alone all of them, we'd *never* create the Model T schools we've inherited from 1893. It's now time for us to embrace and communicate these new bedrock realities with everyone we know who cares about America's future.

③

TOTAL LEARNING FOR TOTAL LIVING

How one learns determines how one lives, which determines how one learns, which determines how one lives . . . This unbroken circle of cause and effect enables us to see the direct parallel between living and learning. To enhance one is to enhance one's capacity to enhance the other.

The new paradigm thinking and realities of the foregoing chapters have opened up a range of exciting horizons for us to consider about the education we want for our children, our communities, and our world. We now recognize that any number of different starting points and strategies would lead us toward very different thinking about learners, learning, life, and education from that which now prevails in our Industrial Age schools. And we also see that if we started with any one of these perspectives or realities, we'd never create the schools we have today. We'd create something far more responsive to what we know about human potential, human learning, domains of living, future conditions, and life performance all rolled into one.

Well, let's devote a few moments to exploring just that possibility. What kind of learning system would we create if we used the best of all the insights we've gained so far but weren't constrained unnecessarily by them? What kind of learning model would exemplify the very best of what our deepest insights allow us to know and experience about human existence and progress? On what kind of foundation would we build that model? And if all we had were blank sheets of paper and our deepest desires for human civilization, what would we design? Here are some intuitive but enlightened guesses about how we'd respond to these four related questions.

First, we'd start with the most optimistic view we could about what makes us human and, therefore, what we'd most want to nurture and cultivate in our children. The most obvious thing that comes to mind is, in fact, *our mind*: This incredible capacity we have to perceive, comprehend, learn, reason, analyze, assess, interpret, organize, plan, predict, design, intuit, create, invent, perform, produce, and construct, and endless variations on these many abilities. Whatever these incredible cognitive/mental gifts are that we possess—whether we call them aptitudes, intelligences, potentials, or capacities—we'd want to identify and develop them to the fullest in all our children.

Second, we're likely to put on the table another fundamental set of human traits related to our ability to create and sustain bonds of affiliation and affection with each other, both as individuals and groups. We care, we relate, we interact, communicate, befriend, value, love, teach, mentor, partner, encourage, nurture, help, support, protect, and do a whole host of related things that enable us to establish close emotional connections and lasting social relationships with each other. Without this empathetic social capacity, stable relationships are not possible on any scale. Consequently, we'd want to nurture and expand these relational capacities in our children as much as we could.

Third, we'd almost immediately put on the table a fundamental reason for undertaking this exercise: our belief that learning/education is important to individuals because it improves, elevates, enhances, and directly contributes to the quality of life they will experience. In fact, if we examined this linkage closely enough, we'd discover that the two are actually inseparable. Learning, for example, is not just about absorbing content from printed material; it's an inherent part of living simply because living is a continuously unfolding array of new input and experiences—things that have to be assimilated, interpreted, and used in some useful way in order for one to function. Similarly, whatever one learns becomes a new resource for living—whether one chooses to live the same way or differently, "better" or "worse."

So if we only went this far in thinking about our ideal design, we'd already have enough to shape the foundation for an enlightening and empowering model of education. Here, in slightly different words, is what we've just established:

- Humans are inherently *conscious* creatures. When fully developed, this consciousness allows us to be aware of both our inner nature and the world around us. This awareness, in turn, enhances our capacity to choose: to be self-directed and "rational" in the choices we make, rather than habitually responsive to instinct or the dictates of others. Having choices and the conscious capacity to expand them is more empowering and fulfilling than not having them.
- Humans are inherently *creative* creatures. This creativity directly embodies and reflects our curiosity, imagination, inspiration, uniqueness, and individuality. It is the inner force that drives invention and change, and it is

expressed in a host of ways—from the things we say, do, and produce to the way we view situations to the way we dress and groom ourselves. In the absence of creativity there is standardization, sameness, rigidity, and tedium.

- Humans are inherently *collaborative* creatures. This powerful interpersonal orientation is the key to everything from the intellectual and emotional development of young children to the creation of stable family structures to the forging of civilizations. We seek loving, caring, affirming contact with others, and in developing that contact us enhance our social skills, develop a sense of self, and learn that these same qualities must be reciprocated for relationships to work.

- Humans inherently seek to be *competent* creatures because environmentally linked skills and abilities are preconditions for personal and societal survival. From effective communication to acquiring food and shelter, to maintaining health, to managing possessions and resources, to executing complex skills, to using tools and technologies, to producing valued products, to providing complex services, competence is a prerequisite to successful living.

- Humans overwhelmingly seek to be *constructive*, for without the positive contributions that we make to each other and the "greater good," the quality and integrity of the environment, society, and culture in which we live would ultimately erode. So to "humanely" enhance and sustain the quality of life and living around them, we willingly care, give, share, invest, contribute, support, safeguard, build, advocate, defend, protect, and even sacrifice—all to benefit something greater than ourselves.

- How one learns determines how one lives, which determines how one learns, which determines how one lives. . . . This unbroken circle of cause and effect enables us to see the direct parallel between living and learning. To enhance one is to enhance one's capacity to enhance the other. Said differently: The richer one's experiences in one arena, the richer one's experiences are likely to be in the other. So if we design education with enlightened, empowering living in mind, it will need to address and cultivate those very qualities in our learners.

- Putting all of the foregoing together leads us to a model of Total Living composed of five essential components: conscious living, creative living, collaborative living, competent living, and constructive living. In the absence of one or more of these components, it's difficult to imagine someone experiencing authentic joy, love, and fulfillment. What's needed to directly support these five conditions? A model of Total Learning composed of conscious learning, creative learning, collaborative learning, competent learning, and constructive learning.

Notice, we started with a view of human potential but quickly linked it to the domains of living and life performance, and before we knew it, we'd also affirmed the nature of human learning. We discovered that humans as a species inherently bring two things to their life experience: thinking and feeling. As they interact with their environment and each other, they're compelled to translate these "inner," conscious capacities into tangible action. So they creatively invent and innovate, collaboratively interact and partner, competently perform and produce, and constructively contribute and support—simply because these four arenas of action are fundamental to making their lives work, have value, and feel meaningful.

Does designing a model of education around these five essentials of the human experience seem too bold, or idealistic, or abstract, or unattainable? It shouldn't if we remember that this is an opportunity to create our future—to clearly express the best of what human existence and progress offer us and our deepest desires for human civilization. This model isn't about school subjects and grade levels, it's about the realities surrounding learners, learning, and life and the new-paradigm vision of education these realities engender.

THE TOTAL LEARNING/TOTAL LIVING FRAMEWORK

We have found it useful to portray the five parallel domains of the Total Learning and Total Living models as a framework that displays the relationships among these domains. That picture is represented in figure 3.1. At the center of this figure lies conscious learning and living, what we earlier called the mind,

The Domains of Total Learning and Living

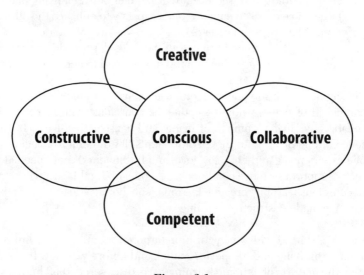

Figure 3.1

awareness, cognitive, and mental attributes of human nature. Everything emanates from this profound perceptive capacity.

The other four components of the model are portrayed in the other sectors of the diagram, which are organized along a vertical and a horizontal axis. The vertical axis reflects the key "productive" aspects of strategic/technical human potential. The *creative* domain at the top of the figure allows us to explore, invent, and express new possibilities for action, while the *competent* domain at the bottom allows us to convert those possibilities into concrete results. This axis relates quite closely to the bottom half of the Life Performance Wheel in chapter 2 and to what Daniel Goleman calls the "IQ and technical skills" aspects of human performance.

The horizontal axis of the diagram represents the key "relational" aspects of social/interpersonal human potential. The *collaborative* domain on the right side of the diagram allows us to affiliate and connect deeply and compatibly with other individuals, while the *constructive* domain on the left allows us to channel our empathy and caring into directly providing benefit or service to the greater human good. This axis relates quite closely to the top half of the Life Performance Wheel and to what Goleman calls the "emotional intelligence" dimension of human performance.

So Total Living is about continuously nurturing and expanding our capacity for conscious thought and for channeling, expressing, and applying it positively in both the productive and relational arenas of life. What, then, is the larger purpose of this ideal educational model that we're creating? To equip, empower, and enable all our learners to "live totally" in tomorrow's challenging world! And what will it take to acquire these capacities? Learning experiences that directly enhance, facilitate, and strengthen each of these domains—experiences we call conscious learning, creative learning, collaborative learning, competent learning, and constructive learning.

The Essence of Conscious Living: Mindfully Developing and Directing Our Inner Essence and Potential

The word *conscious* means "mindful." Together these two words fundamentally represent the perceptiveness, openness, attentiveness, sensitivity, thoughtfulness, consideration, reflection, identity, values, spirituality, commitment to growth, and attention to deeper purpose and meaning that characterize the inner essence of deeply aware people. When allowed to operate fully, this inner awareness—or consciousness—enables us to experience life and all it has to offer in great depth and allows us to choose the kind of experiences we seek.

This is why some psychologists say that fully conscious people are "at choice"—because they are completely aware of the range of options and choices open to them. And it's why they describe so many others as being "stuck on automatic"—because they *un*-consciously and impulsively react to situations as if only one choice or course of action exists. Clearly, then, conscious living is an essential to Total Living because without it life becomes little more than an externally defined, materialistic, unfulfilling, and sometimes frenetic search for personal value, status, meaning, and joy.

Conscious living is a matter of viewing every experience as an opportunity for learning and growth, for enlarging one's understanding, for assessing its potential value in one's life, for considering new possibilities, for reflecting on its deeper meaning and significance, for further expanding one's awareness, and for sharpening one's identity and sense of self. Those who live consciously have nothing to "prove" to others because they fully understand and accept who they are in their own right. They know and value their unique strengths, openly acknowledge their limitations, and neither shoot from the hip nor demean others to inflate their own status. This allows them to comfortably "walk their talk," "talk their walk," and operate in fully ethical ways.

Because of these deeply "authentic" qualities, conscious people attract others to themselves like magnets and counterbalance the materialistic and competitive nature of today's world. No wonder we strongly desire these qualities in ourselves, admire them in others, and seek to cultivate them in our children.

The Essence of Creative Living: Openly Exploring and Expressing Life's Boundless Possibilities

Creative living is what allows individuals and societies to evolve and develop. It is both the source and expression of our curiosity, imagination, invention, and intense desire as a species to explore, innovate, and experience the new and unknown. Unless we live creatively, life becomes little more than an inflexible, constraining, repressive array of repetitive experiences with no higher stimulation, vision, or promise of change.

Those who live creatively approach life with the expectation that they can make something unique and interesting out of every experience. They freely use their imaginations in confronting new situations, they think and act outside the box of convention and conformity, and they consistently entertain and explore possibilities that lie beyond the obvious. Their insatiable and undaunted curiosity about life and new discoveries gives them a unique perspective on how life could be if we'd only consider. . . .

Creative living is synonymous with childhood. The attributes of imagination, innovation, originality, exploration, freshness, and invention that children bring to their lives are powerful assets in a world of continuous discovery and constant change for they allow us to anticipate, shape, and deal constructively with things that are unanticipated or new. To live creatively is to view and address issues, decisions, and circumstances with a strong focus on the future and on what could be, rather than on what has been. And it's also about looking beyond conventional understandings to show the unexplored avenues one might take in the face of challenging situations. In short, creative living continuously expands our horizons and vision of the possible and is an essential in today's rapidly changing world.

The Essence of Collaborative Living: Deeply Connecting with Others to Share Common Experiences

Collaborative living is the wellspring of emotional development, human bonding, and the formation of stable and constructive social units. It is both the source and expression of our deeply felt sense of connection, belonging, loyalty, and love toward others. Collaborative living is essential to Total Living because without it life can be little more than an isolated, alienating, often hostile, and indifferent array of experiences with no trust, love, celebration, or deeper emotional expression.

Everything that we idealize about acceptance, friendship, teamwork, trustworthiness, love, emotional bonding, and loyalty are played out in this essential domain of living. Those who live collaboratively are intensely people-oriented and are masters of interpersonal relationships, the second of the two major domains of emotional intelligence as defined by Goleman. Their decisions are based on the role and active involvement of others because inclusion and close interpersonal/emotional connection and support are extremely important to them. They deliberately interact with others in ways that encourage everyone to share openly and equitably in experiences and the benefits they hold, and they listen actively in all face-to-face interactions, allowing the other parties to fully convey their meaning and intent before responding.

Their win-win orientation to life is reflected in their willingness to (1) carry out their responsibilities as team members conscientiously and fully, and to actively support other team members in carrying out theirs; (2) share pertinent information and ideas openly with others to facilitate and support clear communication and sound decision making; and (3) take the interests and viewpoints of others fully into account in carrying out common endeavors. It's clear that these qualities and abilities counterbalance the often frenetic and impersonal conditions in today's world. And it's no wonder that they are attributes we strongly desire in ourselves, admire in others, and seek to cultivate in our children.

The Essence of Competent Living: Directly Crafting Understanding and Skills into Positive Results

Competent living is synonymous with and essential to the productive functioning and effectiveness of all human endeavors and organizations. It is both the source and expression of our capacity to carry out life's essential roles skillfully and to produce what is needed to sustain and advance our personal and societal welfare. Competent learning is essential to Total Living because without it life becomes little more than a struggle for survival among people with limited skill, understanding, or the ability to function effectively in the world they face.

At their essence, those who fully embody competent living are masters of setting and achieving high expectations, of translating those expectations into attainable standards, and in setting an example of skill and productivity that others can emulate. They are thorough, industrious, reliable, and committed to excellence. Those in careers stand out as experts. Because they value quality and excellence, they view both learning and life as ongoing opportunities to achieve goals, be productive, and make a difference.

Competent life performers diligently (1) apply both their natural talents and learned skills to everything they undertake; (2) use the highest standards and most advanced methods to accomplish projects successfully within agreed upon time constraints; and (3) devote time and energy to updating themselves on the information and skills needed for performing at their best. It's clear that these are essential attributes and abilities in today's global economy where quality is an entrance requirement and success can be fleeting. That's why the ability to perform Competently is something we strongly desire in ourselves, admire in others, and seek to cultivate in our children.

The Essence of Constructive Living: Fully Sharing My Best to Enhance the Greater Good

Constructive living is the pathway to individuals and societies becoming truly "civilized"—that is, where one's endeavors are positive, useful, and valuable to others. It is both the source and expression of our desire to make the world a better place by freely and selflessly sharing what we have—time, talent, insight, resources, compassion—to enhance the well-being of others, the space we occupy, the environment on which we depend, and the quality of life we experience. Constructive living is essential to Total Living because without it life becomes little more than an individualistic pursuit of personal gain, status, and advantage with no regard for its impact on others or the welfare of humankind.

Those who live constructively operate from a bedrock of compassion and caring about the condition of the world, give full attention to significant problems and their long-term consequences, and clearly demonstrate a commitment to enhancing the ultimate welfare of things beyond themselves. They steadfastly advocate for those without a voice, conscientiously address complex problems, patiently facilitate difficult changes, and always show deep empathy toward what people are facing but "hang tough" when the going gets that way. When in leadership positions they are masters of "doing the heavy lifting"—getting the difficult organizational, resource, procedural, political, and personal obstacles out of the way so that things can be or operate better.

It's clear that these are essential attributes and abilities in a world awash in personal, collective, and national insecurity and self-interest. But it's also clear that the compassion that underlies them has a deeper meaning here than simply "wearing your heart on your sleeve." It's about fundamentally seeing your own status as interdependently related to that of others, where to diminish another is to diminish yourself, and to enhance another is to enhance yourself. These deeply humane qualities exemplify what we strongly desire in ourselves, admire in others, and seek to cultivate in our children.

THE ESSENCE OF TOTAL LEARNING

Total Learning is the vehicle we can use to develop in our children the qualities and abilities needed for Total Living in today's extremely challenging world. As we noted earlier, conscious learning fosters conscious living, creative learning promotes creative living, and so forth. What remains is for us to capture the essence of what we need to address in each domain of the framework and to design our learning system to directly develop each essence in every learner. The template for this design is presented in figure 3.2.

As we can quickly see in the figure, the names and locations of the Total Learning domains remain the same as they were in figure 3.1. We've simply added a definitive descriptor to each label indicating what the purpose, focus,

The Essence of Total Learning

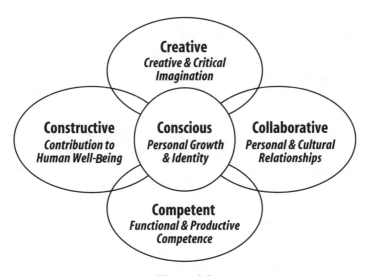

Figure 3.2

or essence of each domain is. We'll look very briefly at each domain in order to consolidate our thinking about what we should do to facilitate this particular kind of learning and living.

Conscious Learning: Personal Growth and Identity

The essence of conscious learning involves personal growth and identity. The instructional strategies needed to support this essence should broaden and deepen learners' awareness of the gifts and potential that lie within them and the unique identity they possess. These strategies should (1) encourage learners to directly explore, develop, use, and affirm all of the capabilities and qualities that lie within them; (2) challenge them to stretch their capabilities in a supportive, low-risk environment; and (3) encourage them to openly acknowledge and affirm the new awareness and capabilities they develop. These affirmations reinforce their learning and deepen their sense of who they really are and what they're capable of contributing to the world.

Consciousness develops when awareness increases, and awareness is fostered when learners continuously assess the nature, meaning, impact, and implications of all new learning and experiences; reflect deeply on those factors; and confirm their significance in their own growth and development. What really happened? Who or what did it affect? What does it mean for me? How does it change me and my understanding of myself? What can I constructively do with this new awareness? What could have been different that would have helped me learn more? These and related questions lie at the heart of the experience/assess/reflect/affirm cycle that strengthens the growth of conscious learners.

Creative Learning: Creative and Critical Imagination

The essence of creative learning involves the development and use of learners' creative and critical imaginations. The factors that foster this essence are: unbounded opportunities to explore, a rich array of resources to explore with, and a set of provocative/challenging questions to address and attempt to answer. The emphasis in this approach is on discovering new possibilities about things that are known and things that are unknown. What is this all about? How does it work? What if this part were missing? What are three better ways of designing this? And on and on.

The key to this process is to tap learners' curiosity and engage them in looking beyond and beneath what's on the surface, stepping beyond routine approaches and conventional models, discovering hidden causes and principles, and exploring how things could work if they weren't defined or put together the normal way. This arena is also where learners can give full expression to ideas, images, and products that embody and reflect their uniqueness, originality, individuality, and deeper essence: who I really am made manifest!

Collaborative Learning: Personal and Cultural Relationships

The essence of collaborative learning involves developing and sustaining personal and cultural relationships that mutually benefit all parties. There are four keys to this process, and each needs to be carried out with great sensitivity. First, learners need experiences that help them see the difference between "personality," motivation, and self-interest on the one hand and roles, role play, and role responsibilities on the other. This enables them to differentiate between personal interests and agendas of various kinds and the explicit expectations and obligations associated with a role. Second, they need extensive guided role-playing experiences, with different expectation, status, responsibility, and interaction parameters built into their roles. This enables them to step out of subjective self into a more objective view of what makes interactions work.

Third, they need a great deal of guided practice in providing and receiving assessments of their different role performances, with an eye to helping them develop criteria and examples of what does and doesn't work in communicating, setting expectations, and interacting in various ways. This "safe" feedback is critical in enabling them to develop a picture of how others see them, what others expect in interactions of various kinds, and how they can improve difficult or problematic aspects of their interactions. Finally, they need a great deal of experience occupying the different roles in working teams and applying the skills developed in the two prior phases of this process. While this process may seem formal and unrelated to "personal attraction" kinds of relationships, it benefits the expectations, communication, and reciprocity aspects of all types of relationships.

Competent Learning: Functional and Productive Competence

The essence of competent learning involves the development and refinement of a range of functional and productive competences. As we'll see later in the chapter, these competences can apply to a wide range of endeavors utilizing the broad diversity of talents and abilities inherent in all of us. The keys to developing them are familiar to anyone who's been involved in technical- or performance-based education of any kind.

Very simply: Learners need clear and realistic standards, expectations, and criteria to work toward; appropriate tools, technologies, and resources to work with; lots of modeling, coaching, and mentoring to establish a sense of what quality and success look like; lots of guided and independent practice; timely, targeted, nonjudgmental feedback on their performance; opportunities to make mistakes as they learn and not be penalized for them; and authentic audiences in a variety of settings and contexts in which to demonstrate what they can do. But most of all they need the encouragement to *try* and to *do*—in all kinds of performance areas with all kinds of technologies and techniques, whether sophisticated computers or hammers and nails. Doing is invaluable!

Constructive Learning: Contribution to Human Well-Being

And so is giving—of time, energy, and talent—to benefit the quality of life of those with less time, energy, resources, or talent. Yes, the essence of constructive learning involves contribution to human well-being—making the world a better place because of what you've done and whose lives you've touched. The process here is simple. Educators need to structure learning opportunities that enable learners to be of service to others in connection with building their conscious, creative, collaborative, and competent abilities. This can take the form of anything ranging from one-on-one assistance of some kind to other learners to large individual or team projects that require extensive planning, design, coordination, implementation, and evaluation in real-world settings dealing with real-world issues.

The difference between a constructive "project" and constructive learning can be considerable, however, if specific goals and expectations aren't set, new learning isn't required, and self-assessment isn't structured into the endeavor. Part of the benefit of this process, like that in conscious learning, is the awareness and affirmation that come from formally, deliberately carrying out a sharing experience, assessing its impact, reflecting on the assessment evidence, and formally affirming the difference that you made. This is not to chalk up "Brownie points," but to internalize the notion that conscious, creative, collaborative, and competent learning can be shallow without the constructive connection. Contribution is the real bottom line of one's learning and abilities, and the more one contributes, the more natural and effortless it becomes.

TOTAL LEARNING POTENTIAL

If we're going to develop the Total Learning abilities of all of our learners and realize the essence of each Total Learning component, then we'll need to take the potential, aptitudes, intelligences, and capacities of our learners into account as well. Why? Simply because learning success ultimately starts and ends with the interests, aptitudes, and experiences that the individual learner brings to the table.

In chapter 2 we described Howard Gardner's pioneering work on multiple intelligences—our diverse capacities to perceive, process, and/or perform things in our lives rapidly and adeptly. Gardner explains that this perceive/process/perform cycle operates in at least seven other ways *besides* the linguistic and logical-mathematical—the bedrock of academic education and IQ measures. He calls these others spatial, musical, interpersonal, intrapersonal, bodily-kinesthetic, naturalist, and "esoteric."

Regardless of what they're called, we want to probe more fully into the abilities that really help some people be good at what they do in the broad range of things that constitute successful and fulfilling living. There are certainly more of these aptitudes than Gardner's nine. In fact, the following list includes twenty-five, some of which are more-detailed dimensions of his broad categories. They're presented in random order to illustrate their variety and range. Feel free to take up the challenge and add even more. The twenty-five are:

- Visionary/Anticipatory: Wayne Gretsky always skated to where the puck was going to be—the master of applying cause and effect.
- Kinesthetic/Physical: Just watch the Olympics or the NBA and marvel at the coordination.
- Recall/Associative: It makes you a big winner on game shows and Game Boys.
- Musical/Auditory: From carrying a tune to writing a symphony, life is sound, rhythms, tone colors, and harmonies.
- Strategic/Systemic: Seeing the big picture and how all the parts move and relate.
- Functional/Operational: "Jack be nimble" with the keyboard, joy stick, levers, tools, buttons, knobs, keys, pedals, wheels, latches . . . .
- Verbal/Communicative: Words create meaning, wars, poems, relationships, joy, and civilization. Don't leave home without them.
- Empathetic/Supportive: Being there fully when the need is greatest, with nothing to gain but your humanity.
- Intuitive/Psychic: Tapping into thoughts and energies that most people ignore.
- Logical/Organizational: The Federal Aviation Agency and FBI Lab want *you*!
- Tactile/Sensory: Experienced massage therapists thrive on it, and the blind read this way.
- Visual/Observational: What do artists, pilots, detectives, astronomers, film directors, and athletes all have in common?
- Openness/Receptivity: Stop, look, listen, and park your ego on the siding.
- Gastronomic/Olfactory: Where cats have it all over people who thrive on fast food.
- Attentiveness/Caring: That glint in the street as you walked by could have been some motorist's nightmare. But now it's in the trash bin.
- Imaginative/Creative: It's noon and you've already thought of six ways to improve the new product your boss announced at nine.
- Social/Affiliative: What? There are people out there who like to do things *alone*?
- Technical/Mechanical: Some people can build or fix anything . . . and it stays built and fixed.
- Interpretive/Diagnostic: In a flash you read between the lines, see the pattern in the chaos, and spot the hidden meanings and agendas.
- Spatial/Relational: Your sales team has just landed in a strange city, and they already know who should drive and who should navigate.
- Selfless/Altruistic: You're the first to volunteer, you carry the heaviest load, and you stay until the lights are out and the door is locked.

- Conceptual/Analytical: Turning information into knowledge, raw data into discoveries, and routine matters into rare insights.
- Mathematical/Quantitative: You just got admitted to MIT and have never used a calculator like your teachers and peers did.
- Representational/Expressive: Translating internal experiences into compelling words, pictures, shapes, sounds, movements . . . .
- Humor/Novelty: Here's tonight's Top Ten List on how to keep the world honest . . . and improve its mental health at the same time.

Clearly this is an expansive array of human potential—capacities to perceive what is happening within and around us, to process it both consciously and subconsciously, and to translate that psychological processing into valued action. Remove any of them from this "starter set" and you diminish our picture of what it means to be human and to develop ourselves "totally."

Let's look at how this array of potentials relates to the five domains of Total Learning, recognizing that some kinds of potential are not limited to a single domain but manifest along the entire vertical or horizontal dimension of the diagram in figure 3.2. It will be simpler to deal first with the outside sectors of the diagram and work our way back to its center.

Creative Potential

Four of the twenty-five potentials just seem to leap into this domain:

- Visionary/Anticipatory
- Strategic/Systemic
- Imaginative/Creative
- Humor/Novelty

Each is about seeing into or beyond what is given in a situation in new, original, expansive, or unconventional ways—seeing novelty or potential that is not immediately obvious. Three other potentials share this essence as well:

- Interpretive/Diagnostic
- Representational/Expressive
- Conceptual/Analytical

They too take information, ideas, possibilities, and feelings and give them unique expression and form—truly creating meanings and things that didn't exist before. Similarly, aspects of Musical/Auditory, Verbal/Communicative, Visual/Observational, Gastronomic/Olfactory, and Technical/Mechanical also fit here because each is a "medium" for channeling one's creative potential.

Since nearly half of these twenty-five potentials can be used as vehicles to enhance our learners' creative and critical imaginations, we clearly enjoy a huge opportunity here for developing every learner's creative potential.

Collaborative Potential

Here too there are potentials that virtually leap into this domain of learning. The most obvious of them are:

- Verbal/Communicative
- Social/Affiliative

Both are strong components of what both Gardner and Goleman call interpersonal intelligence. But at least four others come into play as factors affecting genuinely collaborative relations with others:

- Empathetic/Supportive
- Attentiveness/Caring
- Openness/Receptivity
- Selfless/Altruistic

And all four of these easily group into what Gardner and Goleman would agree is intrapersonal intelligence.

Since six of these twenty-five potentials can be used as vehicles to enhance our learners' personal and cultural relationships, we clearly enjoy a genuine opportunity here for developing every learner's collaborative potential.

Competent Potential

The heart of competent learning is the execution of skills that enable tangible products or results to emerge. Five of the twenty-five potentials gravitate directly into this domain:

- Kinesthetic/Physical
- Representational/Expressive
- Functional/Operational
- Spatial/Relational
- Technical/Mechanical

Five others clearly have a performance or production aspect to them that fit congenially here as well. They include:

- Musical/Auditory
- Visual/Observational
- Verbal/Communicative
- Gastronomic/Olfactory
- Tactile/Sensory

Since ten of these twenty-five potentials can be used as vehicles to enhance our learners' functional and productive competence, we clearly enjoy a major opportunity here for developing every learner's competent potential.

Constructive Potential

Three of the four potentials that help support collaborative learning represent the heart of this category:

- Empathetic/Supportive
- Attentiveness/Caring
- Selfless/Altruistic

All three are profoundly intrapersonal in nature and embody what's commonly called considerate, conscientious, decent, admirable, generous, caring, humane behavior. There are supporting potentials in this domain as well:

- Visionary/Anticipatory
- Strategic/Systemic
- Openness/Receptivity

Those who are instinctively open, who look ahead, and who see the big picture are much more likely to recognize (1) the ultimate interdependence of individuals, groups, and nations across the globe; and (2) that ignoring others' welfare will ultimately jeopardize one's own.

Since six of these twenty-five potentials can be used as vehicles to enhance our learners' contribution to human well-being, we clearly enjoy a genuine opportunity here for developing every learner's constructive potential.

Conscious Potential

At its heart, conscious potential is about how we continuously and mindfully perceive and process our experiences. It's about what we bring into our awareness and how we process what's there. At one level, then, all twenty-five potentials fit that description, which leaves us back at square one. But we can frame this domain by distinguishing between potentials that embody "thought" and those that reflect our basic senses—hearing, touch, sight, and smell/taste. There are five of the latter, and they belong in this category:

- Musical/Auditory
- Verbal/Communicative
- Tactile/Sensory
- Visual/Observational
- Gastronomic/Olfactory

They're important because they're fundamental to basic life functioning.

But so are the highly diverse range of nine potentials called "thinking." As you read through this list, note how differently people function intellectually depending on which of these potentials is stronger or more latent:

- Recall/Associative
- Visionary/Anticipatory
- Strategic/Systemic
- Intuitive/Psychic
- Logical/Organizational

- Imaginative/Creative
- Interpretive/Diagnostic
- Conceptual/Analytical
- Mathematical/Quantitative

And what may be the triggering agent for all of them is:

- Openness/Receptivity

For without Openness, not much "gets through" or "comes up" to be processed via any kind of thinking potential.

There's clearly a huge opportunity here for developing the conscious potential of our young people since on the surface fifteen of the twenty-five potentials can be used as vehicles to enhance their personal growth and identities. But we'd be wise to proceed with caution because not all potentials are created equal when it comes to inner consciousness. Better that we focus on Openness/Receptivity, Intuitive/Psychic, Imaginative/Creative, and Interpretive/Diagnostic and cast the others in supporting roles.

A Skeptical Aside

So here we are with at least twenty-five different potentials that young people bring with them to school. Which of them is unequivocally encouraged and developed by Standards-Based Reforms? Two are unconditional winners:

- Recall/Associative
- Mathematical/Quantitative

Six others appear to be conditional winners because at least some (fairly narrow) aspect of them is demanded or cultivated by the standards, even though large aspects are ignored or suppressed. These conditionals are:

- Visionary/Anticipatory
- Verbal/Communicative
- Logical/Organizational

- Visual/Observational
- Spatial/Relational
- Conceptual/Analytical

That leaves seventeen of these twenty-five potentials either totally ignored or suppressed in the recent reform push. That's not saying much for a country that claims to be the most advanced on the planet.

TOWARD A TOTAL LEARNING COMMUNITY

The ideas in this chapter are natural extensions of the new-paradigm thinking addressed in chapter 1 and the five new research realities described in chapter 2. We've simply put them in a coherent framework here that links learning, living, and human potential. If this integrated framework seems exciting and worthy of widespread development, it is. If it also seems far removed from what we recognize as "the realities of schooling," it is; and the next three chapters will make this contrast look even more extreme.

When we finish looking at the deeper realities of our prevailing system in chapters 4 and 5 and its reinforcing reforms in chapter 6, we will truly stand at a crossroads. One of our key choices at that point can be to declare the foregoing too idealistic and dismiss it. Our other choice is to recognize its intrinsic power and develop it into a new model of education. Those willing to consider this latter choice, even tentatively, will have the opportunity to see a new template unfold in chapter 7, a template organized around five compelling standards that will enable us to directly apply the ideas from many enlightened sources into what we call a Total Learning Community (TLC).

Then it will be a matter of taking the five visionary steps needed for creating a TLC, one critical component at a time. When we're finished, we'll have a culture of Total Professionalism, a foundation of insight and inquiry, a framework of life performance learning essentials, a system of empowering learning experiences, and a strategy for mobilizing the resources that support learning—all in one integrated, seamless, fully aligned model.

Why is this so "visionary"? Because TLCs embody a major paradigm shift; and, as futurist Joel Barker reminds us, when paradigms shift, "everything goes back to zero." Total Learning Communities create a new future for education, and once we discover what they entail in chapters 7 through 12, we won't be able to go back to "school" again and accept what we see as legitimate. You'll see. Just turn the page.

DROWNING IN
OLD-PARADIGM INERTIA

*The form that "school" takes is an educentric iceberg . . . floating in a
sea of ingrained practices and outdated policies. It is this iceberg that
has been institutionalized by educators, legalized by policy makers,
internalized by parents and the public, and reinforced by the press
and media over the past several generations until it has produced the
literally unchangeable educational system we have today.*

For three chapters we've been exploring new paradigms, realities, and models
that have inspired us to view, describe, and create education in an enlightened,
learner-empowering way. But our pathway to a world where learners mean
more than procedures and precedents has its obstacles and perils, and they
compel us to take nothing for granted.

As we think about our own children we can recognize in them many forms of
human potential described in chapters 2 and 3. And we've watched them go
through the human learning process and develop many of the abilities in the Life
Performance Wheel. And we've done our best to prepare them for the domains of
living and the future conditions that await them. And most of all, we've resonated
with the authenticity of the Total Learning for Total Living model, holding it as a
standard for their continued development and fulfillment as well as our own.

What we most want to do is "get on with it" and create a learning system, large
or small, that brings all of these elements to fruition. Before doing that, however,
we must recognize that we face a choice about which route to take to make this vision real. One choice sounds like: "Let's take these ideas and create our own learning community now. We'll easily be able to find others to join us." The other

sounds like: "Let's use these ideas to transform the system we have because it's its only hope for the country's long-term survival. Without an enlightened and empowering public system, we will Balkanize our society even more than it is."

If the first choice is where you are, then you may not find this and the next two chapters your highest priority. Nonetheless, please read them because they reveal the deeper and darker side of the structural properties that get built into educational systems. These properties determine the conditions that the individuals in the system, both educators and students, must deal with, whether they choose to or not. No matter how personalized and humane we try to make a system, it is a system nonetheless; and systems have their boundaries, requirements, regularities, and quirks. So let's use these next three chapters as guidance for what to avoid at all costs in creating our ideal learning system.

But if the second choice is where you are, then brace yourselves for an even deeper look at the inertia we must redirect if we hope to succeed in taking education down the new-paradigm path described in the foregoing chapters. Keep in mind that this is the paradigm of school that our society has institutionalized, legalized, internalized, and reinforced for a century. And, like it or not, it's become *the* way of viewing and doing education in America.

OUR EDUCENTRIC ICEBERG

In the introduction, we began to explore the territory of school in order to prepare ourselves for the challenge of changing it into a different kind of environment. Then in chapter 1 we began to see more of its archaic, closed-system character and the inertial political and institutional forces that keep it in place. Fortunately, we recognized that it didn't have to be the way it was, and chapters 2 and 3 convinced us of it. But in 1983, hordes of influential people chose for this outmoded paradigm of schooling to continue in its present form, even when exciting new-paradigm choices were available.

Now, in 2001, this outdated systemic model is literally being frozen into place for another generation of educators and learners by zealous state reformers who are quite at home with it. As we'll now see, the form that school takes is an "educentric iceberg" (see figure 4.1) floating in a sea of ingrained practices and outdated policies. It is this iceberg that has been institutionalized by educators, legalized by policy makers, internalized by parents and the public, and reinforced by the press and media over the past several generations until it has produced the literally unchangeable educational system we have today.

Notice that the iceberg in the figure has five levels. As we descend into its depths, each layer represents a historical period older than the others. At the top, where 10 percent is exposed to today's winds of change, we find the realities and challenges of the Information Age future conditions that we examined in chapter 2. Below the surface, sheltered from these winds of change and In-

Our Educentric Iceberg

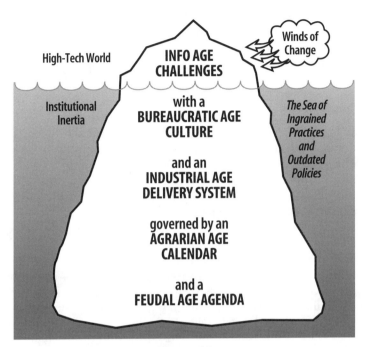

Figure 4.1

formation Age realities, are the iceberg's means-driven Bureaucratic Age culture, which rests on its Model T Industrial Age delivery system, which, in turn, is governed by its 1893 Agrarian Age calendar.

At its base, supporting and influencing everything is the iceberg's Feudal Age agenda—its philosophy of grading, labeling, and sorting students; giving them different kinds of opportunities to advance; and selecting the most able or advantaged for high status by offering them superior credentials and access to more elite educational opportunities. It is there that we must start if we want to more fully understand the territory of schooling and the challenge of change we face, because the thinking, beliefs, and realities of our Feudal Age past are very much alive and well in today's society, schools, and reforms.

OUR FEUDAL AGE AGENDA

The Feudal Age in Europe laid the groundwork for today's advanced societies and institutions. Its key feature: huge differences in the status, wealth, rights, and privileges of various classes or castes of people. In their day these classes were called lords and serfs. We know them today as the *haves* and the have nots. Paradoxically, these major class and wealth divisions either did not exist or were minimized in more tribal and communal forms of society that many First World people today regard as primitive. Is this a way of saying that advanced societies are advanced because they create larger status differences among their members? That thought probably makes all of us rather uncomfortable.

Grounding Beliefs

The tool that Feudal Age societies used to legitimate and reinforce these huge differences in status, opportunity, and, eventually, education was a belief system which asserted that:

1. These differences are part of the natural order of the world and divinely ordained: God wants you to have the status you have.
2. Status, wealth, opportunity, and benefit are in scarce supply, so it will be the fate of some to do without.
3. Those commodities in scarcest supply should go to those with the greatest natural claim on them, as determined by the resources they can marshal to acquire them—education being one of those resources.
4. It is the individual's responsibility to acquire whatever status, wealth, or benefit he can from this natural order of things, because it is also natural that men, being the stronger and more able sex, determine things for their families.

In short, Feudal Age thinking held that life is a competitive struggle, and those with the resources to compete successfully and come out ahead have the natural and legitimate right to capture the prize. Those who lose are obligated to continue struggling, no matter what the odds, because the natural order of things can't be changed and struggle is part of it.

Today that's described as a "Life is hell, and then you die" outlook. Sociologists and philosophers call this pattern of social relations "social Darwinism": competition for scarce resources and survival. Its other popular label is "survival of the fittest," which, paradoxically, biologists now see as the "survival of the most adaptable." Maybe there's a lesson here that hasn't been widely grasped yet.

Nonetheless, since the Feudal Age, the names and details have changed but not this fundamental system of beliefs. Here we are hundreds of years later in what we regard as advanced, modern societies, having institutionalized, legalized, internalized, and reinforced this scarcity/survivalist view of the world in our whole approach to living. And if you wonder whether or not it's working for us, for our young people, or for our schools, just look at the daily headlines across the Western world: crime, hatred, violence, ethnic cleansing, war, social and political polarization of every kind, limited health care for the poor, a seriously deteriorating global environment, and education systems that are failing to educate shocking numbers of their students from low socio-economic families.

And, in America's case—a nation that goes out of its way to applaud its democratic institutions and belief in equality of opportunity—astronomical disparities in wealth between the top 10 and lowest 10 percent of the population persist.

This Feudal Age thinking has created a win-lose view of the world that ultimately does not work, an outcome that we're extremely reluctant to acknowledge on the one hand and persist in perpetuating on the other. It is bad enough that we adults choose to conduct our social, political, and economic affairs this way, but, whether we intend to or not, we perpetuate this win-lose orientation by continuing to educate our children this way in iceberg schools with Feudal Age agendas.

These agendas are a direct manifestation of the four basic beliefs just described. Translated into educational terms, they are:

1. The right kind of talent (academic/intellectual) is in scarce supply. It is our first responsibility to identify it (through standardized testing), then to develop it more fully (by tracking the most capable).
2. The (comparative/competitive) bell curve is the natural standard for defining achievement, success, and opportunity. Not everyone can be excellent, get As, or be a winner.
3. Rewards, credentials, and opportunity are scarce. Some (the less academically intelligent) must go without (get poor grades and fail). Those who want them (the motivated) must prove themselves deserving (by working harder and doing better than others).
4. Those with more learning resources (the academically intelligent from more advantaged backgrounds) deserve more opportunity (because they can do what's required in the time allowed).

So as we further explore this deeper and darker aspect of education's systemic nature, look for evidence of these four agenda items. Keep in mind as well that the numbers game and the five agendas called learning and achievement that we described in the introduction are natural extensions of this Feudal Age, comparative/competitive worldview. And since this agenda is about identifying the fittest and helping them get ahead, keep an eye out for the reactions of those who aren't winners. How do they react when they know that all the spoils go to the victor? What kind of effect does it have on their sense of identity and motivation to be an also-ran day after day, year after year?

Five key things stand out as serious learner-diminishing Feudal Age features of today's schools. They are direct extensions of the four agenda items just mentioned and are intimately connected to the numbers game and the use of points and test scores to define learning and learners described in the introduction. Each of the five is significant because it inhibits the system's ability to empower and genuinely benefit all its learners, and, as a set, they serve as a backdrop to our remaining exploration of the iceberg as a system. The five are:

1. Schools use "bell curve" expectations to impose an artificial quota on learning and success and force win-lose competition among students.
2. Schools emphasize talent selection over talent development and heavily load the scales in favor of the educational "haves."
3. Schools distort and obscure real learning in favor of artificial and meaningless scores and numbers.
4. Schools promote short-term task compliance rather than long-term competence development, giving fast learners a huge advantage.
5. Schools create false definitions of, and incentives for, learning, achievement, and contribution.

Since each of these assertions dramatically influences how schools define and shape learning and achievement, we will examine each of them in the next chapter. In the meantime we'll continue our exploration of the iceberg and how its structural features affect student opportunities and success.

OUR AGRARIAN AGE CALENDAR

We saw in chapter 1 that today's public education system was formed over a century ago in an era when most young people still lived on farms or in rural areas. Consequently, education was institutionalized and legalized as a seasonal enterprise. Summers were reserved for harvesting crops and other agricultural activities. Or for those in urban areas, it was simply a time to enjoy the warm sunny weather and play in the streets.

But in making this arrangement, the founders of our current system set a precedent that has made schools inconsistent with today's modern world. As we saw in Lewis Perelman's writing, we live in a remarkable era unforeseen a century ago, one having the technological capacity to enable virtually anyone to learn anything at any time from anywhere from worldwide experts. Today we can easily translate that into a simple phrase: *unlimited Internet access*!

"Hyperlearning," as Perelman calls it, can occur twenty-four hours a day, seven days a week, every day of the year. Schools, by contrast, operate on a seven-hour, five-day, forty-week schedule. And if you want to learn anything that receives official recognition by the system, you have to do it within the constrained window of opportunity called the school year.

The Great Definer

Keep the term *year* clearly mind as you explore the agrarian territory of the iceberg because in schools virtually everything is legally defined and organized around the nine-month calendar! Time is the Great Definer and constant, and everything else revolves around it.

Said differently, everything in the system is defined and structured around blocks of time which determine how long something is supposed to last, not on what the system is there to accomplish or what actually gets achieved. Or to say it in the language of chapter 1, time is tight and results are loose. Therefore, you'd be wise to think of schooling as a *time-based, calendar-driven* system (see Spady 1994). And if you doubt it, just look at this small list of major calendar-defined and -driven components of schooling

> Curriculum structures, organizational structures, grade levels, courses, instructional access, grades, credits, reporting systems, learning opportunities, promotion and retention, graduation requirements, job contracts and responsibilities, sports eligibility, budgets, and all other segments of the year itself, such as semesters, quarters, and grading periods.

Feel free to add your own examples to this list. And while you're at it, notice how this time-defined, means-based system sends a clear message to all its members, be they students, faculty, or others: Your major obligation is to give a good effort for a given amount of time. If you've done that, then you've done your job and you can't be held responsible for anything more.

Other more explicit ways of saying this are: Courses are nine-month events, not bodies of knowledge. We'll cover as much as we can until the time runs out, then go home. Grade levels are when we make learners of a given age learn particular things in the curriculum. Their level and rate of learning have to match this window of eligibility/opportunity or they're out of luck. You're done when the time block ends, regardless of what you've learned or accomplished. When the time block ends, so does your opportunity to learn and demonstrate it for credit. Good luck.

And listen to the deeper message that these other messages can send to our students: Since school is the only place that learning counts and gives you credits, why bother to learn when you're not in school or don't have to? In other words, as we saw in the introduction, learning only counts when you're "in custody," and the Agrarian Age calendar is the definer of those custodial conditions and custodial credentials.

Of all the many calendar-defined components of schooling, the one with the most serious consequences for students is *learning opportunities*, largely because the system basically closes off opportunities to get credit for learning on the final day of the school year. Because promotion and retention decisions are made at that time, there's little chance to demonstrate what you can do after that date and still get credit for it. Having an arbitrary day when you no longer may get credit for learning certainly supports the school's Feudal Age agenda of sorting and selecting, but it also violates the common sense and sensibilities of those who recognize differences in students' learning rates and want to support learning success on whatever day of the year it might occur.

So, if you want to challenge the status quo while exploring this level of the iceberg's territory, try asking the following questions while making your rounds:

- Why "retain" students based on what they do in early June, when it's their ability to perform in September, when school reopens, that actually matters?
- What about summer? Can't people learn in the summer? Is it poison?
- What about expanding learning opportunities *without penalty* in the summer, whether or not there's an official summer school? And even if there is, who says that the only learning that counts is the learning done under the supervision of a teacher?
- What's wrong with using the entire summer as an "expanded opportunity" period for any student who wants to learn more? Or better yet, what if we operated schools year round, just like life and the Internet? Oops, did I say something wrong?

If this discussion of inflexible time blocks frustrates you, then you see why the Agrarian Age calendar is such a counterproductive definer of schooling.

OUR INDUSTRIAL AGE DELIVERY SYSTEM

In chapter 1 we noted Raymond Callahan's 1964 book, *Education and the Cult of Efficiency*. In this brilliantly argued history of U.S. education, Callahan likens schools to the assembly-line factories of the early twentieth century after which they were modeled. His book clearly describes the philosophy and rationale used in organizing and operating schools the way we have for a hundred years. This happened because we were in the maturing stages of the Industrial Age, and the era was bringing more goods and more prosperity to more people than ever before.

Anything as productive and efficient as assembly-line factories, policy makers reasoned, needed to be emulated in education as well. The thing that attracted them to the factory model was its tight organization, its uniformity of product, and its standardization of process. So they assumed that if they just did the same things in the same ways to everyone, they'd all come out with the attributes they wanted. The thinking of the day was: "Why, with this model our schools could be producing students with the same efficiency and consistency as Henry Ford is producing Model Ts!"

So America has tried for nearly a century to implement Industrial Age delivery systems, but they haven't worked, won't work, never worked, and can't work! Nonetheless, our state policy reformers keep trying to have teachers make them work, sometimes—like today—with a vengeance!

This mechanical, standardized, command and control, Industrial Age model of instruction is profoundly flawed because it's contrary to human potential, human learning, and Total Living. We're not standardized machines, even though the Industrial Age tried to convince us that we were. And, for what it's worth, in the last two decades or so, we humans have been reclaiming the field, creating more and more flexible and person-responsive organizations, thanks to the inspiration and impetus of dozens of books like Tom Peters and Robert Waterman's *In Search of Excellence*. The problem in education is that our policy makers just haven't caught on to the possibility of operating schools any other way.

So, as you explore the Industrial Age territory of iceberg schools, look for the assembly-line nature of curriculum and instruction. The most obvious feature is what we call grade levels in elementary school and courses in high school. They are the line. We put kids of the same age, their teacher, the official curriculum, and their textbooks on the assembly line once a year, in late August or September, and they proceed down the line at a uniform pace, covering the designated curriculum until the line stops in June. If the teachers do it right, they'll start on page 1 in September—the only time all year that it's OK to do the page 1 work— and end the year on the last page of the book during the last week of the school year, except for final examinations and parties, of course.

Note how the Agrarian calendar and the Industrial Age delivery system work together: There's only one possible date when you can start learning, and there's one fixed date when you have to stop. It's a straight, linear, uniform run through the material in a fixed block of time, with everyone doing the same thing at the same time in the same way throughout. Some may think it's efficient, but, based on results, it certainly isn't effective. Those teachers who really try to instruct differently are swimming upstream against a torrent of precedent and inertia.

Ironically—and tragically—what's both inefficient and ineffective is what we do with slow learners who can't keep up with the line. Do we help them catch up or finish during the summer? Increasingly, urban districts have done so, but the recent testing reforms often give them no choice. If the learners fail the test on the designated day, they must start all over again from the beginning next September and do the entire line again in the same way they did it this year— which hardly sounds efficient. The system calls it "retention."

And what about the fast learners who could have started in the middle of the book in September and finished by Christmas? They constantly have to wait and wait to be taught the next thing in the book because there's only one day when they can start and only one instructional pace to maintain. Why? Because it's their *grade level*, and grade levels are defining features of schools!

So be aware that in the dynamic between alleged Industrial Age system efficiency and Information Age learner needs, the learner loses, unless he or she is the one in a million whose learning readiness, learning rate, and learning style actually match the pace of instruction in every subject that assembly lines provide. From the system's perspective, it's the student's job to do the learning on the specific days that it's being offered, not the school's job to help the student learn when he or she is ready and able. Certainly many individual teachers try to overcome this inflexibility with different kinds of "differentiated" instructional strategies that accommodate learner differences, but the system's structural inflexibilities make these approaches difficult to execute.

By this reasoning, Industrial Age schools are providing equality of *instructional* opportunity by giving everyone the same thing on the same days in the same way for the same amount of time from the same book. Otherwise, the reasoning goes, education would be unequal (from a standardization point of view). But from the students' perspective, they are *not* getting equality of *learning* opportunity because they're not receiving the help they need when they need it the way they need it to accomplish existing learning goals.

So, in the last analysis, this dilemma comes down to a profound issue of purpose. And, despite all the rhetoric to the contrary, that means deciphering the school's real job. Is it "delivering curriculum," or is it "ensuring learning"? The advocates of Standards-Based Reforms would claim that it's the latter, but their operating model betrays them. The advocates of our new-paradigm, learner-empowering model would also claim it's the latter. But they have the substance of chapters 7 through 12 to legitimate their claim.

OUR BUREAUCRATIC AGE CULTURE

The two purposes just noted go to heart of what we will be encountering as we explore the territory of the iceberg's Bureaucratic Age culture. According to Terry Deal, one of the world's top experts on organizational cultures, a culture simply manifests "the way we do business around here." And to that add, "when no one is looking." That is, a culture is the combination of beliefs, values, customs, statuses, expectations, and visible symbols of what gets honored by the people in a society that give it its unique character. It's both how people think about things and how they behave in relation to that thinking, and it has a huge influence on how and why organizations operate the way they do. You know you've hit the core of a culture when people treat features of their beliefs and social system as sacred and unalterable. In the real world, those are the things nations go to war to protect and preserve because they are the absolute definers of who they are as a society.

In this case, the Bureaucratic Age culture of our educational system is a direct extension of the layers of the iceberg on which it rests. It simultaneously embodies major features of the Feudal Age, Agrarian Age, and Industrial Age in its unique way of thinking and operating, and it's these combined features that have been institutionalized and internalized over the years into the sacred and unalterable features we regard as school.

As we saw in chapter 1, one of the best windows into the powerful bureaucratic culture of schools comes from Peters and Waterman's 1982 classic, *In Search of Excellence*. In that paradigm-shifting book the authors gave us a whole new way of thinking about organizations, and in figure 1.1 we described the essence of that new paradigm as one in which organizations have a clear fix on their deep purpose and the results they are there to achieve, and use available people, resources, and organizational processes in customer-responsive ways. Function and ends are fixed; form and means are flexible. The operational opposite of this new "excellence" model is the "bureaucracy." In the latter, form and means are fixed; and function and ends are variable.

Managers of Means

To underscore this major emphasis on means within the bureaucratic culture of schools, we'll only have to take a short step back to chapter 1 and revisit the paradigm-shifting list of ends and means elements that we described there. For convenience, it is repeated below:

- Ends rather than Means
- Purposes rather than Procedures
- Results rather than Resources
- Outcomes rather than Programs
- Goals rather than Roles
- Learners rather than Time
- Learning rather than Teaching
- Challenges rather than Content
- Performance rather than Curriculum
- Competence rather than Credits
- Learner Potential rather than Grade Levels
- Possibilities rather than Precedents
- The Future rather than the Past
- Life rather than Schooling

As you review this framework again, note the items from either side of the list that you think are "sacred and unalterable" to educators, keeping in mind the Feudal, Agrarian, and Industrial Age things that define what schools are and have been for a century. And if you were asked to rank the top five from this list, what would they be? Here, in the same order they appear in the list, are eight leading contenders you might choose from:

- Procedures
- Programs
- Roles
- Time
- Content
- Curriculum
- Grade Levels
- Precedents

Yes, all eight are from the means side of the list, and six of them form an interesting constellation around the key concept of "roles." They are: roles, programs, time, content, curriculum, and grade levels. As you reflect on these six concepts, think about how educators' roles are formally and contractually defined around three key things:

1. Areas of subject matter expertise—which connects programs, content, and curriculum.
2. Grade levels—which define the clientele for which educators have responsibility and which further specify the former three factors.
3. Time—which defines the duration of their role responsibility and the basis of their compensation.

So, with no other words to work with at the moment, let's consider the possibility that this constellation of factors not only defines teachers' role responsibilities but their professional identities as well. They are experts in given bodies of content, legally qualified to work with children of a given age, and their contract determines the time parameters of that work. In short, this could easily be their operating definition of being a professional educator.

But we can't forget that a key responsibility of their role is to foster student learning and achievement. And how are they defined? By the five C's described at the end of the introduction: custody, compliance, competition, competence, and content. So, if we took those five components of learning and achievement and incorporated them into this analysis, they would expand the scope of the professional role to being (1) a teacher of content and related competences, (2) a control agent, and (3) an evaluator.

In effect, then, their professional role requires that they do three major things simultaneously: (1) manage instruction; (2) manage student behavior; and (3) manage the reward system. In which priority order they do these three things is unclear, but an educated guess suggests that for talented teachers it's: Manage instruction, and the other two will take care of themselves. But for those less-talented educators, especially in "tough" situations, it's: Manage rewards in order to manage behavior in order to manage instruction.

Now to complete the picture, we need to bring the other two words from our short list of eight into the mix: procedures and precedents. It's easy to see how strongly educators would be inclined to favor and advocate procedures—"how we routinely do things around here"—and precedents—"the way we've always done it before"—that protect this three-part professional role identity.

For those teachers who handle the instruction part of their role with no difficulty, organizational procedures and precedents are of little consequence except when they interfere with their more flexible and innovative approach to working with students. But for those lacking these skills and needing strong organizational support, procedures and precedents can be the difference between coping and chaos. They *need* an organization that is tight on procedures and precedents because it directly supports the more structured and means-based character of their professional role performance!

So if we pulled all of these factors into one giant conclusion about the bureaucratic nature and culture of schools, it would be that educators' role responsibilities, professional identities, and role performances are all tight on means and loose on ends. One set of means factors defines and supports the other in an endless, self-reinforcing, chicken-and-egg, cause-and-effect, dog-and-tail, closed system cycle that manifests itself in the "CBO Syndrome."

The CBO Syndrome

With this reinforcing means-driven cycle as background, perhaps the simplest way to assess the bureaucratic intensity of a school's culture is to give it the CBO test. Over time we have developed ten indicators of whether a school is drowning in the sea of ingrained practices and outdated policies or not. Each of these indicators happens to be spelled with a C word, a B word, and an O word. Hence, CBO Syndrome. If they're drowning, it's a sure bet that their Bureaucratic Age culture is flourishing and that CBO has overwhelmed the organization.

So, since old-paradigm organizations are really into points and scores, you might consider rating any school you're exploring from one to ten on each of the ten indicators that follow. Give them a one if there's "No evidence of this CBO" in what you observe, and a ten if they're "Overwhelmed with this CBO." Here are the ten indicators:

1. Cellular-Based Organization—Boxes within boxes driven by boxes.
2. Calendar-Based Opportunities—"You've got till June to learn this!"
3. Curriculum-Based Outcomes—"Look at that tail wag that dog!"
4. Content-Bound Objectives—"Wow, and that tail's so small, too!"
5. Contest-Based Orientations—"Who can do the most by Friday?"
6. Convention-Bound Obligations—"What do you mean by innovate?"
7. Compliance-Based Obedience—"You know what the rules say!"
8. Custodial-Bound Obsolesce—"You've got to be here to learn this."
9. Convenience-Based Operations—"Who needs staff development?"
10. Conformity-Based Obsession—"But yours will be 'different'!"

Okay now, let's see whose school can score the highest!

5

EXPOSING THE NUMBERS GAME

Because we (falsely) believe that numbers are measures and that everything is worth 100 points, we feel safe in attaching ordinal numbers to components of learning. . . . This wild leap of faith works as long as you think in numbers, but it completely breaks down when you think in substance.

In both the introduction and chapter 4 we have explored how our prevalent model of schooling has been loading the deck against countless learners for as long as we can remember. From its multiple agendas surrounding learning and achievement, to its Feudal Age agenda of sorting and selecting, to the limiting opportunity conditions of its Agrarian Age calendar, to the standardized, assembly-line nature of its Industrial Age delivery system, to the protectionist nature of its Bureaucratic Age culture and CBO Syndrome, the institution we call school is undermining its own effectiveness.

Instead of basing its operations on the excellence paradigm described in chapter 1, the five research realities described in chapter 2, and/or the vision of Total Learning for Total Living described in chapter 3, school remains governed by outdated thinking, counterproductive structures, and an illusory numbers game that have taken on lives of their own. The time has come to address the numbers game and to unmask the many illusions and distortions it has created regarding learning, assessment, and achievement. Only when we see this numbers game for what it is—and isn't—can we create a more enlightened, authentic, and empowering alternative. And not a moment too soon, either.

MODELS OF ACHIEVEMENT

To expose the numbers game for what it is, we first need to take a larger view of what we mean both by "achievement" and by the major factors that determine what it means in education and elsewhere. To understand how achievement is defined and operates in our current system, and how it could be defined in an alternative system, we need to take five key things into account. Let's call them (1) the definers, (2) the standards, (3) the measures, (4) the evidence, and (5) the structures. Each plays an independent role in defining a total model of achievement.

The Definers of Achievement

The simplest way to think about the definers of achievement is to return to our discussion of both human learning and life performance in chapter 2. There we noted that learning was made up of two key components: mental processing and tangible performance. We called them *thinking* and *doing*. At their essence, they're about content and competence, respectively.

At its simplest, *achieving* means "attaining a new/higher level" of something. In our case, "learning achievement" means advancing to a new level either (1) in one's mental processing—"She can make more connections among more (complex) kinds of content"; (2) in one's execution of observable skills, processes, or products—"He can both design and implement a basic marketing plan"; or (3) both—"She can design as well as implement multi-step, multi-tiered marketing strategies."

To keep it simple, let's note one more time that thinking/content and doing/competence are different. You can do very complex kinds of thinking (which is seen as good) with complex content (which is also seen as good) without actually being able to *do* much with that content except process it mentally and carry out basic paper-and-pencil tasks with it (like answer test questions) in rather basic performance contexts (like sitting in a quiet room by yourself). To do more with that content requires learners to develop and continually execute skills, processes, and competences—some of which can be very complex and challenging—in performance contexts that can be very complex and challenging as well.

Keep this basic distinction between mentally processing content and tangibly demonstrating competence clearly in mind as you assess what people mean by "achievement." A competence model of learning and achievement requires far more of learners than a content model alone.

The Standards of Achievement

If achievement is about attaining new or given levels of ability, then some kind of *standard* is required for determining what those recognized levels are.

The standard serves as the benchmark against which the ability or product or performance can be assessed. Although there are a number of ways in which standards are defined and applied, existing models of achievement are based on two main approaches.

The first is *comparative*. This means that the standard is set by comparing abilities, products, performances, or results against each other—almost always in a competitive situation. In this model, the number of allowable "successes" is usually determined in advance, and only that designated number of the best participants are declared winners. The others are declared something else, no matter what the particular merits of their product or performance may be.

For example, in highly competitive models, such as athletics and contests of all kinds, only one may be declared best, and the labels winner, champion, number one, the greatest, valedictorian, and so on are assigned to their acquired status. This leaves labels like runner-up, serious contender, loser, also-ran, and so forth to be assigned to the remainder of the competitors. However, in other kinds of comparative systems, such as college admissions or "grading on a curve," broader quotas may be used, indicating that a given number or percentage are allowed to meet the standard. This expands the pool of those deemed successful but it too leaves major numbers out of the running, no matter what the merits of their individual qualifications or credentials may be.

The driving concept in this model is *ranking* the participants against each other. The key reason for using it is *selecting* and honoring the best.

The other approach to setting standards goes by a fancier name: "criterion defined." A *criterion* is an essential component or quality that a product or performance must have in order embody an accepted standard of excellence. If that component or quality is missing, then the standard is not met, regardless of whose accomplishment may be "better" than others in a group of participants. However, if the necessary criteria/components/qualities are present, then the standard *is* met—and it doesn't matter by how many since, in this model, there is no quota on how many can achieve success.

The criterion model operates with a clear concept of quality in mind. The challenge built into the model is for participants to rise to the standard/level defined by the criterion (singular) or criteria (plural). If they can, they are declared successful, no matter how many of them may do so. This model is used in all kinds of certification and licensure programs where competent performance is clearly defined and essential: driver's licenses, SCUBA and CPR certifications, pilot's licenses, surgery specialization degrees, air traffic control certifications, electronic repair certifications, Scouting merit and honor badges, and every imaginable kind of performance in the military.

The driving concept in this model is *rating* the participants against a clear criterion. The key reason for using it is determining who's *qualified* to perform competently.

The Measures of Achievement

It's easy to think of a yardstick as a measure because it is precisely calibrated with equal intervals denoting the length of things. When you're concerned about the physical size of common objects, then it's a useful tool to have around. But it isn't very good for measuring the speed of an airplane, the intonation of a musical instrument, or a person's ability to solve an interpersonal problem. These phenomena require altogether different kinds of information/data-gathering capabilities for which a yardstick is useless.

So, in one important respect we're back to square one when it comes to measuring achievement because these examples make it obvious that you can't measure what you haven't defined! And this implies that what we mean by *learning* and what we mean by *achievement* need to be precisely defined, *using precise words*, so that we know what criteria are germane to their assessment, what kinds of information or evidence to gather, and what kinds of tools would be most appropriate or effective for doing so. In a nutshell: Substance defines achievement. Without substance—call it *clear criteria*—we really don't know what we're dealing with, no matter what people may call it.

But very often just the reverse is true. We accept the *score* or *symbol* that we attach to some kind of assessment device (such as a multiple choice test) as the definition of what the thing itself is. And we think it is a measure—like our friend the yardstick—because numbers are attached to it. There are some very common but misleading examples in education: intelligence (IQ) scores, reading (at some grade level) scores, and achievement (based on grades and GPAs) itself.

What we must recognize and acknowledge from this point forward, then, is the simple fact that *numbers don't make something a measure*! It's an easy trap to fall into, especially when people calculate them in very precise or complex ways. But numbers are simply symbols that we attach to things we observe, they are not inherent in the demonstration itself. We decide to give a certain number of points to some things and a different number points to other things; and we've been doing it for so long that people think that the points or the scores are the actual substance/learning/achievement that we seek. They are not. They are simply a code—artifacts that we attach to demonstrations of learning because we're looking for a convenient shorthand for describing something that is very complex. Unfortunately, this shorthand code obscures and distorts the real thing. That is, the numbers replace the learning, and the symbols disguise or obscure the substance that defines what the learning actually is.

For now, just keep in mind: There's no substitute for substance—real words that describe the real demonstrations of learning that you want to see. So the next time you see a score or symbol or code about a child's performance, demand to see the substance, the criteria and assessment tool that lie behind it. Only then will you know what the *real* learning is and what you might do as a parent or teacher to help improve it.

The Evidence of Achievement

We commonly think of *evidence* as the information or documentation that is provided to support a decision or judgment. "We should take this course of action because. . . ." "He should be given an A because. . . ." In short, evidence is the *because* stuff, the basis on which a conclusion is developed or drawn.

In the case of learning achievement, however, there is another side to the coin. More often than not in schools, evidence is not just what underlies a decision or conclusion, it's also what actually gets reported as the judgment itself. The clearest example of this is grades. In iceberg schools, numbers, symbols, and codes are used as the measures of achievement. In such a model, grades on assignments and tests are the evidence, grades are what gets reported, and grades are achievement itself. This constitutes a self-defining closed system that is based on points (i.e., code) being the fundamental source of the evidence, a translation of that code into the symbol called a grade, the reporting of that symbol as learning, and then the interpretation of the symbol as achievement.

The legitimacy of this extremely convoluted and ambiguous model lies in our willingness, as parents, educators, and the public, to accept this multilayered translation process as valid. In short, the legitimacy of this model requires us to believe in our minds that:

1. Points are exact and accurate representations of learning.
2. It's appropriate to combine, weigh, and average points that represent very different kinds of learning, performance, and behavior so that the original substance disappears.
3. It's appropriate to arbitrarily establish ranges of points that constitute "levels" of performance (e.g., 93 or above is an A).
4. The one-point difference between 59 and 60, or 69 and 70, or 79 and 80 is, indeed, the one and only clear demarcation line between what we call success and what we call failure.
5. It's appropriate to report these points as an accurate representation of a student's learning and capabilities.
6. It's appropriate to interpret this amalgamation of points and scores as a student's achievement.

If you can't accept these six assumptions as valid, then what's the alternative? What kind of evidence should we be demanding? The answer goes back directly to the previous section: substance—real descriptions, authentic criteria, and tangible evidence of what learners can actually do—real nouns, real verbs, and real examples of what is being demonstrated as evidence of learning.

Fair enough. But this is going to require a different model of reporting than we're used to seeing, one that contains the space available to describe the authentic evidence being described here—something akin to what is known today as "performance portfolios"—a portable physical storage place where learners can keep best examples of their work and performances and where teachers can report directly on the substantive evidence that relates to key learning goals. Clearly a portfolio system like this is a far cry from traditional report cards which, on a single page, only allow enough space in their tiny boxes for a single, permanent symbol or number to be entered for a specific subject or area of learning for a designated time period.

So when we place these two evidence-reporting alternatives side by side, an interesting cause-and-effect, dog-and-tail issue arises. Do iceberg schools employ a number/symbol/code reporting system because it's convenient and embodies what they think learning is, or is it because tiny marks of some kind are the only things that will fit into the tiny boxes provided on report cards? Regardless of which is the tail and which is the dog, this traditional system leaves us with remarkably little capacity to represent learners, learning, and achievement in terms other than code.

The Structures of Achievement

As with these other four aspects of an achievement model, there are two major structural alternatives that dramatically influence how we define and document what we regard as achievement. One is called "cumulative" and the other "culminating." Each represents a different approach to defining achievement, and each typically treats the "opportunity structure" surrounding learning and achievement differently as well.

As its name implies, a *cumulative* model of achievement accumulates as evidence of learning performance virtually everything that a learner does over a designated period of time—often a school year or an entire schooling career—and consolidates it into an overall summary, usually by averaging all the available information into a small number of general indicators. This provides a picture of the overall consistency, quality, and range of work done up through a given date in the learner's career. Because this model takes virtually everything into account from the beginning of the designated time period, it has two major effects on what emerges at the end.

First, since everything is taken into account, based on the time period in which it was done, there is a tendency for any element of learning to be treated as equal to any other element, no matter what its nature or complexity. For example, whatever constitutes this week's grade is treated as the same in the averaging system as what constituted the grade for a week that occurred three months ago. This happens because, in a cumulative model, grades are defined and allocated around *time blocks* of given sizes—days, weeks, semesters. They are not issued when specific learning and performance goals/levels are reached.

A day is a day and counts just as much as any other day in the year. Similarly, a week is a week, a grading period is a grading period, and a semester is a semester.

Second, what is done in the early developmental stages of learning tends to count just as much in the overall achievement profile as that which occurs later—things done in September count just as much as things done in May, and things done in grade nine count just as much as things done in grade eleven. Consequently, if the learner is a slow starter, the model's system of cumulative averaging continues to figure that slow start in with what may be rapid progress and significant success later. This, in turn, means that the learner's ultimate grade (i.e., cumulative measure of achievement) may never catch up with that of someone who started faster—even though they both end up at the same place or level by the designated end—simply because the faster starter has more high grades from the early stages to include in the average.

Keep in mind, then, that in this model, the achievement clock is ticking every minute of every day of every week of every semester. This keeps learners "diligent" and focused on every task and test as it comes up. In short, no letups are possible: *Everything counts!*

Culminating models of achievement operate quite differently. As the name implies, they are primarily concerned with documenting learning pinnacles and ultimate results, not with permanently grading and averaging all the details and practice attempts that were required in order to get there. Their admonition to learners: "Keep at it and see how good you can really get. That's what will ultimately count."

Clearly, Culminating is about the *end*, and the practitioners of this approach begin with that end in mind and meticulously plan instruction "back" from there so that the path to that end is sound and inviting. Because their focus is on encouraging, developing, and assessing the learner's highest possible final result, they treat lessons, tasks, and assessments as necessary steps along a larger path, but not as permanent and unalterable ends in themselves.

This concept comes alive when we see it embodied in a high school's annual spring musical, or an actual game involving one of its athletic teams. These are highly complex demonstrations of learning that require the integration of many different elements, and they come to fruition in the live performances held for the public. From this macro perspective, achievement is the set of abilities and the quality of product that are embodied in these complex, "big picture" culminating demonstrations. These high-level performances are vehicles that allow learners to integrate and apply all of the smaller learning steps and abilities needed for executing them competently. Clearly, these underlying skills and abilities are essential and cannot be dismissed. In fact, without them it would be impossible to execute the higher-level demonstrations that ultimately matter.

But none of these micro skills is the equivalent of a macro demonstration, just as means are not ends and a pile of stones is not a cathedral. Those who implement culminating achievement models are acutely aware of these differences between means and ends, micro and macro, and the stones that constitute the walls of the cathedral and the cathedral itself. The stones by themselves, like individual skills and pieces of information imbedded in lessons and curriculum units, are simply building blocks, not walls, arches, or cathedrals. They must be crafted and assembled with other stones to become components of those larger entities.

Keep in mind, then, that cumulative models of achievement tend to focus on how many stones are being carved each day, while culminating models of achievement focus instead on designing and getting the cathedral built.

Integrating the Five Components

Theoretically there are lots of ways to put these five sets of components together to form an operating model of achievement, but for now let's paint these pictures with very broad strokes. One picture quite accurately portrays the model of achievement that prevails in iceberg schools. It defines achievement primarily as the mental processing of content; its standards are comparative and competitive; its measures are numbers and symbols; it uses points and codes as evidence on conventional report cards; and it is fundamentally cumulative and unforgiving, rewarding consistent short-term performance.

The more authentic and empowering counterpart would embody the opposite set of alternatives. It defines achievement primarily as the active demonstration of competence; its standards are criterion-defined; its measures are defined by substance; it uses authentic criteria and substance as evidence in performance portfolios; and it is fundamentally culminating and encouraging, emphasizing and documenting the highest levels of performance that learners can ultimately reach.

MAJOR MYTHS ABOUT THE NUMBERS GAME

The foregoing has already brought to light a number of major flaws in the purpose and integrity of operating a numbers- and symbols-driven achievement system. But given the stranglehold this system has over American education, it is worth explicitly highlighting seven key myths about the numbers game that go unchallenged decade after decade, even though they make no sense once brought to light. Those myths are:

1. Numbers Are Measures.
2. Everything Is Worth 100 Points.

3. All Points Are Created Equal.
4. Points Define Standards of Success.
5. Points Define Essential Learning.
6. The More Points, the Higher the Achievement.
7. Points Are Incentives for Improved Learning.

Although they are highly interrelated, we'll expose the reality about these seven myths one at a time.

Myth 1: Numbers Are Measures

As noted earlier in this chapter, numbers are not measures of learning, *criteria* are; and criteria are defined by real words that describe the actual components of the desired learning or performance. Numbers are proxies or an artificial code that we attach to elements of a performance. Then after adding up and manipulating the numbers, we represent the numerical solution as if it were a measure of the learning. At best it's a grossly inaccurate proxy. But without this grounding myth, the numbers game could not exist.

Myth 2: Everything Is Worth 100 Points

This is the second great myth that makes the numbers game possible. The blunt truth is: Nothing is worth anything unless we attach value to it, and the implementers of the numbers game have decided to attach 100 points' worth of numerical value to everything in schools that moves, no matter how different it is from anything else that gets 100 points: assignments large and small, tests large and small, presentations large and small, projects large and small, performances large and small, homework on time or late, attendance and deportment, attitude and effort, and on and on. Everything is calibrated against 100 as if it were a magic number.

Now, have you wondered why the number of questions to be answered on assignments and tests almost always divides into 100 evenly? That's so the points can be distributed easily, not because there are four equally important things that constitute an adequate understanding of something, or five, or ten, or twenty. It's so that the arithmetic comes out even when teachers take points off for mistakes. Because of these 100 points and the deductions made from them, the most-asked question in American education on Fridays is "What did you get?" *not* "What did you learn?"

Myth 3: All Points Are Created Equal

Because points are ordinal numbers, educators assume that they differ from each other by equal orders of magnitude. That makes ten just as different from nine as it is from eleven. And because you can perform any kind of basic operation with ordinal numbers you desire, they can be added, subtracted, multiplied, divided, averaged, compared, and ranked against each other just about any way you wish.

Because we believe that numbers are measures and that everything is worth 100 points, we feel safe in attaching ordinal numbers to components of learning. This segment of content is worth this many points, and this specific skill is worth that many. This wild leap of faith works as long as you think in *numbers*, but it completely breaks down when you think in *substance*. That's why no one can figure out the degree of numerical magnitude between the vertebrae in the spinal column and the tallest mountain in South Africa—or how to subtract "describe" from "design."

Nonetheless, educators proceed undaunted by substantive reality, assuming that "these ten points" (whether missing or present) is of the same value as "those ten points" or some other ten points somewhere else. If they're right, then they're justified in making equal achievement trades between the capital of Italy, the longest river in South America, and the number of known planets in our solar system, because each is an item on a ten-item test and each item is worth ten points. Note, however, that it also makes the capital of Italy worth five times more than the capital of New York, because you only get two points for the latter on a fifty-item test in the same geography class.

But this is only part of the dilemma created by this myth. The real truth is that one particular point is of incredibly far greater value than all of the other ninety-nine! It's the point you need to go from fail to pass. It might be the sixtieth point, or the seventieth, or the eightieth, depending on your district's "achievement standards"; but there's no doubt that it's the most valuable and most unequal point of all. The point that moves you from a C to a B is also a lot more valuable than most of the others, as is the one that moves you from a B to an A. So in terms of consequences, not all points are created equal at all, regardless of the naive assumptions we make to the contrary.

Myth 4: Points Define Standards of Success

Every educational jurisdiction in North America has a numerical standard for passing and failing. In most American districts it's the difference between a score of 69 and 70, but in some districts it's 59 and 60, and in others it's 79 and 80. And in Canada, where several provinces follow the British example, it's 49 and 50; but there it's rare for anyone to be awarded more than an 80 for anything, no matter how good it is. So what's correct, proper, accurate, or realistic as a standard? No one knows. *We just make it up* and compel students to live with whatever our particular number is.

At a score of 70, students still can't do 30 percent of what's required successfully, but it's a pass in thousands of places. Too lenient? Well, it all depends on what the 70 and 30 are all about. If airline pilots only had to get 70 percent correct, we'd have hundreds of crashes a day—until we ran out of pilots and planes, of course. And if they had to get 80, that would still leave us with disasters everywhere (the missing 20 could have been the part of the test that covered safe landings). So would 90, 95, and even 99. Now apply that to your own driving success. Allowing yourself two trips a day for a year, how many accidents would you have at 95 percent accuracy? Over 36. At 99? Over 7.

If these realities seem discouraging, then you might want to get rid of the numbers game altogether. How? Start by asking: 70 of what? 80 of what? 95 of what? What's the "real" measure? Don't be surprised if no one can answer you because you're talking substance and they're doing numbers. The two don't match—water and metal. Two different paradigms—no connection. But your questions will get their attention and expose the need for creating a criterion-defined standards system.

Myth 5: Points Define Essential Learning

One example will suffice to dispel this myth, and to do so we'll set our "standard" for success at eighty, which is pretty high by schooling norms. It's now Friday, time for our ten-item test in biology. Our teacher has been reminding us all week about how *essential* this information is to our ability to progress in biology, and this test will prove it. This is a Big One!

What do we need to score in order to pass? Eighty. Eighty is Essential. That means we can miss two and still pass. Okay here goes: Do we need to know the first item to pass? No. It's not essential. Do we need to know the second item to pass? No, it's not essential, either. Well, what about the third? By itself, no. It too isn't essential. "But wait," you say. "Something's wrong here!" "That's for sure," I reply. "Watch closely."

What's success on this test? Eighty points. What does it take to get eighty points? Answer *any eight* items correctly. Of the eight, does it have to be the first? No. Of the eight, does it have to be the second? No. The third? No. Not any of them. When you're playing the numbers game, *no item is essential*. There's no particular thing you *have to* know in order to succeed. But you do have to know *enough* items to succeed; eight of them, in fact—any eight. As it turns out, nothing is *essential* on this biology test, but *enough* is *mandatory*! Our teacher mistook one for the other, and it happens all the time when you play the numbers game. And remember: They call those scores "achievement."

Myth 6: The More Points, the Higher the Achievement

Early in this chapter we defined achieving as "attaining a new higher level of something." This, as we saw, makes learning achievement synonymous with "advancing to a new level" in either mental processing, the execution of observable processes, or both. Now let's take this definition seriously as we examine the case studies of two typical learners. One enters the course with a strong background in it. She already knows a lot, so is at a higher level at the beginning. The other doesn't know much at the beginning but wants to learn it. He starts at a lower level.

Now both the course and the numbers game begin, and the higher-level student immediately begins piling up perfect 100s because she already knows a lot of it, the new stuff is familiar, and her rate of assimilating the new concepts and processes is quite rapid as a result. The other student, on the other hand, is struggling to get his bearings and things are proceeding slowly for him. Poor initial test results and lots of permanently lost points, but he persists. And after some months of determined effort he's getting higher and higher marks on his assignments and tests. He's moved to higher and higher levels of understanding and competence.

Finally, in April he does it. He gets his first 100, and then another and another! Meanwhile his counterpart has been working conscientiously too and continues to get straight 100s. In June they take the final exam and both get 100s. The teacher is elated at their "achievement" and averages up their grades. She gets an A for her straight 100s. He gets a B for his mixed record. Who, by our definition, achieved the most? He did. Who got the fewest points? He did. Who got shafted by the numbers game? You only get one guess, and it's worth 100 points!

Myth 7: Points Are Incentives for Improved Learning

The numbers game is a massive reward-and-punishment system that Alfie Kohn describes and decries in his 1993 book *Punished by Rewards*. As we saw in the introduction, school is a place where educators and students are locked in a battle of control and compliance. The students *have to* be there whether they want to or not, and the teachers *have to* get them to learn the things in the official curriculum, whether the students find them interesting and valuable or not. As it turns out, points, grades, and credit are the commodities of exchange in this dysfunctional system: If you do what I ask, you'll get points and credit for it. Without points and credit, you're in deep trouble. Seen more closely, it's a tradeoff between compliance and the avoidance of humiliation and punishment—things called failure, retention, and discipline.

Add the ingredients supplied by the previous six myths, and students come to believe that points, scores, and grades *are* their achievement, success, and passports to the future. For those highly motivated to move on into higher education, maximizing their points is one of the key ways of enhancing their chances of attaining a high GPA, a high class rank, and admission to college. How do they do this? By "protecting" their GPA their final year. It's done by avoiding the most challenging courses where the risk of not getting an A is high and settling instead for easier alternatives where As are more likely. Does their achievement increase? No, but their points do. And that's what ultimately matters when learning degenerates into a numbers game.

ADDING INSULT TO INJURY

The foregoing makes clear that the numbers game of schooling distorts and degrades the authentic nature of education, learning, achievement, learners, and educators. And, as we saw in chapter 4, it is the driving force in implementing the Feudal Age agenda of schools. There we argued that this archaic, deeply entrenched agenda/game/achievement model diminishes learners and the opportunities education affords them to fully develop themselves as Total Learners in five key ways. We can now see that those five factors add further insult to the injuries just described. They are:

1. Using the "Curve" to Create Failure
2. Sorting and Selecting the Advantaged
3. Using the Code as False Measures
4. Achieving Short-Term Compliance
5. Offering False Incentives

We'll examine each of these five insults here in light of myths about the numbers game that we've already exposed.

Insult 1: Using the "Curve" to Create Failure

Schools make successful learning a contest that only some can win. They do it by setting up a comparative standards system as noted above, and by using a mathematical device called the "bell curve" to justify things like tracking, grading, and class rank. The curve is the statistical graph of how often things are likely to occur under "natural" or "neutral" conditions—things like inches of annual rainfall in an area, average daily temperatures over a ten-year period, and so forth. Its shape looks somewhat like a bell; there are not many occurrences out at the high and low extremes of the distribution, but there are lots more piled up toward the middle. The curve has become religion in psychological measure-ment circles and crept heavily into education since its discovery/creation in the early part of the twentieth century.

The curve is a perfect device for misapplying statistics and for reinforcing the Feudal Age, "sort and select" agenda of schools. First, the curve's advocates assert that it represents the "natural order" of things in which there are only so many really smart individuals, excellent performances, high-level successes, or top grades possible. These desired attributes are simply declared to be in scarce supply, and from that all else flows. Notice, for the curve to work, people have to *believe* that only so much "good stuff" is available. With this scarcity mindset in place, there's no possibility of more than "normal," limited amounts of good occurring, even with proper intervention, teaching, or support.

Second, in this Feudal Age, "natural" order of things, the small number at the top "deserve" the highest grades (As) and the most and best education. It's only "fair" because only they have the talent and/or attributes to properly take advantage of the (limited) opportunity available! That's why schools have curriculum tracks: To give students with different levels of "capacity" the curriculum they deserve.

Third, the curve also indicates that there's an equally small number of truly inferior performers down at the other end, and it's only appropriate that they be graded (with Fs) and educated accordingly. They have their special track in the curriculum as well, and it assures that they never get the good or hard material to learn. That leaves a huge pile of "average" people in the middle (to get Cs), and smaller groups of above average (to get Bs) and below average people (to get Ds) on either side of them. Remember, many believe that to alter this pattern is to distort that which is normal, natural, inevitable, and desirable.

With only a limited amount of success available and a comparative standards system in place, students are placed in a win-lose competitive learning situation in which, if they want to succeed, they're going to have to do better than lots of other people, no matter what it takes. If you win, they lose. If they win, you lose. It's just how the game is played. Who you are in your own right, or your originality and contributions, or friendship and caring, or insight and leadership in their own rights disappear from sight once the curve, the numbers game, and the school's Feudal Age agenda get activated and translate who you are into a GPA and class rank.

Insult 2: Sorting and Selecting the Advantaged

Schools are in the business of finding out who's got what it takes to get the most points, not helping everyone get all the points possible. Consequently, if you want to end up at the top end of the curve, you've got to bring four key assets to the table. Without them, it's going to be an extremely tough go. If you doubt it, just go back and review Myth 6.

First, the most important thing is being a *fast learner*. The faster you are, the more likely you will be to keep up with the pace of instruction and do all your assignments on time. Since there are daily grades for everything, being "on time" is what gets you points because those points get averaged into your weekly grade and then your reporting period grade, and then your semester grade, and so on. To be slow is to be late, and late means fewer points.

Second, you've got to *be smart*. That means *never make mistakes*. Every mistake you make will mean points off and bring down your average. And, since the grades are in ink, that means they're "permanent mistakes," even if you correct them later. That's really why teachers use ink when they grade: to find out who's smart enough to do it right the first time. Anyone can learn if you take the time to help them. This is about seeing who's smart enough to learn with only limited help—both today and by Friday!

Third, you've got to enter school *knowing how to read*. If you come to school expecting the school to teach you how to read, you'll be placed in the Parakeet group, and that's like "permanent remedial." There are only two abilities that are guaranteed "point attractors" in school: reading and math. Everything else is incidental. Reading counts the most because without it you can't do any of the other content work, and content is the lifeblood of school. It is really too bad if you, like many children, have a reading problem or learning disability because, if you do, you can look forward to twelve years of struggle, tons of missing points, and a permanent home in the bottom quarter of your class.

Fourth, as we saw in Myth 6, to win the points contest you've got to *already know a lot of it* beforehand because the game is rigged in favor of those who do. It's simple. Those who come in already knowing a lot start way ahead of those who are there to learn it. Because our grading system averages everything—beginning, middle, and end—those who already know things can start off getting maximum points. And since they'll probably keep getting maximum points week after month, their final average is going to be "max." Those not already knowing a lot probably won't do well at first. And that means *losing points*. And since all points are permanent and get averaged with everything else, *they can never get their missing points back*.

Insult 3: Using the Code as False Measures

As we have seen throughout this chapter, iceberg schools operate on an achievement code of symbols rather than on substance. Points, scores, percentages, grades, and credits comprise the core of that code. This entire system of symbols operates on the false assumption that everything that students do can be translated into points that have equal meaning and value. We've already explained that this key assumption is not true, and all we need to support our position is to focus on the substance of the learning we seek to develop. It requires us to use real words, and real words possess no inherent mathematical values or properties. They can't be added, subtracted, multiplied, divided, averaged, or squeezed into tiny boxes on report cards. Code is a distorted short hand. Real words tell the story, especially when used accurately.

Despite these realities, the system feels justified in "translating" real learning down into a single number (grade point average [GPA]) that has no substantive meaning, and then ranking everyone on that number. Furthermore, to give this bogus exercise the illusion of scientific precision, the system calculates GPAs to the third and fourth decimal places—as if something of value is to be gained by having a very precise indicator of something with no substantive meaning. This counterfeit "measure"

- "satisfies" the requirements of college admissions officers who don't want to admit anyone of "inferior rank" to their campuses
- simplifies record keeping and communicating with those interested in student records by reducing everything down into a common code that fits efficiently into tiny little boxes on single pieces of paper
- makes the choice of this year's student graduation speaker "objective," unless there are ties
- takes thinking, ambiguity, and complex decision making safely out of play by letting the numbers speak for themselves—no one can be blamed for showing bias or playing favorites

If these four "reasons" don't impress you, the next time you're confronted with code, demand to see the real substance, the real criteria, and the real performance evidence that underlies it. The more you persist, the sooner the system will have to come to grips with the factors that constitute authentic learning, and the sooner we'll be able to reach the place where learners mean more than numbers.

Insult 4: Achieving Short-Term Compliance

Cumulative achievement models, the numbers game in general, the realities of Myth 6, and Insult 2 combine to emphasize short-term task compliance over long-term competence development. How? By giving *time* greater priority than *learning* in the distribution of points. This makes sense when you look at teachers' record books. They're not designed around higher-order learning goals or ultimate outcomes; they're organized around days, weeks, and semesters, with boxes and pages designating each.

From this perspective, it's easy to see that points and grades, the coin of the realm, are issued not for kinds of performance, as is claimed, but for performance on *given dates*. All those tiny boxes in the record book are an open invitation to place something in them. Otherwise, it might look like nothing "happened" that day or week. So with a "daily grade" at stake, there's pressure on the student to do something "good" every day, primarily because the points given for that day are in ink. Ink means permanent, and permanent means eternal. Today is the only day you can get today's points, and whatever they are, they'll be there forever, probably to be averaged with countless other points from 179 other days.

What we're describing here, largely because of the ink, is a structural feature of schooling called "constrained opportunity." Your chance to do things (well) is determined by a block of time. Opportunity exists until that block of time ends. If it's short, so is your opportunity. If it's longer, opportunity expands, but only until that block ends, because that's the day the ink appears. All of this sends a profound message to students: If you want to succeed, you've got to meet each day's demands *on time*. Fooling around will cost you.

If this sounds a lot like the structure of work on an assembly line, you've got it right. Where do you think we got the idea? And what do you think we're preparing students for?

Insult 5: Offering False Incentives

The essence of this fifth insult is portrayed in our response to Myth 7. By holding out points as the key definition of achievement and success, schools inadvertently undermine the value of challenge and continued growth. This is true not only for high achievers who find that they have a GPA and class rank to protect, it's just as true for slower, less-advantaged, nontraditional learners and low achievers who realize that the numbers game is stacked overwhelmingly against them and that there's no legal way that they can "win," get recognition, or retain their dignity by playing it. They aren't fast learners at what schools require they learn, they make mistakes like most of us, they didn't know how to read English before entering school, and they don't know much about the courses they're required to take. So those destined for the bottom half or the bottom quarter of their class ranking are also being punished by what educators think are the rewards inherent in the numbers game.

And how do they respond? Some act out against what they see as a no-win system and become continual discipline problems. Many others just go through the motions because they know they can't catch up in a cumulative achievement model that has been averaging everything they've ever done since they walked in the door. Short of a miracle, they know they'll never end up in the "top half" of their class where the credentials, real rewards, and future opportunities are overwhelmingly loaded. Still others eventually give up and leave with a bitter taste in their mouths. Given our Feudal Age agenda and its accompanying myths and insults, can we blame them?

6

BOXED IN BY REFORM

If they persist, Standards-Based Reforms will most certainly leave us with public schools that are even more "change-proof" than they have proven to be over the past thirty years and that serve only one segment of the public well: the children of the well-educated who have a head start coming in and can get all the extra help they need at home.

From chapter 1 on, we have been dealing with two different realities. One is the legacy of over a century of institutionalized educational practice being played out in schools and reforms. The deeper we probe into that set of realities, the more it reveals about the profound flaws and limitations that are built into our current system, and the more it evokes in us an urgency to eliminate those serious negatives before they further diminish the potential and motivation for authentic learning that reside within our young people.

The other realities relate to the higher aspirations we have for our children's education, development, and future success in a complex world of continuous discovery and constant change. Those realities reflect the insights we have shared and consolidated as a people regarding the deeper and more fulfilling nature of human learning, development, living, and growth. They give us an inspiring foundation and template for educating our young people, one where the unique potential residing within every learner has the opportunity to be discovered, nurtured, and developed to the fullest in a setting we've called a Total Learning Community.

The dilemma posed by these two realities is clear. One has been institutionalized, legalized, internalized, and reinforced to such a degree over the past century that most Americans simply regard it as a given, something they cannot imagine being different from the way it is. The other, by contrast, offers a compelling invitation to move completely beyond what now exists and to create the kind of education our children and civilization desire and deserve.

THE STANDARDS-BASED REFORM MOVEMENT

Standing in the way of taking this bold and exciting move forward is not only the massive inertia that has built up around the existing system but also the impetus and legal force that are being placed behind what are called Standards-Based Reforms (SBRs)—reforms that reinforce and lock in place virtually every negative, counterproductive feature of the iceberg and numbers game that we've examined in the previous two chapters; reforms that ignore and/or reject all five new research realities and our vision of Total Learning for Total Living described in chapters 2 and 3.

Yes, here we stand in the twenty-first century with more ideas, tools, knowledge, and strategies at our disposal for designing and implementing enormously positive, large-scale breakthroughs in educational practice than ever before in history, facing huge armies of politicians, business leaders, citizens, educators, vendors, and curriculum and testing "experts" marching at us shouting and carrying banners that say "Higher Standards," "Greater Accountability," and "Test Scores Forever." What we don't see, however, is what's written on the backs: "Onward to 1893," "Long Live *A Nation at Risk*," and "Parents for Better Icebergs," among others.

This is the coalition of educational critics that formed in 1983 in support of *A Nation at Risk*, and since then they have forged a genuinely awesome political alliance that has both the existing system and us enlightened citizens boxed in by the narrowest and most mechanistic assembly-line set of "educational" prescriptions imaginable. By 1999, over two-thirds of the states had officially joined the march, each demanding some kind of periodic standardized testing of public school students in order to force their schools to change and improve.

Unfortunately for them, however, they're only going to get one of their two desired prizes, because the thrust of their SBRs will actually put all of the iceberg features of schools in an even deeper freeze than now. They may get their version of improvement in the form of *higher test scores*, but they'll never get *change*. Only the *rhetoric* of this movement is about change. The operational reality is status quo: more (of what we're already doing), harder, and better! The iceberg will remain frozen in its current form, the numbers game will be stronger than ever, and the seven myths and five insults will go unchallenged. This promises to be educentrism's finest hour, and we'll all pay a big price if we don't find a way to get beyond these counterfeit reforms.

The Galvanizing Myth

A powerful galvanizing force in this movement is its appeal to achieving higher standards by "raising the bar." But not just any standards or bar will do. To really "count," they have to be *academic* standards because the word *academic* projects an aura around two related concepts that lie at the core of American values and mythology: rigor and expertise.

The word *rigor* evokes images of quality and thoroughness, something people could count on back in the good old days as prerequisites to achievement and success. And *expertise* evokes the words *exceptional* and *mastery*, qualities that lie just beyond the grasp of most mortals but which fuel their ideals and aspirations nonetheless. Knowing this, the advocates and implementers of the school's Feudal Age agenda got into the act early in the twentieth century and seized the high ground, declaring academic courses, academic programs, and academic tests to be the exclusive arenas where rigor, quality, thoroughness, expertise, exceptionality, and mastery were developed and proven. And for a century this association has been reinforced over and over in everything schools do and communicate to their constituents.

In simplified form, the chain of reasoning goes like this: If it's academic, it's rigorous; and if it's rigorous, it's for smart kids. Dumb kids can't handle rigor; hence, dumb kids can only do *nonacademic* things which require no rigor. The hidden concept here is the word *abstract*. When we add it, we can see the additional loaded words and implications that creep in: Academic work is abstract and, therefore, requires rigorous thinking, which is of high value. Applied work is concrete and, therefore, "only" requires manual application, which is not valued. So who in their right mind would want to build a reform movement on nonrigorous, applied standards that are not valued?

What this deeply entrenched myth fails to take into account, of course, is that practical, technical, applied, inventive, useful, inspiring, relevant, active, challenging, creative, imaginative, and exploratory learning and performance can be just as rigorous and infused with expertise as abstract academic learning can, if not more so. Just look at Bill Gates, the Information Age's most famous college dropout—an exemplar of nonacademic, practical, technical, applied, inventive, useful, inspiring, relevant, active, challenging, imaginative, creative, and exploratory learning and performance at its all-American best!

So the SBR movement that we're about to examine in more depth treats an invalid myth about Academic content and courses as sacred and unassailable. And in the process it's forcing American education into the narrowest learning and achievement "box" it has experienced since its founding. We can surrender to this Academic juggernaut, or see the word Academic as the dictionary does: Scholarly, abstract, cold, merely logical; of no consequence to things real.

Reform's Rigid Boxes

As the foregoing implies, the current SBR movement is wholly an "inside the box" approach to educational improvement. Everything that we described in chapter 1 concerning the narrow-band, closed-system, means-driven, educentric focus of the *Nation at Risk* reforms of 1983 is manifested in spades in SBRs. That leaves us with boxes within boxes driven by boxes within boxes.

In fact, there are at least seven rigid "reform boxes" severely constraining educators and undermining any incentive they might have for initiating genuine innovation and change. And, as boxes do, they (1) establish a fixed structure within which people think and operate, (2) put fixed boundaries around things that severely limit options and choices, (3) limit people's vision so they can't see what lies outside the box, and (4) constrain opportunities for creative or divergent thinking and problem solving. These seven boxes include:

- The Control Box
- The Curriculum Box
- The Standards Box
- The Grade-Level Box
- The Testing Box
- The Achievement Box
- The Accountability Box

Although these seven boxes and the issues they represent are tightly intertwined, we'll deal with each of them in the order listed and make the needed connections as they arise.

The Control Box

In nearly forty of our states, it's quite evident that state-level policy makers have completely lost faith in public education, public educators, and the public in general because they've chosen to take all significant educational matters into their own hands. The reforms they are implementing suggest the worst about the capacity of educators to operate as professionals and the public to make enlightened judgments.

A varied coalition of governors, state legislators, state superintendents, and state boards of education have chosen the force of law as the mechanism to directly control everything in education that they think matters. They define the curriculum, set the standards, approve the materials, devise and/or approve the tests that students take, determine what constitutes an acceptable performance on those tests, determine the criteria for student achievement and advancement, determine the consequences of various levels of testing results, and in some states ultimately determine who's allowed to remain employed as an educator in which schools and which districts. They would probably do the teaching, too, if there weren't so many classrooms out there to cover—and if they actually knew the same things they're expecting every student to know, which is certainly doubtful.

So state policy makers have created a hypercontrolled system that's ultimately defined at the capital and reinforced through statute and regulation in which the stakes for the participants are very high. State bodies control the ends of education and also stipulate the means. They define the game, determine the ground rules, bring the balls, deploy the players, serve as the umpire, and determine who gets what at the end of the game. What are these state officials really seeking? Improvement? Probably. Compliance and dtandardization? Absolutely! Just look at the lower right sector of figure 6.1.

State policy makers have created a very tight and rigid Control Box for local educators, and it leaves them with few choices if they want to keep their jobs.

As we can readily see, the structure of figure 6.1 parallels that of figure 1.1 in chapter 1. So does its substance. The difference lies in the words in the four sectors of the new diagram. Instead of saying "Excellence Paradigm," the upper right corner of this figure is labeled "Purpose-Focused," the approach we'll be taking in creating Total Learning Communities. The lower left sector has also been renamed from "Bureaucracy Paradigm" to "Procedure-Focused," the prevalent pattern of control in iceberg schools. But Standards-Based Reforms have plunged into the control game with both barrels blazing. With "tight"

Patterns of System Control

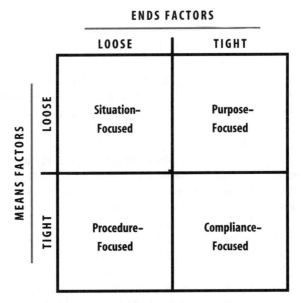

Figure 6.1

control on both ends and means, they are giving local schools no wiggle room at all. Simply stated, it's a very Industrial Age, top-down, command and control, old-paradigm, assembly-line model.

This compliance-focused Control Box has an enormous influence on the size and character of virtually all the other six Reform Boxes because what the state wants, it's going to force the locals to deliver. If this sounds too harsh, then feel free to circle as many as apply:

- You don't live in California, Massachusetts, Michigan, New York, Texas, or Virginia
- You don't know any public educators or local board of education members
- You have fond memories of the job you once had at a factory
- You cherish the 1893 antiques you bought in 1983
- You're a state policy maker and haven't been in a school since you were seventeen

The Curriculum Box

When we last discussed it, curriculum was defined as a means, not an end. Yet in the SBR movement, the academic curriculum framework of 1893 is the tail wagging the dog of twenty-first-century learning. It consists of separate, boxed-in subject areas called language arts, mathematics, social studies, science, and so forth. They go by the very erudite-sounding name, the "academic disciplines." In the traditional credit systems of the past century, each discipline and each subject/course within it was "boxed" separately and treated in isolation from the others—even though students needed math skills to be successful at science and language skills to be successful at everything! That formal segregation is further reinforced in the SBRs.

What matters most in these segregated curriculum areas is *content*, largely because differences in the nature of content is what created the disciplines/curriculum areas in the first place. Virtually every major subject area has a national organization dedicated to providing professional support to educators who work with its particular content. With the best of intentions—and lest they be seen as "behind the times" or against the national goals and standards that the president and the National Governors Association were pressing so hard to implement in the late 1980s and early 1990s—these subject-matter associations scrambled to develop standards for their respective curriculum areas. In the process, they created ends for their means!

Each association appointed a distinguished, blue ribbon committee of mainly college professors and high school teachers from among its members to carry out this process. Given what they were asked to do, it's no surprise that these content experts produced standards that are about what you need to know or do to be a *top student* in a *specific curriculum area* at a *specific grade level* in school. By acting in the interests of their career expertise and identities, these committees of content specialists produced standards that seemed to be saying to students: "This is the content we know well, regard as important, and teach. And this is what you need to know to be good at it. Once you learn it all, you'll probably end up the valedictorian of your class and get admitted to the college of your choice!" And they could have also added: "The nation's politicians will be happy, too, because they'll have higher test scores to show other nations and each other."

Overwhelmingly, then, today's standards are about school curriculum, not about the life performance competences described in chapter 2. And to appear "rigorous," most of these standards have taken the form of "content overkill." Each subject area has notebooks and manuals filled with detailed goals and objectives about what students should know and do in their particular subject at particular grade levels to thoroughly demonstrate mastery of the curriculum in that area. They need to learn this, then this, then this, then this, then this . . . and the lists go on forever, confirming that subject-based content is truly the alpha and omega of SBR thinking and practice. Persuasive evidence of this content overkill is provided in Susan Ohanian's *One Size Fits Few* (1999).

The Standards Box

If academic curriculum content is the bedrock of the standards, then these content-based standards are certainly the bedrock of these pervasive reforms. Especially in states where extensive "high stakes" testing programs have been developed to assess their accomplishment, standards are the driving force of everything in the system: curriculum design, instructional priorities and processes, materials purchases, accountability conditions, testing and reporting, student program placement and status, and on and on. If something doesn't directly address or align with these standards, don't expect schools to give it any attention. They're already overwhelmed with the pressure to achieve the existing standards and don't need anything else on their plates.

While it's easy to argue that it's about time schools had standards which they took seriously, it's just as easy to argue that as long as they're taking them so seriously, it would be even better if the standards had merit and relevance beyond themselves. Standards for the sake of standards keep you . . . well, in a box! Here are four very disturbing "realities" that undermine the alleged merits of the current standards frameworks.

1. *These standards are highly unrealistic.* They are written for the best student the design committee members *wish* they had ever had, but that student hasn't shown up in school yet. Very simply, when you take the entire volumes of the standards across all the different subject areas and stack them up, they've never had a student who could, or would want to, memorize all of this stuff. The standards might best be considered "academic ideals," or high-level expectations for people who want master's degrees in some of these curriculum areas.

But when you consider that some states are expecting *every student* to meet *all* of them in *every subject*, they cease to be ideals at all. With hundreds of them to learn per subject area per grade level, they look to be more like either a bad joke or ridiculous farce than something all Americans can or should learn to be successful after they finish school.

2. *These standards are hypocritical*, simply because almost no well-educated, successful adult knows or can do them—including teachers. For example, it would be the extremely rare high school teacher in America who can pass *all* the Standards in *all* the subjects, because high school teachers, like college professors, are subject specialists, not generalists. Specialists don't know the other specialized stuff their colleagues down the hall are teaching. And who leads the list of those who can't pass them? The governors, state legislators, and corporate leaders who so eagerly embrace and endorse them as "essential" for everyone else. Are there any parents out there who want to try to pass them with their personal future at stake? Hello? Parents? High stakes testing, anyone?

Yet we expect high school students to do so; otherwise they won't receive diplomas that "qualify" them for entry-level jobs. It sounds like we're dealing with hypocrisy here: "The kids need all this stuff, but we don't. We're already successful and in control." Eventually a truly informed public will overlook the potential merits of these standards simply because there's too much here to absorb that isn't essential to successful living, and because they're beyond the desire and capabilities of young people to achieve.

3. *These standards ignore the greater realities of life* and living as creative, contributing human beings. Standards are all about mastering basic skills and specific academic content, but there's very little of that content which directly enhances the complex competences adults need in their career, civic, and family life roles. Traditional curriculum content relates to only a couple of the multiple intelligences described in chapters 2 and 3, and hardly any of the domains of living, future conditions, or life performance abilities described there, either.

Based on the new research realities and the importance of the Total Learning for Total Living model, we're deluding ourselves to believe that the more traditional academic content we know, the more competent and effective we'll be in our complex life roles. Therefore, the more time and energy we spend obsessing over this Standards Box, the more we'll short change the development of these deeper, more essential qualities and abilities in our students.

4. *These standards are costing us a fortune*—in dollars, time, resources, and opportunities lost. Any testing program that attempts to fully address and assess all of them will cost a fortune, waste billions of person-hours of educational time, fail most of the students, jeopardize their futures, diminish our collective vision of learning and achievement, and prove nothing that the teachers and parents of these students don't already know about their academic abilities and standing. But it will give the newspapers tons of numbers to report and schools to rank and the critics of public schools more ammunition for criticizing them.

Armed with "proof," the latter group can, without reservation, encourage parents to abandon their public iceberg schools for private iceberg ones down the street that have higher standards and test scores.

The Grade-Level Box

The Grade-Level Box is a structural feature of iceberg schools that brings their Agrarian Age calendar and Industrial Age delivery system together into an operating reality that we've called the assembly-line approach to instruction. This is truly a multidimensional "box" in which the age of the students, a body of curriculum content, and the pace and style of the teacher's instruction are squeezed together for a prespecified nine-month block of time.

Think of grade levels as "windows of eligibility," where eligibility is determined by when we *let* students have the opportunity to learn particular things in the curriculum and by when we *make* them learn it. The grade level, then, is the block (box) of time in which we "offer" students of a given age a prescribed body (box) of curriculum. In an inflexible grade level system, they're eligible/scheduled to study that box of curriculum at a particular time, so that's when they *must* study it and prove they know it. That box of time defines what the system means by "opportunity."

The overriding assumption of this constraining model of opportunity is that the great majority of "capable" children of a given age will be able to learn and assimilate a given body of material at a uniform rate within the amount of time allocated. If any of them can't, they are retained in that curriculum box and forced to repeat the entire body of material and experiences again (and again) until they *do* get it. Those who can are promoted to the next Grade-Level Box, where this process is repeated for the next chunk of curriculum and block of time. The model "works" because the system ignores all but the very largest differences in student learning rates, learning styles, backgrounds, aptitudes, and interests. The *regularity* of the system is what matters most. Significant learner differences create major inconveniences.

What gives this already inflexible box even greater strength and rigidity is the insertion of these new content standards as the key condition for promotion or retention. If students are going to advance through the system, they are obligated to meet these standards, and on the designated schedule. Local requirements may supplement them, but they are the gate through which all must pass via the only accepted means available: a state-designed and/or state-approved standardized, paper-and-pencil test.

The Testing Box

Unfortunately, three quite different educational words and concepts have gotten badly entangled and distorted over the years. They are evaluation, assessment, and testing. *Evaluation* is a process of comparing a given body of evidence against an existing standard or set of criteria and making a judgment regarding the acceptability or quality of the evidence at hand. Words like good, poor, acceptable, not acceptable, pass, and fail are associated with that term, and decisions are made accordingly. The SBR movement is obsessed with evaluation.

But in order to evaluate, you need to gather relevant evidence in the first place, and that process is called *assessment*. "Authentic" assessments ask subjects or performers to generate evidence that directly matches a clearly known goal, objective, outcome, or standard. If this match/alignment doesn't exist, the performer is "shooting blind," and the assessment misses the target and is thus invalid. So there's really only one kind of valid assessment, and it's called "authentic and aligned."

For example, depending on how a desired outcome is defined, its authentic assessment might require performers to write, describe, explain, design, plan, organize, lead, persuade, negotiate, teach, model, implement, demonstrate, perform, build, or produce something. In virtually all of these cases, they'd be required to execute one or more of these complex processes, often with other people and materials involved, and to generate evidence that they had done so. Because of the processes involved, *testing* as we know it would not be a valid approach to assessing performer competence in any of these cases unless it were what testing experts call "open-ended." And even then, except for written passages, paper-and-pencil tests can't assess psycho-motor, strategic, operational, productive, or interpersonal processes—though they're the very competences that constitute the majority of what people *do* to be productive and successful in their lives and careers.

So the kinds of objective, paper-and-pencil testing employed in the SBR movement are valid and useful for assessing only a narrow range of abilities, primarily those involving the mental processing of content and concepts. Apart from the mental processing—remembering, understanding, interpreting, analyzing, and inferring—the primary skills required on a paper-and-pencil test involve marking the correct box on a score sheet and placing words, numbers, or other notations on answer sheets. By focusing exclusively on "objectively" assessing these mental processes in a standardized, paper-and-pencil way,

> Standards-Based Reforms are eliminating most dimensions of human potential, almost every competence in the Life Performance Wheel, and almost all aspects of being a Total Learner from consideration as priority learning and achievement.

That's an awful lot to lose for what you get: a score that fits in a tiny box based on a single test that determines your educational future, your school's resources and reputation, and even your teacher's and principal's careers. But that single score in that tiny box satisfies state policy makers that you and your school have been made accountable, and in the long run that's what matters to them the most. For penetrating analyses of this misapplication of standardized testing methods, see James Popham's article "The Mismeasurement of Educational Quality" (2000) and Alfie Kohn's book *The Case against Standardized Testing* (2000).

The Achievement Box

Almost everything we might discover about the Achievement Box has already been exposed in chapter 5. Everything about the myths and insults of the numbers game holds here and should be brought directly into this part of the discussion. We need only note that in the SBR movement, numbers, scores, symbols, and code are treated as the learners' learning, abilities, and achievements and their schools' effectiveness with no questions asked, even though the unreliability of these tests is well-known. For example:

- Tests can be designed to tap everything from the basic recall of simple facts to the complex analysis of relationships among sets of factors affecting a potential outcome. How can a single score and a single pass/fail mark accurately reflect the diversity of abilities that might lie behind the answers provided? They can't, and they never have. Just because a test is taken by thousands of students, is scored by a big computer, and yields numbers that can be manipulated and compared in all kinds of fancy ways, doesn't make it an accurate measure of anything.
- The professional literature and press are filled with articles showing major discrepancies between students' scores on SBR state tests and the demonstrated quality of their classroom work. From the SBR perspective, in cases like this, the test is right and the classroom teacher's criteria are off the mark simply because tests are "objective" and teachers are "subjective." That response is akin to: "We're lost, but we're making great time!"
- Student scores vary considerably from test to test in the same learning areas depending on how the designers create the test. There are thousands of relevant pieces of information associated with any learning area. We must recognize that only a given, small number of them are chosen to represent this huge range of possibilities on any official test. Why those particular items? Do they represent a broad cross-section of material, or probe one area in more depth? Would a different set produce a different result for individual students? No doubt that it would. Is one set superior to any other set? It depends on what you're trying to measure, but only the people who designed the standards and tests think they know, and they're not telling.

To break out of this unproductive box, ask the following twelve questions again and again of educators and policy makers. They get to the heart of the matter and will compel testing advocates to come to grips with the issues raised here and in chapter 5 about the myths surrounding tests, scores, and standards.

1. Exactly what, in precise words, does this test measure?
2. Exactly what, in precise words, does this test *not* measure?
3. Exactly what, in precise words, does this test *not* measure that is essential to students' success in tomorrow's world?
4. Why don't we measure and report that instead?
5. What exactly does a particular student's test score mean?
6. Is this one test score the student's total learning and achievement?
7. Which score clearly indicates that the student is competent?
8. Does one point less indicate incompetence?
9. What does this test or a given test score prove about the student, the school, or the district?
10. What exactly does this test score indicate about the student that needs to be improved?
11. What exactly does this test score indicate about the school or district that needs to be improved?
12. What does this test score indicate about a student's learning that her or his teachers don't already know?

We could go on with critical points like these for a long time, but the larger issue has been joined. SBRs about assessing the capabilities of individual students and the quality of their teachers and schools on the narrowest of measures at a single point in time using a very questionable assessment device in order to generate a single do-or-die score that can be easily manipulated statistically to prove whatever needs to be proven. But there's even more. Everyone affected by these reforms is going to be made accountable if they don't clear their state's standards bar!

The Accountability Box

Let's give the architects of state-driven reforms credit for seeing iceberg schools for what they are: bureaucracies. And, as explained in chapters 1 and 4, since bureaucracies are tight in managing their means, and loose with respect to their ends, their natural "accountabilities"—what they really *have to do*, or else!—also gravitate around their means. But these means-based accountabilities weren't producing the results/ends that policy makers were seeking, so they decided to force the issue and make educators accountable for ends/learning/results as well. Hence, Standards-Based Reforms.

In principle, this was a step in the right direction, but the SBR designers unfortunately locked in on standardized tests as the way to define and achieve ends-based accountability. Because they are standardized—which means that everyone is being assessed on the same thing in the same way at the same time—the results that emerge from the tests are presumably comparable. And because we've all been subjected to plenty of these tests over the years, we've created the illusion of understanding what their scores mean. And since scores are visible, concrete, objective, and quantitative, people understand and value them as measures of desired kinds of learning.

Bolstered by this almost-universal acceptance of test scores as legitimate measures of achievement, policy makers gave the tests teeth by attaching significant consequences to them. If the scores aren't high enough, then students can fail, teachers and principals can be fired, funding can be reduced, and/or local districts—school board and all—can be taken over by their state's department of education. And, no matter what else, the scores will be published in the newspaper so that a massive exercise in finger-pointing or back-slapping can begin.

This leaves educators "boxed in"—on two fronts, both means and ends—with no professional discretion or judgment left. With their jobs and reputations at stake, they are being told *what* to teach, *when* to teach it, *how* to teach it, and *how well* to teach it by a certain date, regardless of whom their clientele are. And the students are subject to the same constraints: *what* to learn, *when* to learn it, *how* to learn it, and *how well* to learn it by a certain date, regardless of differences in their learning rates, learning backgrounds and home languages, learning styles and talents, and career interests and aspirations.

The apparent goal of all this is standardized achievement, a standardized curriculum, standardized instruction, standardized tests, standardized opportunities, standardized students, standardized educators, standardized schools, and a standardized system for a standardized America that has simply become far too diverse as it is. And notice, some policy makers are saying, "It's long overdue!" But writers like Susan Ohanian (1999) and Peter Sacks (2000) are urging us to view this obsession with standardization as extremely destructive to everyone caught in these layers of legally enforced bureaucratic constraints.

HIGH-STAKES CONSEQUENCES

Clearly, SBR efforts vary a lot from state to state. Thankfully, not all states have gone as far down the standardization path as others. But in states with "high-stakes" testing programs—states such as California, Massachusetts, Michigan, New York, Texas, and Virginia—the word *stake* has come to mean "stake in the heart." Test performance in those states has turned into the only outcome that matters, and when that happens you create a pervasive climate of fear and a loss of both professionalism and talent.

The fallout of these reforms is distressing, and the long-term implications for our education system are even worse. Today's newspapers, educational publications, and National Public Radio programs are filled with stories describing how:

- Out of fear, countless teachers have narrowed their curriculum focus and teaching methods to stress what's going to be tested, period. It's called "drill and kill," and it's become the universal method of choice, even among teachers once regarded as innovative and inspiring. If things aren't likely to be tested, they aren't likely to be taught, no matter how interesting or valuable they may be to students. Lots of relevant, interesting, valuable, and applied things aren't getting taught anymore, and student talents of all kinds are being ignored. Students recognize this and are speaking openly about it in interviews and articles on the reforms.
- Educator morale has plummeted, and excellent veteran teachers are resigning because what is expected of them is so narrow and limiting that it runs counter to their beliefs and professional ethics. They simply won't remain in a system that diminishes and demeans themselves and their learners so severely. As you might expect, pride and motivation among our most imaginative and talented teachers are sinking fast because they're being treated like hired hands and replaceable cogs in an uncaring machine. Who will replace them? Conscious, creative, collaborative, competent, and constructive Total Professionals? Guess again!
- Principal and superintendent vacancies go unfilled because no one applies. States are demanding compliant managers who will unfailingly carry out their mandates—cogs in the bureaucratic machinery, not leaders with vision and imagination. Local initiative, flexibility, and innovation have been replaced by state (legislative) control and standardization. Smart people don't want the hassle and don't want to manage what they regard as an immoral system. They can find far better ways to improve the world than to manage a system that denies everything known about learners, learning, effective instruction, and the future. Across the country the leadership "pool" has all but evaporated.
- Students of all ages are displaying serious stress symptoms because of the pressure on them to produce on the tests and the stigma that results if they don't. They report to physicians, counselors, and psychologists that school is no longer relevant or interesting since almost all their time is spent intensively drilling for tests.
- Students by the carloads are failing the tests. Most of them come from low-income or non-English-speaking families—the very population the reforms claim to be helping. But the casualties also include a host of non-traditional learners, as well as highly successful students who have done well in the very same subjects that they've failed on the tests. As noted earlier, this has led critics to question why the tests depart so significantly from sound classroom work and why some of them contain things that no

one will ever see or use again outside of very specific coursework. Consequently, many high achievers and their parents have begun challenging
and boycotting the test administrations.

- Dropout rates and hostile behaviors are increasing as students experience shattered self-esteem and opt out of a system in which they find little recognition, little relevance, and no hope for success.

Given these consequences, it's no surprise that some educators, parents, students, and even policy makers are up in arms over the SBR movement. At some
level, they believe, reform is supposed to make things better—besides the test
scores themselves. But these indicators suggest that *they're making them
worse*! In addition, they're reinforcing an archaic approach to schooling that
should have been abandoned in the eighties when both the handwriting and the
new blueprints were already on the wall.

CHANGE-PROOF SCHOOLS

Those inclined toward conspiracy theories could have a field day with SBRs.
We've had a Democratic president, major corporate leaders, eager Republican
governors, one of the major national teacher's organizations, many zealous Republican state legislatures, and leading academic reformers arguing for the
same things in varying degrees: *iceberg reforms*—visible attempts to improve
public schools at the margins but leaving their fundamental organizational and
operational features unaddressed and unchanged.

If they persist, SBRs will most certainly leave us with public schools that are
even more "change-proof" than they have proven to be over the past thirty
years and that serve only one segment of the public well: the children of the
well-educated who have a head start coming in and can get all the extra help
they need at home. The other children will simply have to fend for themselves
in a highly competitive environment made even more competitive by the reforms themselves.

> They are taking an iceberg that is already out of date and out of sync with
> today's highly dynamic world and making it three times bigger and three
> times colder and denser than it now is. How can such a thing ever melt?

Given the six consequences we just noted, conspiracy theorists might offer
the view that this entire SBR exercise is a ruse—that it was not intended to significantly improve public education at all but to make it so incapacitated, outdated, and ineffective that it will simply drive those with a choice elsewhere.
Without question, it's driving both talented administrators and teachers from

the system. Who will replace them? In addition, learners of all kinds are suffering "shell shock" from the pressures they face as "high-stakes" students. Their symptoms are an impetus for them and others to leave; either for another school or for the streets. And what will the SBRs do with the huge backlog of failures as kids get retained and retained by the thousands because they don't "deserve" to be promoted to the next higher assembly line?

At this rate we may end up with three parallel systems: (1) public iceberg schools for those with no choice; (2) private iceberg schools for those *with* a choice; and (3) empowering, future-focused Total Learning Communities for those attracted to the realities and models described in chapters 2 and 3.

The first alternative is simply the natural extension of what's already happening: iceberg public schools being driven by a very narrow vision of learning and an even narrower methodology for achieving it. They will be attended by the very students the reforms are now trying to reform the most—the children of the poor and less educated—because they'll have nowhere else to go. They'll be taught by teachers who are paid lousy wages but have a deep sense of commitment to working with the disadvantaged.

The second alternative will also be an iceberg system, but for the children of the educationally advantaged who have everything to gain from an iceberg operation that's not cluttered up with nonachievers. With or without vouchers, well-educated parents who want the same kind of education for their children that they had will enroll their children in private or charter iceberg schools that will operate just the way today's reformers would like: with rigorous academic standards and tests driving a Feudal Age agenda, an Agrarian Age calendar, an Industrial Age delivery system, and a Bureaucratic Age culture. To them, it's "school"; it worked well, it gets you into good colleges, and it gives you the credentials you need to have a successful career.

The third alternative will actually be called the "alternative system." It will be for all children whose parents want a more personalized, future-focused, enlightened, and learner-responsive education for them. You readers and people like you will work within your states and communities to establish the kind of models described in the remainder of this book. You'll be motivated by an intense desire to have your children develop all of the unique talents and interests they manifested as preschoolers and to leave education as truly conscious, creative, collaborative, competent, and constructive human beings with the abilities and qualities to shape their careers and world in healthy ways. You'll call your creation a Total Learning Community because that's what it will be, a place where everyone learns, children and adults alike.

7

CREATING STANDARDS FOR
TRANSFORMING EDUCATION

*These standards define the bedrock essentials of a new-paradigm
learning system, from now on called a Total Learning Community.
This TLC has a positive, growth-oriented culture; a powerful and enlightened rationale for planning and implementation; a future-
focused framework of life-performance learning expectations, an
open-access, learner-responsive instructional system; and a rich infrastructure of people and resources on which it regularly draws.*

We've spent the last three chapters exploring the outmoded and counterproductive features of the educational system we've inherited from the past. And
we've seen that the recent Standards-Based Reforms are counterfeit because
they further reinforce and entrench, rather than change, these negative features of our system; severely box in our thinking and options; and create negative consequences left and right for students, educators, and the system as a
whole—damage from which many will never recover.

But we've also seen that there are fundamentally more enlightened and empowering alternatives open to us—whole new ways of grounding our thinking
about learners, learning, and education. These new-paradigm alternatives
emerged because we were willing to expand our vision beyond the educentric
constraints of conventional thinking and practice. In the process we considered
five research realities in chapter 2 that continue to evolve and expand. These
new knowledge bases reveal exciting possibilities about expanding and literally
transforming our notions of education as we have known it. With them and our

Total Learning framework as a working foundation, we're now ready to create a profoundly more enlightened, empowering, and future-focused way of educating our young people—one that will come together in the remainder of the book in what we call a Total Learning Community (TLC).

THE VISIONARY GOALS OF TOTAL LEARNING COMMUNITIES

So here we are: intelligent, concerned, and enlightened parents, business leaders, educators, and citizens who have no organized lobby, or bully pulpit, or media clout, or special ties to the politically powerful. But we share a deep awareness that iceberg schooling and the reforms that are now reinforcing it no longer make any sense to us and that the country's future depends on our melting the iceberg and replacing it with a far more enlightened, new-paradigm model of education. We also know that our young people need an education that will:

1. Equip them for a future of continuous discovery and constant change—not for an Industrial Age past that is now behind us.
2. Prepare them to lead totally fulfilling lives—not just qualify for more advanced schooling.
3. Foster the kinds of complex abilities needed to succeed in and shape tomorrow's dynamic and complex world—not master curriculum and standards that one only encounters in schools and on tests.
4. Encourage students to be producers of their own knowledge and products—not passive consumers of content from teachers and texts.
5. Develop the kinds of orientations and abilities needed to remain a self-directed learner throughout one's life—not limit learning to what is taught in school subjects or formally tested and scored.
6. Nurture the many dimensions of learning and talent that reside within all human beings—not just the verbal and mathematical skills needed to pass paper-and-pencil tests in academic subjects.
7. Respond sensitively to differences in student learning rates and the unique challenges many learners face when confronted with abstract, lecture-type instruction—not assume that a uniform rate of covering the material is the same as teaching.
8. Focus on achieving the ultimate level of competence possible for each learner—not on the time blocks in which courses are typically offered.
9. Respond positively to the emerging possibilities that the new research on learning, human development, and the future is continuously revealing—not lock students into routine grade-level/assembly-line content, instructional methods, and learning opportunities.

10. Welcome and implement promising innovations that advance future-focused learning—not stick to old habits and time-honored practices.
11. Create a culture in which everyone learns from everyone—children and adults alike—not only in age-determined teaching-learning roles.
12. Establish ways of continuously assessing and improving everything it does—not embrace familiar, routine practices for their own sake.

We recognize these as the twelve learner-empowering goals stated at the end of chapter 1, but they have a deeper meaning now because of the many discoveries we've made in the intervening chapters. And as we focus on the tremendous differences in approach embodied in each goal, we're accomplishing three key things: (1) strengthening our vision of the paradigm of education we advocate; (2) clarifying the features of the old paradigm that make it counterfeit in today's world; and (3) engaging in the process described in chapter 1 as wide-band thinking—thinking that extends beyond the narrow, closed-system scope of past experience and fixed beliefs.

CREATING A NEW PARADIGM OF STANDARDS

To achieve these twelve new paradigm goals, we'll need to create a set of criteria that guide us to this new way of operating, remembering from chapter 1 that in this ends-based approach, there may be multiple ways to accomplish any given goal. If we do our job right, these criteria will serve as the standards around which we can design our new model and against which we can assess our implementation progress and success.

The remainder of this chapter explores five such standards that have the power to guide and shape the kind of learning system we want to create. We regard these five criteria as *essential systemic components* of such a model; that is, they are the five major things we absolutely need to put in place to assure that our new learning system will function properly and accomplish these new paradigm goals. If any one of the five is overlooked or is poorly implemented, this systemic model will be seriously compromised. Consequently, we are committed to designing and implementing a model that consistently and systematically:

1. Creates and sustains a culture of integrity, inquiry, and continuous improvement in which all participants contribute and share.
2. Designs and aligns everything it does around the five new research realities: human potential, human learning, domains of living, future conditions, and life performance.
3. Develops in all learners the unique qualities and complex life-performance abilities each needs for success and fulfillment in life.

4. Ensures that all learners receive continuous, stimulating learning experiences and support from any qualified source in developing and documenting these qualities and abilities to/at their highest levels.
5. Seeks out and utilizes all available people, resources, technologies, and approaches in providing these continuous, stimulating learning experiences.

These standards define the bedrock essentials of a new-paradigm learning
system, from now on called a Total Learning Community. This TLC has a positive, growth-oriented culture; a powerful and enlightened rationale for planning and implementation; a future-focused framework of life-performance
learning expectations; an open-access, learner-responsive instructional system;
and a rich infrastructure of people and resources on which it regularly draws.
The nature and character of each component supports the others and provides
the conditions that enable the twelve learner-empowering goals to be achieved.

But note, TLCs aren't "prescriptive" or "canned" models. Tightly prescribed
models immediately create boxes that limit thinking and structural options, and
we're not going to fall into that trap. Instead, our model has clear standards
about the kinds of operating conditions that must be developed and implemented to have integrity and be successful, but it does not prescribe the form
that those essential conditions must take.

For example, first, these standards do *not* demand that a TLC have a specific
form or physical structure that would limit sound implementation options. Second, they do not say that learners need to be a given age or go to a specific location on a specific schedule in order to learn. Third, they do not say that learning
must take place in specific rooms of a specific size with a specific number of other
learners in attendance. Fourth, they do not say that you must develop a specific
framework of unique learner qualities, implement a specific framework of life-
performance abilities, or develop and document them in a given way. Fifth, they
do not say that continuous, stimulating support must take a given form, or that
people, resources, technologies, and approaches be utilized in a given way.

So take the list of means described in chapter 1—curriculum, courses, semesters, programs, grade levels, textbooks, and so on—and put them aside for
the time being. They're all constraining boxes and form, and we're not going to
let those specific tails wag our dog.

As we address, design, and implement each essential component, we'll be
stepping out of the conventional boxes of schooling and taking enlightened
strides toward a new reality—the reality that Peters and Waterman offered in
1983 and which the new research realities now suggest was right on the mark.
And with each daring step we take beyond familiar old "comfort zones," we'll
be showing that iceberg schools and Standards-Based Reforms are neither inevitable nor desirable. In fact, we'll show that *reforming* education is the wrong
mission. *Transforming* it is what's actually required, and these five standards
will be the template for that long overdue "remodeling."

LEADING TRANSFORMATIONAL CHANGE

If we're daring to undertake the transformation of America's time-honored educational paradigm, then we've volunteered to lead an enormous adventure into the unknown regions of something called "systemic change." And for that we need a quick introduction to the territory of leadership and change before jumping in with both feet. Fortunately, we've got the key ideas and wisdom of a hundred of the world's leading experts of leadership and change at our disposal in the form of the book *Total Leaders: Applying the Best Future-Focused Change Strategies to Education* (Schwahn and Spady 1998).

What we discovered in our comprehensive analysis and synthesis of this highly significant body of work, is that:

> Leadership and change are inseparable. You can't have one without the other.

Leaders lead change—because there's nothing else to lead. If you're not leading change—moving beyond current conditions and taking your people where they wouldn't go on their own—you're administering or managing the status quo. Moreover, purposeful and lasting change doesn't happen by accident. It requires significant leadership initiative, skill, and persistence.

More importantly, however, we discovered that there are five major approaches to describing the essence of leadership and change. Each of these five approaches, or schools of thought, turns out to be a critical component of an even larger model, one we call "Total Leadership." The five domains of Total Leadership performance are called Authentic, Visionary, Cultural, Quality, and Service, and each domain has its major champions, gurus, exemplars, and body of research.

Moreover, each domain has a key set of abilities and performance roles associated with it, and these abilities are critical for establishing a particular condition that enables change efforts to be successful. We call these five conditions "pillars of change" because, without each pillar, change efforts—the attempt to create and sustain something new—inevitably collapse. Very simply put, purposeful, productive, and lasting organizational change does not happen by accident; it's the result of the skills of Total Leaders who create new ways of operating by building and sustaining these five key pillars of change:

1. A deep and compelling organizational purpose for the change.
2. An inspiring, future-focused vision of the change operating at its ideal best.
3. Inclusive involvement of and ownership by everyone in the change process.

4. The capacity and know-how to implement the change and sustain its continued evolution.
5. Solid support structures for the change process to start and continue indefinitely.

Without these five pillars, organizations and their members lack a compelling reason to change, a clear picture of the change, the deep commitment to change, the tangible ability to implement the change, and the opportunity/ assistance to make the change happen—five critical factors in shaping the success or failure of any new initiative.

The challenge of establishing and sustaining these five pillars will be as true for us as for the leaders of any other kind of change effort. The steps we take in the following chapters will assist us enormously in establishing these pillars.

THE ESSENCE OF OUR NEW TRANSFORMATIONAL STANDARDS

Up to this point in the chapter, we have used the terms *new-paradigm learning system* and *Total Learning Communities* interchangeably because one *is* the other. TLCs are direct manifestations of wide-band, future-focused, open-system, new-paradigm thinking that answers the question, If we could design a learning system based systematically on the best insights currently available on human potential, human learning, domains of living, future conditions, life performance, effective instruction, and today's technologies, what would we create? The answer is a learning *system* that has all the characteristics of a Total Learning Community.

It would be defined and organized around the future instead of the past, promising possibilities instead of established precedents, Total Living instead of more schooling, Total Learning instead of content areas, a deep and compelling purpose instead of formalized procedures, learning results instead of time, life-performance abilities instead of test scores, and learner potential and interests instead of grade levels. In short, we would transform conventional schooling concepts and practices into a model that fully utilizes the latest research on learners, learning, and authentic performance to develop in all learners—adults and children alike—the full extent of their capacities as conscious, creative, collaborative, competent, and constructive human beings who lead joyous, productive, and fulfilling lives.

To accomplish this broad ideal, TLCs transcend the serious limitations and boxes of the old system, thereby enabling any learner to learn anything of relevance at any time from any expert or resource at any location that works for them—and be formally acknowledged for it whenever it happens. This requires enormous flexibility in thinking and operations, something that can only realized when a system's ends and purpose are clearly established and focused, and its means and procedures are learner-responsive and adaptable—the very characteristics we've referred to again and again in previous chapters.

In order for this model to function optimally as an integrated system, our work suggests that it must contain five basic, interrelated components:

1. An inquiry-based *rationale* around which everything is explicitly designed. The sound research, values, beliefs, perspectives, principles, and mission/purpose embodied in that rationale are the foundation for all of the model's planning, decisions, and actions.
2. A framework of future-focused *learning/performance essentials* that appropriately challenges and empowers all learners. These essentials are derived directly from the rationale and serve as the prime focus and operating purpose of everything the model does.
3. A rich, continuously available array of stimulating and challenging *learning experiences* that directly facilitate the accomplishment of the learning essentials. These experiences offer learners expert assistance and feedback whenever they need them at whatever level of challenge they're prepared to undertake.
4. An *organizational culture* that embodies the model's social "climate," moral tone, health, and expectations. A culture committed to deep reflection, active exploration, personal growth, quality performance, and continuous accountability is essential for the model to function effectively and realize its purpose.
5. An infrastructure of tangible and human *resources* and supports that is used both directly to implement the model's learning experiences and indirectly to coordinate and facilitate its functioning. Without these resources, the model could not function properly or hope to achieve its instructional mission.

Given the "design back from where you want to end up" nature of this design process, everything in the model flows from the rationale. Hence, it needs to be clear, powerful, compelling, and future-focused.

Second, the rationale serves as the foundation for the model's statement of what it is there to accomplish: relevant, empowering learning and performance success for all its learners. So getting a clear, powerful, compelling, and future-focused learning/performance framework in place is our second critical design step. Once we establish our picture of these learning essentials, it then becomes the driving force in designing the rest of the model, especially the kind of learning/instructional system needed for achieving it.

Third, the heart and soul of the instructional function of the model is carried out through the learning experiences, but we can't appropriately design them until we have our rationale and framework of learning essentials solidly in place. Once we do design them, however, our design must assure that all learners will get the assistance and support they need to develop and advance consistent with their unique potential and interests.

Fourth, only after we've developed these prior three components will we be ready to explicitly design the kind of support systems we'll need to implement and sustain them. These are what we've called organizational culture (the more intangible supports) and resources (the more tangible ones). These will ultimately be the supports that sustain the model's purpose, intended outcomes, and learning system.

Now with these clarifications in place, it's fairly simple to make the link between each of these five critical components and the transformational standards that will guide the rest of this book. However, there is one change in the order in which the standards are listed that deserves explanation. The first standard states: "Creates and sustains a culture of integrity, inquiry. . . ." But culture is the fourth component in the model, not the first. Why the discrepancy?

It becomes clear if we recognize that the standards are listed in the order in which we need to take our explicit design steps, rather than by the design logic just described. Establishing a "culture" or set of agreements and under-standings about how we're going to operate, treat each other, make decisions, delegate responsibilities, recognize and support what is done by others, grow and learn, and deal with a host of other interpersonal issues has got to get clear and in place before we have any hope of taking the other design and implementation steps necessary for generating and operating our model.

So with this in mind, let's now formally map out the connections that we're proposing:

1. *Culture* is directly addressed and established in Step 1/Standard 1. From this point on we'll call them "Establishing a Culture of Total Professionalism."

2. *Rationale* is directly addressed and established in Step 2/Standard 2. From this point on we'll call them "Laying a Foundation of Insight and Inquiry."

3. *Learning essentials* are directly addressed and established in Step 3/ Standard 3. From this point on we'll call them "Defining Life Performance Learning Essentials."

4. *Learning experiences* are directly addressed and established in Step 4/ Standard 4. From this point on we'll call them "Ensuring Empowering Learning Experiences."

5. *Resources* are directly addressed and established in Step 5/Standard 5. From this point on we'll call them "Mobilizing Resources to Support Learning."

We'll briefly describe the essence of each of these transformational standards in the sections that follow, then deal with them in more detail in the final five chapters.

Standard 1: Establishing a Culture of Total Professionalism

The foregoing clearly indicates that there's more to a model of education than curriculum, instruction, and assessments. What the people in that system do to keep it healthy, alive, future-focused, and professional is vital to how well its instructional mission is carried out.

Those attitudes, values, principles, beliefs, expectations, norms, rewards, sanctions, symbols of honor, and behaviors come together into what researchers call an "organizational culture." A culture is carried in the often informal agreements people in a society or organization make with each other about what they value and honor. How effectively, congenially, and openly an organization functions—what many people call its "climate"—is a direct reflection of its culture and the strength of the moral foundation that bolsters it. It is imperative that our Total Learning Communities model embodies a culture of unassailable integrity—one that we call "Total Professionalism."

Our society offers few accolades more revered than to call someone a "true professional." And by that we usually mean that those people are exceptionally competent, consistently perform at very high levels (even on bad hair days), show their finest colors when the circumstances become the most challenging, place the well-being of their clients or constituency far ahead of their own, go the extra mile to meet agreements, work harder than most to continuously improve what they already do exceptionally well, exhibit genuine humility in the face of great accomplishment and adulation, never lose their composure, and are completely trustworthy.

Clearly professionalism is more than talent and competence. It's the capacity to operate from a moral grounding of contribution rather than wanting, learning rather than knowing, and openness rather than opinion. In an extension of our leadership analysis in *Total Leaders*, we describe how Total Leaders embody and demonstrate the qualities of Total Professionals. In short, Total Professionals are ethical in their judgments and actions, cutting-edge in their approach to their work, collegial in their interactions with peers and clients, expert in the execution of their craft, and dedicated to making the most positive contribution they can.

But these admirable attributes are no "accidents" of personal virtue. They are the result of a principled way of approaching life and their work. As we demonstrate in *Total Leaders*, true professionals are guided by a set of principles that serves as the standards for manifesting who they are as people, that shape their view of the world, that guide all their decisions, and that determine their actions—especially in the face of adversity.

But a culture of professionalism is more than having individuals choose to behave professionally. It happens when there is *collective agreement* among the members of a social entity that their decisions and actions will be guided by a common set of principles, ones that shape their decisions and actions in ways that make them ethical, cutting-edge, collegial, expert, and dedicated. Ten such principles characterize the professionalism of Total Leaders, and in *Total Leaders*, we show how those same ten can enhance the professionalism of any entity, including school boards. They are:

1. Connection
2. Inquiry
3. Future-Focusing
4. Clarity
5. Inclusiveness
6. Win-Win
7. Accountability
8. Improvement
9. Alignment
10. Contribution

Consistently applying these ten principles to everything they do will allow TLCs to meet the first transformational standard: "Creating and sustaining a culture of integrity, inquiry, and continuous improvement in which all participants contribute and share."

Standard 2: Laying a Foundation of Insight and Inquiry

Laying a foundation of insight and inquiry that will drive a new-paradigm learning system is going to require significant work because it means providing people with a whole new rationale for doing what they do. Building that rationale requires enlightened and committed endeavor in four key areas.

First, we'll need to assist people over a long period of time with developing a wide-band, open-system, ends-based, future-focused way of thinking and conversing about educational matters. Old habits die hard, and the means-based vocabulary that surrounds educentric schooling must be replaced by words, frameworks, questions, and examples that help people shift their frame of reference toward learners, learning, life, and the future.

You'll need to sit down with others and review the examples in this book again and again—for example, the means-ends comparisons and the CBO Syndrome at the end of chapter 2, and the myths of the numbers game in chapter 5. Another helpful device is using catchy slogans, like "We're in the learning business, not the curriculum business." Whatever tools you use in solidifying this shift, remember that a Total Learning Community will only be as strong as the paradigm foundation on which it rests. What your constituents see and say is what you'll get.

Second, the rationale we develop must be built on a continuous and insightful review of the evolving five new research realities: human potential, human learning, domains of living, future conditions, and life performance. They are the *reason* anything in a TLC exists, and they must be kept front and center in all planning and implementation. The bottom line is that your people must be able to say, "We're doing what we're doing because:

1. It's totally consistent with the best we know about this particular new research reality.
2. It's vital in preparing learners for success beyond school.
3. We're committed to honoring, utilizing, and expanding this knowledge base in our work."

Third, our new paradigm rationale will include what we referred to above as a "moral foundation"—often called a "philosophy" or "guiding ethos." This foundation/ethos will be made up of four kinds of elements: beliefs, values, priorities, and principles. Beliefs are the fundamental assumptions on which the organization operates, its "articles of faith," the tenets and premises that it assumes to be true about learners, learning, life, and so forth. A key example is "All children can learn and succeed, but not on the same day in the same way."

Values are things we believe in, honor, revere, strongly prefer, and respect in ourselves and others. An example is "Honesty and forthrightness, rather than manipulative half-truths."

Priorities are "things that matter most" in our lives and work. They're reflected in where we place our time, attention, and resources and in the things we choose over others. In many ways, they're our values expressed. An example is "Whether students learn something successfully is more important than when and how they learn it."

Principles are standards for making decisions and pursuing courses of action that rise above personal interests, inclinations, or convenience. They both invite and compel organizational members to operate on a higher plane of awareness and concern regarding the meaning and consequences of their decisions and behavior. The ten principles that define Total Professionalism were listed above.

Finally, the fourth key component that constitutes a TLC's rationale is its purpose statement—the short, compelling expression of why the organization exists and what it is there to accomplish. Powerful purpose statements capture and embody many of the other elements in the rationale, and in doing so they set a clear direction for the organization, make clear what the organization sees as its top priority, and motivate people to achieve it. A succinct but powerful example is "Equip all learners to shape their changing world." Let there be no doubt, as we saw in figure 6.1, TLCs are purpose-driven entities.

Taken together, then, these four elements form a TLC's Rationale and serve two key purposes: (1) they publicly declare what the organization stands for and intends to accomplish; and (2) they serve as a screen through which all decisions and actions must pass. The more concrete and compelling these elements are, the more direction the organization's members have for carrying out their responsibilities with confidence and integrity.

Standard 3: Defining Life Performance Learning Essentials

We've emphasized throughout this book that the model of learning that guides our new-paradigm learning system is a far richer and more complex one than defines typical school performance. As we saw in chapters 2 through 6, if we want to bridge the major gap between school success and life success, we'll need to look at life performance learning in a far more complex way than is offered in traditional models of school achievement.

As we noted in chapter 2, the key notion that takes us to this new level of understanding is called a "role performance." Roles are complex configurations of abilities that individuals carry out using a broad range of content, and in a broad range of situations, circumstances, conditions, and challenges in their lives—things we called "performance contexts" earlier. Figure 2.3, the Life Performance Wheel, gave us a very useful example of a role performance framework that incorporates both essential strategic/technical competences and interpersonal/relational competences. Another vehicle for portraying an even richer version of these kinds of abilities was the Total Learner/Total Performer frameworks described in chapter 10.

The key issue here is that these two sets of frameworks have a direct grounding in the human potential, human learning, domains of living, and future conditions research realities described in chapter 2. This makes them excellent examples that TLCs are free to use as they develop their own unique learning essentials framework, using a process called "strategic design" that we'll describe in chapters 9 and 10. Once they do, that framework will be the driving force in everything else that happens in their TLC, including:

1. Deriving from it a framework of supporting/enabling competences—the building-block skills needed to accomplish these more complex life performance essentials.
2. Developing and implementing a comprehensive authentic assessment system that validly measures, records, reports, and credentials learner accomplishments on these life performance essentials as they emerge.
3. Designing and implementing a comprehensive and engaging array of learning experiences that directly facilitate both these life performance essentials and the supporting competences that underlie them.
4. Developing and employing the kinds of cutting-edge strategies, tools, techniques, technologies, and resources that best facilitate these life performance essentials and supporting competences.
5. Marshaling and providing the expertise and assistance to advance learner progress on these life performances and supporting competences whenever and for however long or frequently it may be needed.

6. Determining the qualifications and abilities of those engaged to help learners' achievement of these life performance essentials—including those community experts not formally certified as teachers.
7. Determining the best settings for learners to develop and demonstrate these life performance essentials—including business and community contexts.

Clearly, then, this third standard is the centerpiece of a Total Learning Community's operations, and it can't be addressed with too much diligence. Its bottom-line message to everyone involved your TLC is: This is the kind of person we're committed to sending out the door, and this is what it's going to take for us to accomplish it.

Standard 4: Ensuring Empowering Learning Experiences

This fourth standard involves what are traditionally called *curriculum* and *teaching*, but those terms evoke too many educentric images. TLCs address this standard from four perspectives.

First, they use their framework of life performance essentials and determine the kinds of experiences their learners require in order to develop and demonstrate them successfully. This is what is traditionally called "curriculum design"—but this is not about books and content as they are defined and boxed in traditional subjects. It's about how the learners will themselves generate and deeply engage with the content relevant to the domains of living, future conditions, life issues, and challenges they'll be facing once they finish school. The overriding design issue here is called "alignment"—making sure that each element in a model perfectly reflects and matches the other. The design rule: If it doesn't align, it won't support the end you're seeking, so alter it until it does.

Second, using their life performance essentials framework as the grounding, TLCs determine the kinds of cutting-edge instructional strategies, techniques, tools, technologies, and resources that best facilitate the learning they're trying to achieve. Since these essentials are fundamentally about competence, and competence develops from doing, they focus particularly on methods and strategies that facilitate skill-building and performance abilities. We'll explain one highly relevant and powerful approach in chapter 11. This, of course, is where "advanced technologies" come into play, and they are used not as "silver bullets" but as the nature of specific learning essentials dictates. Here too the design and implementation concept of alignment is critical.

Third, TLCs are committed to the "anyone/anything/anytime/anywhere/any expert" philosophy described in Chapter 1. Consequently, their design and implementation are focused on assuring that learners will get the kind of help they need when they need it from whatever source of assistance is most appropriate. They call it "continuous opportunity and assistance." This clearly implies breaking out of traditional delivery and opportunity boxes and creating a much more flexible and learner-responsive approach to instruction. It also places an enormous premium on staff collegiality, collaboration, creativity, communication, competence, and coordination. TLCs don't foster the cellular work and opportunity structures found in iceberg schools.

Fourth, an additional aspect of the "anyone/anything/anytime/anywhere/any expert" philosophy is what TLCs call their "open access and advancement" structure. The essence of this element is the belief that there should be no limits on how much students can learn and achieve, nor on their advancement through a program. They are not to be boxed into the rigid grade levels, narrow windows of eligibility, conventional time-based grading and averaging systems, or calendar-year promotion arrangements described in chapter 6. In TLCs, learners are simply moved to more difficult and challenging learning experiences when they show the ability to handle them without frustration, and when their levels of maturity and mastery indicate that they're ready to move forward, no matter which week of which month of which year it happens to be.

It's apparent from these four elements that this standard embodies the heart and soul of a TLC's open-system, wide-band, new-paradigm character.

Standard 5: Mobilizing Resources to Support Learning

TLCs bring five key sets of resources together to support the flexible, learner-responsive nature of their empowering learning experiences. Their design process includes these five specific steps:

1. Extensively Involving Our Constituents—because TLCs know there is power, insight, and expertise within their constituencies and communities that are invaluable to their instructional efforts, and they want their learners to reap the benefits of learning from these people.
2. Attracting and Using Qualified Personnel—because the qualities and abilities needed to facilitate life performance essentials and to work in a future-focused, collaborative, flexible, learner-responsive instructional system are far different than those needed for conventional instruction and classroom responsibilities.
3. Marshaling Appropriate Material Resources—because developing life performance abilities requires a far broader range of experiences, processes, materials, technologies, and environments than that required by conventional, "in your seat" instructional programs.
4. Modeling Open Communication—because timely, accurate, widely shared information is indispensable to the effective functioning of the

kind of highly interactive, collaborative, flexible, learner-responsive system that TLCs advocate and implement.

5. Making Data-Driven Decisions—because the system cannot be genuinely learner-responsive without accurate, timely information on each learner's unique attributes, interests, aptitudes, and performances which directly supports instructional planning, implementation, and opportunities.

From the perspective of the Total Leaders model, mobilizing, coordinating, and utilizing these resources require the special skills of those called cultural, quality, and service leaders, and these skills are needed in every person who participates in a Total Learning Community.

GETTING THESE TRANSFORMATIONAL STANDARDS IN PLACE

Putting these five transformational standards in place in working models is now our key challenge. As noted earlier, each standard is linked to a concrete step we can take using a systematic process called "strategic design." The following chapters demonstrate, step by step, how this process works and how an authentic Total Learning Community can be created.

As visionary and unique as these steps may seem in light of the impetus surrounding Standards-Based Reforms, they are clearly manageable. And once we've taken them, like Roger Banister's breaking of the four-minute mile, the floodgates to a new educational future will open and we can help our country and communities move beyond counterfeit reforms and test scores to the paradigm realities that have been staring them in the face since 1983.

8

STEP 1: ESTABLISHING A CULTURE OF TOTAL PROFESSIONALISM

The principles that we establish and get our constituents, communities, and colleagues to formally endorse should both invite and compel them to operate on a higher plane of awareness and concern about the meaning and consequences of their decisions and actions than they might otherwise do. This higher plane enables everyone to operate in a more consistent, trustworthy, and professional way.

Beyond Counterfeit Reforms is the first step in carrying out a process called "Strategic Design." It enables educational communities to design and ultimately implement all five of the critical components of a learning system—components that are directly linked to each of the five transformational standards described in chapter 7. The design logic of this process is: *why* drives *what* drives *how.* Translated, this means: Your rationale determines your instructional system, which in turn determines the kind of support system you'll need to put in place in order to be successful.

For over a decade, communities of all kinds and sizes have used this Strategic Design Process to define and develop the kind of new-paradigm learning system we're committed to creating. However, we've learned that Strategic Design is not a silver bullet if communities and constituents do not have a compatible way of engaging with each other in the process. Some fundamental understandings, beliefs, and agreements must be established first so that the other steps of this process can, in fact, proceed effectively. These agreements allow a "culture" of expectations and priorities to develop that will sustain the integrity of the process when disagreements or difficulties arise.

The Power of Cultures

As we saw in chapters 4 and 7, organizational cultures are the direct manifestation and extension of the values and principles that their members endorse and embody in their everyday activities. Although they are intangible and sometimes invisible to outsiders, organizational cultures have enormous influence on how individuals address and carry out their responsibilities—ranging from resistance to enthusiasm. This is largely because organizational cultures embody the system of both formal and informal expectations that define what's "okay" and what's "not okay" for organizational members to do.

We can only anticipate, then, that the culture of a Total Learning Community will decisively influence how it is likely to define and carry out its key functions. In short, its culture greatly affects *how* its members think of and carry out the "business of learning."

Iceberg schools and Standards-Based Reforms define the learning business one way, but we'll have the advantage of defining it differently. This difference allows us to approach this first step in our system creation process with a constituency of like-minded people who are ready to create the changes described in this book. We'll be people who resonate deeply with the five new research realities described in chapter 2, the Total Learning for Total Living framework described in chapter 3, and the notion of a Total Learning Community being an entity where *everyone is a learner*, regardless of age or experience.

The participants in this process will be parents, business leaders, and community members who want far more for our young people than they'll get from the current system and its regressive reforms. And they'll be educators whose sense of professionalism and commitment to learners and life performance learning leaves them frustrated and disillusioned with the assembly-line nature of current practice. Many will join once the opportunity to coalesce around a larger vision is made available. But they will need a way of operating together in order to get this first standard in place.

That pathway can be opened by establishing what we referred to in chapter 7 as the principles of professionalism—standards of decision making and action that enable people to get beyond personal interests, inclinations, and convenience to honor and foster the greater good—the principles by which ethical, cutting-edge, collegial, expert, and dedicated professionals consistently operate. By agreeing on a set of principles that will serve as the criteria on which we and our constituents become accountable to ourselves and each other, we'll be able to establish a sound way of operating as we engage in this joint endeavor for change. Without these guideposts and criteria, we run the serious risk of inviting personal agendas to disrupt the cohesion we'll need to succeed.

ESTABLISHING OUR OPERATING PRINCIPLES

The principles that we establish and get our constituents, communities, and colleagues to formally endorse should both invite and compel them to operate on a higher plane of awareness and concern about the meaning and consequences of their decisions and actions than they might otherwise do. This higher plane enables everyone to operate in a more consistent, trustworthy, and professional way. In *Total Leaders* (Schwahn and Spady 1998), we describe how ten such principles seem to consistently and successfully guide the actions and decisions of leaders involved in significantly changing their organizations. These compelling principles of Total Professionalism are:

1. Connection
2. Inquiry
3. Future-Focusing
4. Clarity
5. Inclusiveness
6. Win-Win
7. Accountability
8. Improvement
9. Alignment
10. Contribution

Here's what each means and why it directly facilitates the kind of design and implementation process we've chosen to undertake.

The Connection Principle

Connection may be the most important of the ten principles because, without it, "the wiring isn't complete," "no one is home," and the impact of the other nine principles is seriously undermined. Very simply, connection is about showing up without your "personal baggage"—being there with all your internal and external sensors turned on, tuned in to what is happening, paying full attention, listening carefully, open to new information and perspectives, and participating fully in what is taking place. At its core it's about being involved—focusing on ideas, information, issues, circumstances, points of view, and feelings as if you were encountering them for the first time. And it's about monitoring how your own words and actions are affecting others.

Robert Cooper and Ayman Sawaf's 1996 book *Executive EQ* is truly about connection, but they, like Daniel Goleman (1998), call it "EQ" instead. They view EQ (emotional quotient) or connection as the emotional and relational equivalent of IQ. At its core, they see EQ as (1) awareness of the many dimensions of human talent and existence, (2) respect for the exploration and development of these dimensions in self and others, and (3) sensitivity to both the similarities and differences among people along these dimensions. Most of all it involves responding, in words and deeds, positively and empathetically to the expression of these dimensions in oneself and in others.

Implementing the five standards in our model will be virtually impossible without a strong EQ/connection principle because it compels people to pay attention to and acknowledge what is going on within themselves and the people they interact with. Connected people are "with it" and "on it" all the time, which is why Woody Allen says that 90 percent of success is about showing up!

The Inquiry Principle

Both professionalism and the operation of TLCs are unimaginable without inquiry as an operating principle. Inquiry entails the conscious and deliberate search for the soundest, most credible, most pertinent information possible that bears on the situation at hand. Its antitheses are impulsiveness, being opinionated, and "shooting from hip." Inquiry is about research, respect for sound knowledge, looking beyond surface issues and misleading symptoms into the true nature of complex issues, and being open to all that is out there.

Inquiry stimulates an honest search for personal and organizational purpose, developing a rich and broad perspective on complex issues, and a deep understanding of ideas and possibilities. It also encourages deep personal reflection about, and a rigorous analysis of, purpose and meaning, information, theory and research, ideas, beliefs, and values.

True professionals think of inquiry as both a state of mind and a way of operating. It prevents people from making snap decisions, from getting boxed in by outdated precedents and practices, and from missing out on newly discovered processes or technologies. It encourages studying and learning, testing theories, knowing and applying the research that most impacts your field, and listening to recognized experts with an open mind. It also allows everyone to become aware of all the options that are out there before making important decisions and to identify insightful and creative opportunities for productive change.

The Future-Focusing Principle

Professionals are inherently future-focused—as are TLCs. Professionals are always looking beyond the tried and true to discover the most advanced ways of doing whatever their job and personal responsibilities require. In this case, future-focusing is synonymous with staying on the cutting edge of one's field—the motivation that defines the progressive thinking, decisions, and actions of genuine professionals. Since future-focusing is inherently creative and imaginative, it fosters thinking and acting outside the box of conventional experience and ways of operating, and it represents a commitment to exploring, discovering, and creating new paradigms, frameworks, models, and options for more effective action.

In our case as leaders of TLCs, future-focusing involves a thorough and consistent study of the trends and future conditions that are redefining the career, social, and political conditions our learners are likely to face in today's rapidly changing world, and taking a visionary, far-reaching view of the emerging possibilities, potential innovations, and promising strategies that we can incorporate into our new model. Future-focusing is the critical first step in effective vision-building, and it asks, encourages, and even compels everyone in a TLC to becoming a trend-tracker, futurist, and lifelong learner.

The Clarity Principle

As a principle of professionalism and way of operating in our new model, clarity embodies the open, honest, complete, and easily comprehensible communication of ideas, information, and possibilities to all organizational members and constituents. At its essence, clarity is about making important information and viewpoints known and accessible to those who depend on them to carry out their responsibilities and accomplish their goals.

In short, clarity pertains to the intention, substance, and impact of all personal and organizational communication. It is rooted in a strong desire to be both honest and understood, and it is the antithesis of manipulation and deceit. Clarity requires that we as professionals consistently communicate proactively with all colleagues and constituents in crystal clear language that can be understood by everyone with a stake in our TLC's success. Consequently, as true professionals, we need to be continuously assessing and improving our communication skills—including the touches of humor that keep our contact with others engaging as well as informative.

The Inclusiveness Principle

At its core, inclusiveness is a people-focused principle and the lifeblood of our model's commitment to empowering all its learners. Inclusiveness is about caring, outreach, communication, recruitment, acceptance, involvement, and the development of ownership and sense of belonging among all organizational members and constituents. Its opposite is the separation and divisiveness inherent in interest-group politics and decision making.

Inclusiveness is embodied in the consistent commitment of professionals to maximize (1) the range of opportunities for input and success available to organizational members, (2) the number of people included in relevant and meaningful organizational decisions, and (3) the level of member and constituent participation and input in decisions that directly affect their welfare.

As inclusive leaders, we're committed to involving all our colleagues and constituents in our planning efforts and operational decisions as much as possible because we want to take advantage of the broad range of expertise, ideas, and possibilities they will inevitably suggest if given the opportunity. We're also committed to inclusiveness because we know that people's commitment and willingness to implement new things, support of others, and gaining of genuine meaning from their work all directly flow from their having a genuine role in what the organization plans and does to bring about change and improvement. Inclusive professionals recognize that people have something to offer—something that will enhance the outcome for everyone involved.

The Win-Win Principle

As we've seen in recent Standards-Based Reforms, the hardest thing to accomplish in the world of competitive, control-oriented, interest-group politics is a win-win orientation to policy making and implementation. Win-win embodies a commitment to achieving and experiencing *mutual benefit* in the agreements people make, the relationships they establish, and the rewards they obtain from the contributions they make. Our model cannot succeed without a win-win culture.

Like the constructive living domain of our Total Living framework, win-win emanates from, and projects a view of, human nature as positive, caring, cooperative, and deserving of dignity and recognition. Its antithesis is selfishness, insensitivity, exploitation, and win-lose—which almost inevitably degenerates into lose-lose as people within and outside organizations counterproductively compete against and undermine each other for what they assume to be the scarce resources of influence and status available to them.

The very good news about win-win as a principle of professionalism is that it leads to more win-wins. People who have gotten a fair and profitable shake from a person or organization quite naturally want to come back for more of the same—the essence of a healthy organizational culture and genuine "learning community." At its core, win-win is about enhancing one's status and well-being by sharing with others, publicly recognizing and honoring the value of others' efforts and contributions, and defining self-interest and success in terms of the common good.

As enlightened leaders, we recognize that win-win is the heart and soul of healthy relationships and is the driving force in organizational cultures that evoke trust and make people want to be involved and contribute. We also recognize win-win from Stephen Covey's famous *Seven Habits of Highly Successful People* (1989).

The Accountability Principle

Accountability is another of the fundamental definers of professionalism, but not the way it is being applied in the political and reform arenas. True professionals see themselves as inherently accountable, period. For them, accountability is a given—a natural process of taking responsibility for the content and process of the goals they set, the decisions they make, and the outcomes that result from the actions they take. Accountability is about being cognizant from the beginning about the need to make agreements and engage in activities with the full expectation that they must be carried out in the most competent, high-quality, conscientious manner possible. And it's also about making sure that those agreements are kept in a timely manner—as in the very process we're describing.

At its essence, accountability is inseparable from the deepest meaning and implications of what society calls integrity. Its antitheses are blame, excuses, and unreliability. As enlightened leaders and professionals, we recognize that accountability applies to us as individuals at a personal level, to us as team members at a collective/group level, and to us as members of larger entities. We further recognize that genuine accountability emanates far more from within the individual or group as a matter of collective consent than from the outside as a tool for threatening and sanctioning others.

Hence, *we should not confuse accountability with compliance*. Accountability isn't about meeting external standards and demands. It's about generating high-quality standards of performance *from within* and expecting to accomplish those standards consistent with these other nine principles. Consequently, we believe that the significance of what we do and the quality of what we produce are so important that we want our learners, colleagues, and widest constituency to know what our standards, expectations, goals, and accomplishments are. In this way, accountability and clarity go hand in hand. We want others to know what we exist to do and how well we do it.

The Improvement Principle

Improvement represents a commitment to getting better and better at everything you do in a world that is constantly changing and demanding more of everyone. As a principle, improvement is about continuously enhancing (1) the quality of both our personal and professional performance, (2) the processes and methods we use to generate our results, and (3) our results themselves. Embracing and applying this principle implies that standards exist (or can be defined) toward which TLCs and their members can direct their sights and efforts. In our case, this includes the five transformational standards around which we're now designing and implementing our TLC. So clearly defining and openly communicating with our constituents about these new standards is a key avenue toward continuous improvement.

Underlying this improvement principle are a commitment to quality and excellence, a belief that everything our TLC does and produces can be done better or more effectively than it has been to date, and a belief that continuous improvement and achieving quality both result when we carefully monitor the constantly rising expectations of our constituents and the challenges emerging from our external environment.

Consequently, by adhering to this principle, we'll ensure that quality standards are developed for all our TLC's significant processes, services, and outcomes; clear and focused feedback loops are established that inform all our members and constituents about how well our quality standards are being met or exceeded; and this feedback will be used to continuously improve both how we operate and the results we achieve.

The Alignment Principle

As we noted in chapter 7, alignment is about making something totally congruent or parallel with something else: actually doing what you said you wanted to do and consistently "walking your talk" and "talking your walk." For leaders this means being consistent, logical, and straightforward in getting planning, policies, decision making, and actual implementation all to precisely match each other. Alignment will happen for us when we purposefully and directly get all our TLC's decisions, resources, structures, and processes to be totally consistent with the elements in its rationale and its life performance essentials— things we'll formally address and develop in steps 2 and 3 of this Strategic Design Process. Alignment requires the same kind of strong personal conviction and analytical orientation as the inquiry principle.

Without alignment, both policy implementation and change efforts are likely to be inconsistent, illogical, unrelated, and/or haphazard—an unfortunate but prevalent state of affairs in education. In fact, without alignment among an organization's vision, processes, policies, programs, and structures, you can't really expect desired results to happen. But you can when things are carefully designed to accomplish and reflect what you declare to be your key purposes, priorities, and intended results. This is called vision building, and it's the process we're now initiating.

For example, what do we want to create, and how do we want it to function? The sheet is blank, and the learning future we've always dreamed about is in our own hands to create and shape. Now's the time to design it and align it!

The Contribution Principle

Contribution means freely giving and completely investing one's time, attention, talent, and available resources to enhance the quality and success of meaningful endeavors. At its core, contribution manifests caring, selflessness, responsibility, and dedication. It's also about giving your best all of the time, with no anticipation of special rewards or recognition. Excellent examples of contribution might include the offensive linemen on football teams who only get noticed when they *miss* a block, and nurses who tend to the sick day after day with little or no recognition. They give their best selflessly because to them it is simply right to do a good job in the face of whatever challenges may exist.

In a word, contribution is inseparable from what it means to be a true leader and professional. It occurs most naturally when people simply pay close attention to what is happening around them (connection) and respond as competently and responsibly as possible (accountability) either when new opportunities arise or things go awry. When crises occur, it's contribution, not simply employment or participation, that spells the difference between failure and success. In the face of such circumstances, few organizations would sustain themselves without the extra investments of time and talent by contribution-motivated people.

By example and by emphasis, genuine professionals work within their organizations to create a culture that makes contribution an expectation and a norm. And they reward it by recognizing and honoring those who go out of their way to selflessly make things work—actions that are consistent with the esteem and self-actualization levels of Abraham Maslow's famous "hierarchy of needs" (1954). We must be prepared to do likewise as we carry forward this Strategic Design Process.

Lead Decisively

As we boldly stated in chapter 7, *leaders lead*! And they do it by taking their people places the people fear going on their own. In this case the fear that we must transcend is not the fear of creating the kind of learning system we want, it's the fear of being clear and decisive about how we'll operate in getting there. Taking the time to forge a clear, explicit, written set of principles on which everyone *formally agrees* to operate—whether it's these ten or some other set—will pay off a hundredfold as our process unfolds. There is nothing more empowering than to have a principled, rather than regulated, way of operating. So feel proud of the fact that in framing a set of operating principles, we'll also be shaping the lasting character and culture of our TLC.

CREATING A CULTURE OF LEARNING AND IMPROVEMENT

Establishing principles that enhance the professionalism of an organization's operating processes has two enormous benefits. First, the processes themselves work extremely well. Second, these principles provide a backdrop and set of expectations regarding everything the organization does. Its culture becomes both professional and principle-driven. If professional means ethical, cutting-edge, collegial, expert, and dedicated, then there's no way that individuals will consistently manifest those qualities without being encouraged and supported by a culture that expects and honors continuous learning and continuous improvement in both individuals and the organization as a whole.

TLCs are able to operate as genuine "communities of learners" because their members establish and share positive expectations that totally support all five of these qualities: ethical decisions and actions (conscious living); cutting-edge thinking and improvements (creative living); collegial and healthy personal relationships (collaborative living); expert knowledge and performance (competent living); and dedicated service to the organization and its clients (constructive living). These are the core attributes of an organization capable of continuous learning, growth, improvement, and change, and they reflect two fundamental realities:

1. In a world of continuous discovery and constant change, personal and organizational learning, growth, and improvement are the keys to survival, fulfillment, and Total Living.
2. Learning and enlightenment are the great rewards on the pathway to personal empowerment and fulfillment.

This requires that all of a TLC's members—including those traditionally called students—be committed, self-directed learners who are eager to support and acknowledge each other's learning, simply because public acknowledgment of someone's learning and growth further encourages everyone else in the organization to learn. As leaders and shapers of this vibrant, positive way of operating, we will need to assure that five key sets of expectations and accompanying strategies are established. They involve deep reflection, active exploration, personal growth, quality performance, and continuous accountability. If we do our jobs well and get these five empowering factors in place—once we've taken Step 2 and established a formal rationale for our TLC—we'll enjoy being part of an exciting and rare "Totally Professional" organization.

Deep Reflection: Considering the Truth Within

TLC members openly acknowledge that all learning and improvement begin *within*—within the individual and within the organization. This inner search is called "reflection"—the quiet, introspective, honest, and empathetic search for deep purpose and meaning in what one experiences. Reflection is the key to the development of the conscious learner in everyone.

To establish and sustain a culture of Total Professionalism, TLC members individually and collectively openly engage in this kind of reflective search and collectively support the candid and affirming dialogues they hold about the genuine status of things people discover within themselves and their TLC. They also openly acknowledge the insights people have about themselves and their TLC and the recommendations people make about what their TLC could improve and ultimately become.

In short, then, deep reflection is what TLC members do as a matter of course. Encouraging it, communicating openly about it, and honoring it are what they do as a matter of personal and organizational health. We'll be operating as a *reflective* Total Learning Community when our organization:

- openly declares reflection and inquiry to be core organizational values and makes all decisions consistent with them
- regularly holds open forums to which all our members are invited to reflect deeply on and discuss matters of meaning and significance to themselves, the organization, and their professional roles
- periodically invites all our members and constituents to openly examine our core values, fundamental beliefs, and operating principles and strengthen them if necessary
- encourages both formal teams and informal groups to meet, reflect deeply on our organization's functioning, effectiveness, and health, and recommend things that would improve both
- publicly applauds our members for sharing their feelings and insights about ways our TLC could better apply its core values and principles and create deeper meaning and fulfillment for people in their work

As leaders, it's our responsibility to ensure that these five critical processes get carried out in a quality way.

Active Exploration: Always Searching for Better Ways

A culture of Total Professionalism will exist when the commitment of TLC members to look within is complemented by their equally strong desire to look beyond. Like all true professionals, and because they are self-directed learners, they are active explorers of new ideas and ways of doing things that can make their work better and more effective, especially the insights emerging from the growing body of new research realities that are currently redefining centuries-old notions of learning and education.

As Total Professionals they collectively encourage and welcome an open, thorough, and stimulating search for possibilities that lie beyond either their current awareness or existing patterns of educational practice. And they both acknowledge the potential merits of these new possibilities whenever colleagues introduce them and readily attempt to apply them in their day-to-day practice.

This openness to what lies beyond the tried, true, and familiar will strongly reinforce our TLC's future-focused orientation and the other research realities that underlie its rationale. It will also encourage members to continue expanding their vision of how good our TLC could actually become when operating at its ideal best. We'll be operating as a *visionary* Total Learning Community when our organization:

- openly encourages our members to regularly study the latest research on the future conditions affecting learning and life and actively translates their explorations and discoveries into alternative scenarios for program redesign and implementation

- periodically assigns teams of members and constituents to review our future conditions and life performance essentials frameworks in light of these scenarios and makes needed changes
- regularly studies the latest research on human potential, human learning, and life performance and recommends "best case" instructional strategies for members to try out and evaluate as they work with learners and each other
- clearly acts on the new information we receive by continually updating and improving the substance, strategies, resources, and structuring of our empowering learning experiences
- regularly invites outside experts to describe cutting-edge advances in their fields and the implications of those advances for improving our life performance essentials and empowering learning experiences

As leaders, it's our responsibility to ensure that these five critical processes get carried out in a quality way.

Personal Growth: Continuously Expanding Personal Boundaries

Personal growth is the continued expansion of a person's capacities for success and fulfillment as a conscious, creative, collaborative, competent, and constructive learner—the five dimensions of the Total Learning for Total Living framework. Deep reflection and active exploration are the keys to this growth. In fact, it is the intense sense of fulfillment that comes from continuously expanding one's awareness, understanding, and performance abilities that will motivate TLC members and learners to keep stretching their range of endeavors beyond familiar boundaries.

What helps fuel this desire for continuous growth and improvement is the TLC's collective support and open acknowledgment and celebration of the new learning, insights, and skills members acquire and the positive contributions those new capacities make to others' successes. In other words: Improved learning and performance are contagious! They are giant win-wins for everyone in the TLC since all benefit and are enhanced when someone learns more and performs better. We'll be operating as an *enriching* Total Learning Community when our organization:

- requires members to continuously invest in their further learning and development as persons and professionals, with an emphasis on expanding their understanding of the new research realities
- conducts a strong, active program of enlightening professional and personal growth experiences for all our members that contains a "coaching for

implementation" component directly tied to our life performance essentials framework

- conducts a strong, active program of enlightening professional and personal growth experiences for all our members that contains strong components on how to continue strengthening all of the elements, resources, and strategies imbedded in our empowering learning experiences
- establishes an active personal and professional growth plan with each member that is closely aligned with the paradigm thinking, new research realities, core values, priorities, and purpose statement in our TLC's rationale
- consistently endorses and facilitates collaborative learning, planning, and work efforts among our members that foster a climate of sharing and collegiality

As leaders, it's our responsibility to ensure that these five critical processes get carried out in a quality way.

Quality Performance: Conspicuously Rewarding Growth and Excellence

The capstone to creating and sustaining a culture of Total Professionalism is the TLC's open acknowledgment and rewarding of both individual and team high-quality performance. A key factor in securing this collective endorsement of excellence will be the members' belief that they have an obligation to develop and demonstrate their skills and abilities at levels that meet or exceed existing standards of high-level professionalism. Professionally committed members go out of their way to make these ideals, and the criteria that underlie them, highly visible throughout the organization. In addition, they work to define the essence of these ideals, demonstrate what they mean and look like in practice, and hold them up as standards to which all members and learners are expected to aspire and against which they can regularly assess themselves.

The other key factor in this endorsement of excellence is that TLCs openly acknowledge and celebrate the successes of their members and learners. This, more than anything, sends signals throughout the organization that quality performance is more than a slogan—it's an exciting, rewarding, and intrinsically fulfilling way of doing business. We'll be operating as a *performance-enhancing* Total Learning Community when our organization:

- openly declares excellence and improvement to be core organizational values
- develops clearly defined standards and expectations for learner achievement on our life performance essentials that we regularly assess and make public to all members and constituents

- develops clearly defined standards and expectations for member, team, and organizational performance that we regularly assess and make public to all members and constituents
- consistently uses assessment results on all our life performance essentials and supporting competences to evaluate the strengths and weaknesses of our instructional efforts, and makes sure our members know how to use this feedback to make needed changes
- consistently acknowledges and honors the outstanding accomplishments and contributions of the learners, members, and constituents who help us achieve our life performance essentials and our declared organizational purpose
- recognizes the personal and professional growth, improvement, and accomplishments of our members through formal recognition, financial awards, career advancement, professional opportunities, and greater organizational influence

As leaders, it's our responsibility to ensure that these six critical processes get carried out in a quality way.

Continuous Accountability: Daily Responsibility for Staying the Course

Total Learning Communities are distinguished by living out their core values, principles, and declared organizational purpose to the fullest. This requires each member to take personal responsibility for embracing, advocating, and living out—in word and deed—the spirit as well as substance of this highly professional code of ethics.

While TLCs are free to determine the specific values and principles that they choose to guide their decisions and actions, several are universals. You can find them in all TLCs because they are the glue that holds the operational pieces together. These moral pillars include reflection, honesty, openness, commitment, excellence, teamwork, inclusiveness, win-win, accountability, and alignment. As we noted earlier in this chapter, alignment is the compass and the standard: Are we being completely consistent with what we said was important? Does this really match what we said we wanted to accomplish?

Accountability, on the other hand, is the attitude and deep sense of responsibility that enable people to care, pay attention, note when things go awry, and willingly intervene to make them right. Accountable people are conscious and connected—aware of what's happening, attentive to the emotional and ethical aspects of situations, and trustworthy in keeping agreements and pulling more than their share of the weight. TLCs work because they foster a climate of continuous accountability in which people are present, caring, and willing to give their best to make something good happen for others, not just themselves. An ethos of this kind doesn't happen by accident. Totally accountable leaders need to both endorse and consistently model it.

Based on this ethos of caring and commitment, we'll be operating as an *accountable* Total Learning Community when our organization:

- formally establishes a set of agreements among all members, learners, and constituents about how the organization should look when operating at its ideal best and translates these agreements into clear expectations about personal and group performance
- regularly holds meetings to discuss the status of these expectations, to collectively resolve situations where they have not been met or upheld, and to celebrate the organization's open and supportive way of doing business
- openly and spontaneously acknowledges people when they act accountably, particularly in the face of difficult or problematic circumstances
- directly supports and encourages people who have difficulty meeting these expectations by explaining and modeling how they might handle various kinds of situations in a more constructive or supportive manner

As leaders, it's our responsibility to ensure that these four critical processes get carried out in a quality way.

SOLIDIFYING KEY CONNECTIONS

As we have proceeded through this chapter, the interconnections among the key elements in this book begin to make themselves increasingly clear. One of those dimensions is the Total Learning/Total Living/Total Professionalism framework. The fact that so many things overlap with its five major domains reinforces its universality. Hence, the more you can legitimately connect other things to it, the more compact and robust this entire design process will become. Instead of there being dozens of things to keep in mind and process, we'll be seeing that they are actually variations on a very few profoundly powerful underlying factors and dynamics.

Another of these universals is what we've called the moral foundation, philosophy, or guiding ethos of an organization. Clearly many of these ethos elements connect directly with the five domains of the "total" framework, as they should. But these elements also need to be seen in their own right because they do indeed guide the thinking, decision making, and actions of people both inside and outside their formal organizational roles. They are powerful because they are the moral rationale underlying just about everything that happens in an organization. Therefore, they can't easily be overlooked in any aspect of what an organization does or how it does it.

Once we take this first major design step and get agreement around and endorsement of the principles of professionalism and five major cultural elements described here, our Total Learning Community will enjoy a sound, healthy, self-renewing culture that encourages reflection, new ideas, personal growth, competent performance, and responsible action on the part of all members. This will provide us with two enormous benefits: (1) we'll have a sound moral and psychological foundation on which to carry out the remaining four steps in our Strategic Design Process; and (2) our TLC will have a positive, growth-friendly culture that encourages all members to perform at their professional best and contribute enthusiastically to the success and fulfillment of every learner.

STEP 2: LAYING A FOUNDATION
OF INSIGHT AND INQUIRY

. . . creating powerful and compelling reasons why we have chosen this specific course of action and not another. . . . is akin to constructing four interconnected, mutually reinforcing weight-bearing walls that must be capable of withstanding the storms of criticism that are bound to blow our way because we've dared to leave the illusory safety of the iceberg and the Standards-Based Reform parade.

We have just learned what it takes to forge a network of committed lifelong learners into a genuine learning *community*, and we have laid out a number of operating criteria that will help us bring this first step in our Strategic Design Process to fruition. Now it's time to explore how we can lay a foundation for that community of learners to become a fully functioning learning *organization*—one capable of continuous evolution and improvement in what it does because it consciously seeks out the best pertinent research available and deliberately integrates it into its structures and processes. Said colloquially, learning organizations know that insight and inquiry are the "breakfast of champions"!

Laying this foundation of insight and inquiry is step 2 in our Strategic Design Process, and it puts in place standard 2 of our transformational model. This is where we formally forge the rationale on which everything else we'll eventually do as a Total Learning Community ultimately depends. It's where we declare the kind of business we are in and *why* we're in that business: It's what we're here to do and the reasons we've chosen this mission and this way of pursuing it.

FOUR WEIGHT-BEARING WALLS

At the simplest level, a rationale is made up of the conscious reasons that underlie a given decision we make or a particular course of action we pursue. If this rationale is genuinely to become the foundation on which everything else in our TLC rests and depends, then we're obligated as its leaders and architects to make it as robust and stable as we can. And that means creating powerful and compelling reasons why we have chosen this specific course of action and not another. This is akin to constructing four interconnected, mutually reinforcing weight-bearing walls that must be capable of withstanding the storms of criticism that are bound to blow our way because we've dared to leave the illusory safety of the iceberg and the Standards-Based Reform parade.

As we think about what those four walls must be, four essential reasons for designing and operating a TLC come to mind. In the absence of any one of them, the strength and integrity of our transformational reform effort is going to be weakened. The four are:

1. Reasons that emanate from the *beliefs we hold* about things: what we assume to be true—our paradigm perspectives.
2. Reasons that emanate from our *knowledge* about things: what we have evidence is true—our research realities.
3. Reasons that emanate from our *philosophy* about things: what we prefer to come true—our values and guiding ethos.
4. Reasons that emanate from our *deep purpose*: what we are trying to get to come true—our mission and reason for being.

As we think about the analogy of having unshakable walls on which to construct our model, we recognize that walls have three essential components: (1) the inside surface—how they appear and are used by those inside the structure; (2) the outside surface—how they appear and what they mean to those outside the structure; and (3) the actual composition—the materials and supporting structures that actually determine their strength and durability and allow them to function as foundation walls.

Let's assume for the moment, then, that the four things that really matter to us inside the walls that enable our TLC to function optimally are the paradigm perspectives, research realities, guiding ethos, and reason for being that will guide, inform, and motivate us. Those are the names we'll place on the inside of the four walls so that we can keep our bearings as we carry out our work. Figure 9.1 provides us with a picture of these relationships. Let's also assume, then, that a parallel set of signs will go on the outside of each wall, indicating to our publics in less-technical terms what each wall represents to them. These external signs will say beliefs, knowledge, philosophy, and purpose, respectively. Finally, let's assume that our job is to supervise the design and construction of each wall so that it has

The Weight-Bearing Walls of Our TLC's Foundation

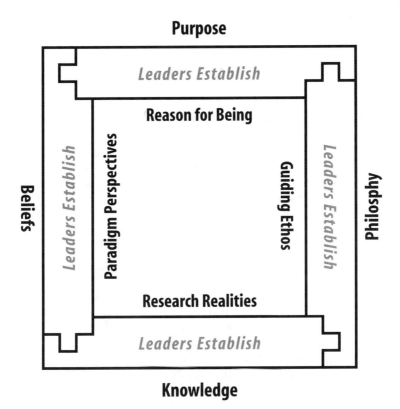

Figure 9.1

the substance and integrity needed to serve its essential function as the foundation of our model. This means that we'll be required to establish:

1. An insightful and compelling set of paradigm perspectives that we can translate into powerful statements of belief about learners, learning, life, and education.
2. An insightful and compelling set of research realities that we can translate into powerful knowledge bases about learners, learning, life, and education.
3. An ethical and compelling guiding ethos for decision making and action that we can translate into a powerful operating philosophy.
4. An insightful and compelling reason for being that we can translate into a powerful purpose statement against which we can assess our effectiveness and improvement.

With these four components of an insightful and compelling rationale in place, we'll have the sound foundation we need for building and operating an enlightened, empowering TLC. Getting them in place is the key leadership challenge of step 2 in our Strategic Design Process.

A NEW PARADIGM OF GOVERNANCE

What we're doing by laying this enlightened and strong foundation for our TLC is taking yet another giant step away from the old-paradigm approach that dominates education. How? Because we're *leading* change, not *mandating* it, and that requires a profoundly different dynamic of influence, governance, and motivation. The hundred books that we summarize in *Total Leaders* ultimately say that creation efforts such as ours must start by involving people and helping them establish a purpose and direction that they "own" and that give meaning and value to their efforts. Very simply put, for a proposed design or change to "take" and be successful in the long run, it has to have the consent and support of those involved in and affected by it.

As we can see in figure 9.2, this professional leadership approach is a paradigm apart from the political forms of influence exercised by those in legal authority, i.e., those in control of Standards-Based Reforms. Figure 9.2 is divided into two halves, the upper half representing the key top-down mechanisms of influence at the disposal of those with legal control, and the other reflecting the bottom-up moral legitimacy of individuals who lead.

At its essence, legal control is external, positional, hierarchical, top-down, and institutionalized. It relies on three key mechanisms for assuring compliance with its mandates: policies, regulations, and sanctions. *Policies* offer broad guidelines within which people and organizations are required to operate. *Regulations* are usually more specific and detailed applications of the policies and limit the range of permissible behavior even more. *Sanctions* are the punishments that will be meted out for violating either the policies or the regulations. Note how strongly the elements in this half of the figure are embodied in the ethos and provisions of the SBR movement as described in chapter 6: It's all about hierarchical control and extrinsic compliance.

On the other hand, we find ourselves squarely in the moral legitimacy sector of the figure, faced with the challenge and opportunity of leading our people somewhere they've been reluctant to go on their own. Notice the profound difference in the terminology here. This sector is about personal involvement, intrinsic motivation, and collective agreement around three key mechanisms of individual and group consent: purpose, philosophy, and principles—key elements in our proposed rationale.

Purpose is the mission and larger end toward which everyone is working. *Philosophy* is the set of values and priorities that people embrace as they pursue that

Two Paradigms of Control

Political

Legal Control   **External Mandates**
Hierarchical Authority   *Top-Down Compliance*

Sanctions
Regulations
Policies

Principles
Philosophy
Purpose

Bottom-Up Consent   *Collective Agreement*
Moral Legitimacy   **Leadership Guided**

Professional

Figure 9.2

larger collective purpose. *Principles*, as we saw in chapter 8, are the standards that individuals and groups apply to all aspects of their conduct and decision making. They're where philosophy gets converted into tangible action.

Together these three elements form the *moral* elements of our rationale. They are our collectively developed statements of what we stand for, what we want to accomplish, and how we will conduct ourselves both in designing and in implementing our new learning community. It is these and the other key components of our rationale that will direct and motivate our people, not formal rules and regulations and the coercive legal controls that underlie and reinforce them. Therefore, from this point on, everything we do to address these five new standards will flow from and manifest this morally grounded rationale.

ESTABLISHING OUR PARADIGM PERSPECTIVES

The biggest challenge we face in establishing a rationale for our new model of education is to get the people we're working with to get their thinking and perspectives about education completely outside the educentric boxes that have defined schooling for the past century. We'll all need to create a new educational reality for ourselves—a reality defined by different thoughts and perspectives, different words and vocabulary, and different choices and actions. It is this combination of factors that researchers call a paradigm—an internally consistent pattern of perceptions, ideas, interpretations, and actions that literally define a person's way of viewing and dealing with the world.

Our Paradigm-Shifting Tools

To create a new paradigm of education, we'll need to shift the meaning and value of many familiar things from one grounding or foundation to another; from what we've educentrically viewed as learning and education to a more "natural" and "authentic" way of perceiving them. What's required? Only that we turn off our automatic pilot when dealing with educational matters and deliberately consider:

- the range of perspectives open to us before forming an opinion
- the words available to us before asking questions or offering comments
- the range of options open to us before making decisions or taking action
- the ultimate, deeper purposes that education could serve

When we do stop, think, look, listen, and ask why, we'll discover that we don't need to *take on* some artificial perspective or new way of acting at all. We just need to think of learners as human beings, not as students; of learning as a richly diverse aspect of all life experience, not as curriculum mastery; of education as a natural process of discovering and enhancing people's inner potential, not as iceberg schooling; and of education's deeper purpose as enhancing one's capacity for Total Living, not as qualifying for more education.

These are the natural, authentic ideas, words, and meanings that have been there all along in our lives. We just need to consistently, confidently, and precisely use them in creating our new TLC. The key is consistently urging your people to think, discuss, and focus on:

- The future rather than the past
- Total Living rather than more schooling
- Life performance essentials rather than curriculum standards
- Open-system thinking rather than closed-system thinking
- Everyone as learners rather than students as learners
- Personal empowerment rather than hierarchical control
- Maximizing human potential rather than delivering academic content
- Authentic substance rather than points and grades
- Life-challenge learning rather than discrete-subject content
- Learner-initiated rather than teacher-directed

- Facilitative coaching rather than assembly-line instruction
- Authentic self-assessment rather than paper-and-pencil testing
- Expansive opportunities rather than age-graded opportunities
- Continuous development rather than lock-step promotion
- Contribution as success rather than scores as success
- Total professionalism rather than mandated compliance

And it will be up to you to keep that focus on the words, ideas, and practices on the left side of this list in everything that happens from this point on.

But note, there are similar lists in this book we can draw on to reinforce and expand this new paradigm perspective. Let's think about adding to this list the dozen other similar pairings in the ends-means lists in chapters 1 and 4 as well as the five alternative components of defining achievement explained in chapter 5. Together they'll give us a very rich set of paradigm-shifting tools to use in establishing a transformational paradigm perspective for our TLC. Our job will be to continuously say: "Okay, gang, let's remember that we're in the (left side of the list) business, not the (right side of the list) business."

We'll need to sound like broken records for a long time on this topic because we've got a century of educentric paradigm inertia to overcome. And we'll need to carefully monitor all our planning and designs to be sure that right-side elements don't accidentally creep into what are supposed to be left-side ways of operating. In doing so, you'll discover that the people on the two sides of this paradigm split also ask fundamentally different questions about education that reflect inside-the-box versus outside-the-box thinking and wording as well. Your job is to stretch that thinking and wording outside the box as far as possible and to reframe the questions that are driving the discussions. For example, it is highly likely that:

> You'll be hearing: What courses should our students be required to take and pass in order to graduate?
> But you'll be asking: What major challenges will they face in tomorrow's constantly changing world?

> You'll be hearing: What content should they be required to learn for the state's standardized tests?
> But you'll be asking: What complex abilities will they require to meet these life challenges successfully?

> You'll be hearing: Which textbooks will best prepare them for these tests?
> But you'll be asking: What challenging learning experiences and environments will they need for developing these complex abilities?

> You'll be hearing: How can we find a faster way for our best students to advance to higher levels in the system?
> But you'll be asking: Which instructional practices will really help *all* our students develop these complex abilities to a high level?

You'll be hearing: How high should the test scores be for students to advance
to the next grade level?
But you'll be asking: What kind of expanded access to high-level learning
must we create for all our students?

As these patterns repeat themselves by the dozens, each incident will offer
you an opportunity to see this open-system paradigm in a new light and its
enormous potential for helping our colleagues and constituents move beyond counterfeit reforms to an enlightened, empowering, future-focused
TLC.

Stating Our Basic Beliefs

The proof of the pudding in this most important paradigm-defining
process is to then translate our key perceptions, tenets, and articles of faith
about what we *assume* to be true about learners, learning, life, education,
and anything else pertinent to the operation of our TLC into explicit belief
statements for our various publics to read, acknowledge, and endorse. These
statements will be our open declaration of the things we take as givens in our
work—bedrock beliefs that lead us to choose certain alternatives over others
in every aspect of what we do and that help define who we are and what we
stand for.

Since *belief* drives *thinking*, *emotions*, *self-concept*, and *action*, being explicit
about what we believe sets the direction for the actions we're likely to take to
confirm our beliefs as true. For example, if we believe that all learners possess
valuable kinds of talent, we're likely to search for those unique areas of talent,
treat those learners as talented individuals, and cultivate those areas of talent
when we identify them. But if we believe that only some have talent, or that talent is genetically determined and unchangeable, then we're likely to search out
those who we believe have it and invest more heavily in developing them than
those who we believe don't.

Identifying our beliefs opens the door to describing them, which leads to assessing their validity, which leads to evaluating their implications and consequences, which leads to letting go of those that are recognized as false and
counterproductive. So one of our biggest leadership challenges will be to create a safe space in which people can reflect deeply, identify, and then acknowledge their most fundamental—often subconscious—basic beliefs about the
four things that are most likely to affect the character and success of our TLC:
learners, learning, life, and education.

Since there are potentially dozens of factors to consider in any of these
four areas, we've got to work hard to zero in on the beliefs that we believe
are most central to determining the nature and operational character of what

we ultimately design and implement. Why? Because a long "laundry list" of statements will overwhelm people and lose their impact. So let's use just one of these four focus points—learners—as an example and lay out some basic belief statements that clearly direct how our TLC should operate. For example:

- All learners are born curious and seek stimulation and challenge in order to develop and grow.
- All learners are born with many different kinds of learning and perform-ance potential that are useful in their lives.
- The different dimensions of human potential and talent can be identified and developed.
- Any kind of potential and talent can be expanded and enhanced through encouragement and stimulating learning experiences.
- Aptitude is the rate at which learners develop in these different areas, not their inherent ability to develop.

If we considered just these five basic belief statements about learners and turned them into criteria for planning and implementation, what would we be compelled to do? First, assess and diagnose each learner for a broad range of talents and interests. Second, continuously give them stimulating and challenging learning experiences that cultivate these various aptitudes and encourage them to explore how all their aptitudes connect to different domains of living. Third, encourage them to monitor their own development on these aptitudes and abilities and identify where their greatest strengths lie. Fourth, structure learning experiences that have no deadlines which might limit learner opportunities or incentives for improving given areas of learning/performance.

Our challenge, then, is to translate our paradigm perspectives on learners, learning, life, and education into similarly focused and powerful belief state-ments that enable us to respond to any "Why are you doing that?" question with a clear and succinct set of compelling reasons that we can ultimately back up with convincing research and results.

ESTABLISHING OUR RESEARCH REALITIES

If we intend to create a model of education that is both a learning community and a learning organization, then there is no component of our rationale more essential than this one. Learning organizations are organizations that learn, and they learn by insightfully inquiring into the key bodies of research that under-lie their existence. In chapter 2 we examined five such knowledge bases because, as a group, they enable us to address the four fundamental issues that drive any transformational model of education:

- Who are the learners we're dealing with, and what's their potential for growth and development? (Human Potential)
- What will those learners encounter once they leave our TLC for which we are obligated to prepare them? (Future Conditions and Domains of Living)
- What will they need to be able to do successfully to thrive in the face of these real-world conditions? (Life Performance)
- How can we best facilitate the development of these essential abilities? (Human Learning)

These five new research realities compel us to directly derive and align the key components of our TLC from them, even as these knowledge bases themselves continue to expand. To do that we'll need to continually (1) ask probing questions about each one, (2) integrate the answers we get into our Strategic Design Process (SDP), and (3) look for innovative implications that arise form these new findings. Here are examples of the questions we need to ask and answer at the initial stages of our SDP in order to build this wall of our foundation. Then we need to re-ask and re-answer them again and again every few months:

- What does the most insightful research available suggest about the different arenas of human potential and how can each best be developed and maximized for learners of different ages and genders? How can we best integrate this information into our life performance essentials framework and the empowering learning experiences we make available to all our learners?
- What does the most insightful research available suggest about the different arenas of human learning and how can each best be developed for learners of different ages, genders, and language backgrounds? How can we best integrate this information into our life performance essentials framework and the empowering learning experiences we make available to all our learners?
- What does the most insightful research available suggest about the different domains of living that people carry out in our complex world and the major challenges and opportunities they face in those respective domains? How can we best integrate this information into our life performance essentials framework, the empowering learning experiences we make available to all our learners, and the resources we mobilize to support their learning?
- What does the most insightful research available suggest about the future conditions our learners are likely to face when they finish their education,

for which we must prepare them? How can we best integrate this information into our life performance essentials framework, the empowering
learning experiences we make available to all our learners, and the resources we mobilize to support their learning?

- What does the most insightful research available on life performance suggest about the qualities and abilities adults need for success and fulfillment
in today's complex world? How can we best integrate this information directly into the design and implementation of our empowering learning experiences and the resources we employ to support them?

While this may seem like a formidable set of questions to have to ask to get
our SDP started, remember we're not tinkering around with an existing model,
we're creating a new one from the ground up, unencumbered by the inertia of
iceberg schooling and Standards-Based Reforms. And this requires both a systemic and a systematic approach to creating what we really want. There are no
shortcuts to defining something that genuinely operates on the cutting edge of
development and practice. It only seems formidable in relation to the far more
routinized process most schools go through to design their instructional programs. Instead of focusing on traditional content areas and mandated standards, we're focusing on five ever-present research realities, using a remarkably
straightforward logic: If this is true about (a particular research reality), then
here's how we can apply it to benefit student learning and success.

But if we really want to have a rock-solid research base from which to operate, we'll need to apply this same inquiry process to the research on the five
major components of our TLC so that we can also continually upgrade how we
operate. Here are the questions that will make that possible:

- What's the most insightful research we can find on what constitutes a powerful and compelling culture of Total Professionalism and on how to create and sustain one? How can we best act on this information to
strengthen our culture?
- What's the most insightful research we can find on what constitutes a powerful and compelling rationale for a learning organization and on how to
develop and strengthen one? How can we best act on this information to
strengthen our rationale?
- What's the most insightful research we can find on what constitutes a powerful and compelling framework of life performance learning essentials
and on how to develop and strengthen one? How can we best act on this
information to strengthen our rationale?
- What's the most insightful research we can find on what constitutes a powerful and compelling system of empowering learning experiences and on
how to develop and strengthen one? How can we best act on this information to strengthen our rationale?

- What's the most insightful research we can find on what constitutes a powerful and compelling system for mobilizing resources that support learning and on how to develop and strengthen one? How can we best act on this information to strengthen our rationale?

If this sounds a bit like the game Twenty Questions, rest assured that it's not, for if we combined the two sets of questions and eliminated overlapping items, we'd discover that there are really only ten uniquely different questions driving this process. There's one for each research reality and one for each standard, giving us ten. But the life performance question in both sets is nearly identical, allowing us to reduce the number to nine. Then following each of these nine, there's a key tenth question that's asked over and over: How are we really going to use these new insights to improve what we're doing?

So maybe we should just put the issue this way: Would you rather focus your endeavors on these ten questions or slide back into educentrism and iceberg schooling? Ah, there are knowing smiles breaking out across the land!

ESTABLISHING OUR GUIDING ETHOS

Some people are bound to recoil from the term "moral" because it conveys to them either a religious or judgmental view of living linked to specific social or cultural taboos. In our case, however, the term refers more broadly to things people strongly value, prefer, honor, respect, believe in, and use as guideposts in conducting their lives, things that they perceive as symbolizing and enhancing the greater good. Consequently, they see particular things as being right, fair, honorable, important, worthy of emulation, and/or ethical.

When we genuinely honor and value things deeply in ourselves and others, we willingly set personal inclinations, impulses, and convenience aside and choose a course of action consistent with these valued things. When that happens, we have placed those values or criteria into our personal "decision screen" and acted ethically according to the criteria in the screen—our *ethos*. Those who consistently act in accordance with their ethos in the face of trying circumstances are said to possess or demonstrate *integrity*.

Having decided to create a model of education that uses the knowledge bases of human potential, human learning, domains of living, future conditions, and life performance as major starting points, we have, in effect, declared ourselves as valuing these five "realities" as guideposts for education over the subject-content "realities" advocated by Standards-Based Reforms. In effect, then, we are openly stating our strong preference for developing learners, learning, educational experiences, and educational results of a given kind, rather than the way conventional education develops them.

Total Leaders describes two related sets of things used by organizations to establish this guiding ethos. One of them many different leadership gurus call "core values." The other one we've already described in detail in chapter 8; it's called "principles of professionalism." *Core values* are things that people throughout an organization widely understand and endorse as things they collectively prefer and honor. *Principles*, as we have seen, are more-explicit standards on which people base their decisions and actions.

Although we have already addressed half of this particular leadership challenge in chapter 8 by specifying the principles that allow us to create and sustain a culture of Total Professionalism, there remains the task of identifying and endorsing what will be our TLC's core values—the things we collectively say we stand for, that really matter to us, and that will guide us as we design and implement our new learning system. As a reference point, let's consider the ten core values that Total Leaders consistently advocate and personally embody as they carry out major change efforts in their organizations. They are:

• Reflection	• Commitment
• Honesty	• Excellence
• Openness	• Productivity
• Courage	• Risk-taking
• Integrity	• Teamwork

A brief glance at these ten words might suggest that many of them are personal attributes rather than values, but that's where the lesson lies for us. Yes, openness, for example, is a personal attribute that some might even call a psychological trait. But notice what happens to it when we collectively say that we prefer it, will honor it, will reward it, will expect it, will hire for it, and will evaluate people based on their consistent demonstration of it in their professional activities. *Then* it becomes a core value, something that we have collectively agreed to formally recognize and deal with as *right* and *proper* for our colleagues to consistently embody and exemplify. So here, for our consideration, are the ten core values of Total Leaders:

- Reflection and thoughtfulness, rather than shooting from the hip.
- Honesty and forthrightness, rather than manipulative half-truths.
- Openness to new ideas and experiences, rather than rehearsed opinions.
- Courage and candor in the face of challenging issues or circumstances, rather than going along with the crowd.
- Integrity of purpose and principle in dealing with problematic situations, rather than yielding to convenience or favoritism.
- Commitment and active involvement in challenging endeavors, rather than going through the motions.

- Excellence and high quality as standards of performance, rather than just acceptable effort and results.
- Productivity and contribution as standards of success, rather than routine participation.
- Risk-taking and initiative as approaches to complex problems, rather than precedent and caution.
- Teamwork and willing collaboration in undertaking projects, rather than plays for individual attention and control.

We would do well to use this framework as a starting point for developing core values that apply to our colleagues, our learners, our constituents, and—most of all—ourselves. Once we have a framework that we can enthusiastically endorse, we can combine it with the ten principles of professionalism to construct a powerful organizational philosophy (i.e., guiding ethos) that proudly states what we stand for, encourage, develop, and support in every member of our TLC. Build this third weight-bearing wall, and they'll come running. Embody it over time, and they'll be breaking down the doors to get in.

ESTABLISHING OUR REASON FOR BEING

The terms *reason for being* and *purpose* are virtually synonymous in the literature on change. As we have noted earlier, purpose is fundamentally about ends, goals, intended results, ultimate priorities, deep meaning, an organization's most essential function, and "the business it is in." But for us, both personal and organizational purpose are about our reason for being—what we are most essentially here on the planet to do and contribute. Deep purpose is why we truly come to work in the morning, and what most affects our sense of well-being, joy, and fulfillment as a conscious entity.

To the host of organizational gurus who strongly advocate what we call "authentic" leadership, there is nothing more essential to a healthy, learning, change-friendly organization than a compelling, client-focused purpose—one that everyone in the organization knows and can state and explain at the drop of a hat. A clear and compelling purpose statement is an essential direction-setter and motivator—something that organizational members internalize, embrace, and consciously embody in their everyday decisions and actions. If it's not on the tip of their tongues, then it might as well not exist because it can't possibly be conscious, internalized, or explicitly directing their thinking, choices, and behavior. If this viewpoint seems too bold, then imagine asking, "What's your organization's driving purpose?" and being told, "I'm not sure, but I can look it up. There's a copy of it right here in my files."

Making Purpose "Real"

Many people confuse purpose statements with mission statements. They differ. A purpose statement is a short, hard-hitting, compelling expression of the organization's reason for being that clearly distinguishes it from other related reasons. Its power and brevity allow it to be internalized and "real." Mission statements can also be powerful, but they generally are considerably longer and assert broad goals and key ways the organization intends to accomplish them. One is pure essence, the other is its elaboration. Unfortunately, the elaboration is often set aside or forgotten because it is simply too long to remember.

As a rule of thumb, purpose statements should be no longer than ten words. Each word should really count by saying something definitive and unique about the organization's reason for being. If they are any longer, people won't remember the words even though they might embrace the general idea. Our experience suggests that remembering each word is critical because each word conveys explicit substance, direction, and intent.

A purpose statement becomes real and members adhere to it when its specific words can be directly linked to its operating standards—such as the five that are driving this Strategic Design Effort—and to a deliberately constructed and implemented tool called a "decision screen" (see figure 9.3).

A decision screen serves as the "moral filter" through which all of an organization's decisions must pass. The sensors in the filter are the organization's purpose, philosophy, and principles. If potential choices and courses of action don't successfully pass through the screen by directly "aligning" with or matching these three criteria, they don't get pursued, no matter what the surrounding circumstances—simply because they're inconsistent with the screen. When used in this deliberate and enlightened way, decision screens can be powerful tools for staying on track, cohesive, and genuinely professional.

Constructing a Purpose Statement

Given everything that we've encountered in this book so far, what could we say is an appropriate purpose statement for a Total Learning Community? What's its reason for being in a world of continuous discovery and constant challenge and change? How should our model's purpose be stated? Here are some key things to consider.

First, powerful purpose statements begin with powerful action verbs relating to the organization's relationship to its learners, not its programs. Note that our choice of verb has major implications for how we'll address and implement all five of our defining standards. Some strong examples include equip, empower, develop, and mentor. But there are certainly other possibilities as well.

Second, who should our TLC be equipping, empowering, developing, or mentoring? In very strong purpose statements, the most common direct object

Making Purpose Real

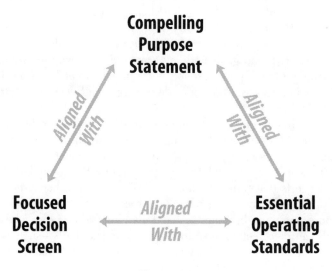

Figure 9.3

of their strong action verb is usually *all learners*. And in our case that will mean adults and educators as well as students.

The implications of these two words are enormous because once a TLC commits itself to doing something active and positive for all learners, then it is formally abandoning all prevalent notions and practices related to iceberg schooling. The comparative-competitive practices of its Feudal Age agenda; the constrained time factors in its Agrarian Age calendar; the impersonal, standardized flow of its Industrial Age (assembly-line) delivery system; and the self-constraining boxes of its Bureaucratic Age culture are all inconsistent with doing something of significance for *all* learners.

Third, if we stick with this train of development, our purpose statement is going to have to address the capabilities we want our learners to develop, where or how we want those capabilities to be carried out, and to what end our learners will apply those capabilities. All this with only seven words left? Well, here are just a few of many possible examples:

... to shape and enrich their changing world.
... to improve our stressful world.
... to succeed in our technological world.
... to contribute constructively to the greater good.

Regardless of which one of these four hypothetical examples we might consider more fully, it's immediately apparent that each defines the real world to be the target context of application for learning and development, not school subjects. In addition, the first three examples use a single adjective to denote the nature of that real world, and each of those adjectives—changing, stressful, technological—has huge implications for the kind of empowering learning experiences that will be needed to enable our learners to successfully encounter and begin to master that real-world context.

Moreover, the first, second, and fourth statements directly imply that whatever abilities learners develop be channeled in a positive, contributing, beneficial way that enhances the human condition. In other words, our learners are to be *contributors*, not just individualistic *achievers*. And this, of course, reinforces the constructive learning and living domain of our Total Learning for Total Living model.

So let's put some examples together and begin to imagine the paradigm perspectives, research realities, guiding ethos, and spirit of educators who come to work each day knowing and feeling that their TLC's reason for being is:

- Equipping all learners to shape and enrich their changing world
- Empowering all learners to improve our stressful world
- Developing all learners to succeed in our technological world
- Mentoring learners who all contribute constructively to the greater good

With the tremendous doors of possibility that open with statements like these, we can anticipate them wanting to be the first to arrive in the morning and the last to leave at night, with no ambivalence about why they are there and what they are there to accomplish. And the cherry on top: they'll be able to confidently state and explain their TLC's ten-word purpose at the drop of a hat!

And our constituents? Build this fourth weight-bearing wall, and they'll really come running. Embody it over time, and there won't be any doors to have to break down.

(10)

STEP 3: DEFINING LIFE PERFORMANCE LEARNING ESSENTIALS

Life performance essentials become our TLC's operational purpose. They are the main reason we come to work in the morning. To strengthen and achieve them for every learner in our TLC, including ourselves, is our reason for being—period! Everything else is secondary, and all the rest is details.

With a totally professional way of operating and a rock-solid foundation of insight and inquiry for our Total Learning Community now established, we're ready to take the most important step in our entire Strategic Design Process. It requires us to address Standard 3 and define the framework of life performance essentials (LPEs) that will shape and drive everything that we implement from this point onward.

As we noted in chapter 7, these LPEs become our TLC's operational purpose. They are the main reason we come to work in the morning. To strengthen and achieve them for every learner in our TLC, including ourselves, is our reason for being—period! Everything else is secondary, and all the rest is details. They'd better be exactly what we want and can enthusiastically support because what we teach, how we teach, the kinds of empowering learning experiences we provide, and the kinds of opportunities and resources we marshal to get this job done will all be derived directly from them in design Steps 4 and 5.

Because we're about to engage in a fairly detailed and complex process here, it will be wise to see what lies ahead from two different perspectives: (1) how the foundation we laid in chapter 9 directly relates to this step in our process; and (2) how our notion of life performance fits into the larger scheme of performance learning. We'll look at the big design picture first.

THE BIG PICTURE OF STRATEGIC DIRECTION SETTING

The foundation of insight and inquiry that we established in chapter 9 was the first of two key strategic steps needed to set a clear and compelling direction for our TLC. This step is the second. As we constructed the four weight-bearing walls of that foundation, we were setting a clear direction for our TLC: Our paradigm perspectives put us squarely in the future-focused learner empowerment business; our research realities reinforce that direction with a heavy dose of life performance added; our guiding ethos directs us toward the core values and principles of Total Professionalism (of people performing in the real world); and our sample reason for being, or ultimate purpose, statements are expressed in unequivocal "life empowerment" terms. Clearly, then, our TLC is headed in a future-focused life performance empowerment direction.

Now we face the question, What does that direction really look like in terms of tangible and observable learner qualities and capabilities? Show us what this direction means in terms of learning results. We'll be able to do that if we rigorously *derive* our life performance learning essentials *explicitly* from the foundation we've established. How that looks in very broad terms is shown in figure 10.1.

At the center of the diagram lies the framework of LPEs we'll be establishing in this third Strategic Design step. As the arrows indicate, they will embody

The Big Picture of Strategic Direction Setting

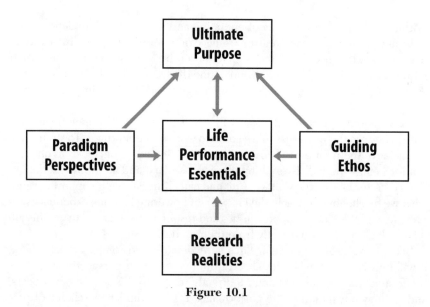

Figure 10.1

key elements of our research realities, our paradigm perspectives, and our guiding ethos. We'll explicitly implement these connections in this chapter. As we just suggested, the figure also shows that our LPEs and our ultimate purpose are one and the same. Ideally, each should directly mirror and embody the other. Finally, it explains that our paradigm perspectives and guiding ethos also have a direct bearing on how our ultimate purpose is stated.

CLIMBING THE PERFORMANCE MOUNTAIN

From chapter 2 onward we've been making the case that learning is far more than just "knowing" and "understanding." It's the ability to do something creative, collaborative, productive, and/or constructive with what you know and understand. We've also emphasized that intentional forms of doing are actually performances, even though learners may not be on a literal stage with a live audience sitting there. Nonetheless, they are demonstrating things in some form of performance context, and that context adds varying degrees of complexity and challenge to what must be done.

When we step back and think in the abstract about doing, demonstrating, executing, and/or performing, we realize that they take many different forms, and these forms vary greatly in scope, magnitude, complexity, and challenge. Some of these forms are quite narrow and specific, and we typically associate the word *skills* with them. Others are broader and more complex, and we often call them *competences*. Still others are even broader and far more complex in nature. We call them *role performance abilities*. The diagram of the "performance mountain" in figure 10.2 shows this range of forms using names typical of what these different forms represent.

We can readily see in the figure that the forms at the top of the mountain— things we've been calling life performance abilities—are the most macro, complex, and context-grounded kinds of performances, while those at the bottom of the mountain are the most micro, narrow, and specific. What we must keep in mind as we undertake this next Strategic Design step, is that we are first going to focus on what's at the top of the mountain—the ultimate life performance abilities we want our learners to develop—then ask what kinds of things from lower on the mountain they will need as stepping stones for reaching the mountain's peak.

In taking this approach we'll be applying an insight from Warren Bennis's classic, *On Becoming a Leader* (1989). Bennis reminds us that mountain climbers always plan their climb from the peak back. That's how they know they'll ultimately be able to reach the top successfully. We call it "designing down" or "building back." It's the ends-based approach to design and implementation.

The Performance Mountain

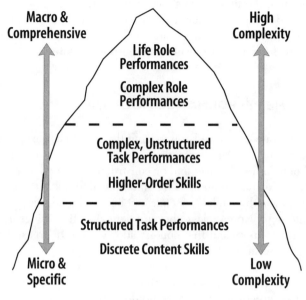

Macro &
Comprehensive

High
Complexity

Life Role
Performances

Complex Role
Performances

Complex, Unstructured
Task Performances

Higher-Order Skills

Structured Task Performances

Discrete Content Skills

Micro &
Specific

Low
Complexity

Figure 10.2

ESTABLISHING OUR DESIGN TEMPLATE

The process we're about to undertake evolved over the course of a decade into the template that follows. Its basic features, however, have been stable from the outset and follow the structure described in figure 10.1. The process has been shaped and driven by a series of questions that were originally designed to break the entrenched educentric thinking around curriculum, instruction, and learning. Our initial experiences with asking and answering these questions in school districts of all sizes and kinds from coast to coast in both the U.S. and Canada clearly indicated that they did.

Defining the Future Context of Success

They key paradigm shift in this entire process is to get a large cross-section of people in a district or community to define learning in terms of what is required in the future for which they're preparing their young people, not simply what's important in school. Two key paradigm-shifting strategic questions open this door to the future:

1. In what domains of life and living do you want your children to be successful and fulfilled after finishing school?

2. Within each domain, what are the key challenges, problems, conditions, and opportunities they are likely to face (for which they'll need to be prepared)?

Note that this first question relates directly to the domains of living described in chapter 2. When people address and answer it, they are simultaneously describing what's really important in life, defining the contexts in which learners will be operating as adults, and providing a non-educentric way of organizing the content that's essential for students to learn (i.e., the content related to what they're actually going to be dealing with in their lives). That's a lot to accomplish with one opening question.

In chapter 2 we identified eight major domains of living that have been central to a number of Strategic Design efforts in North America. Using that framework as a starting point, a Strategic Design team in Australia's Northern Territory came up with a similar framework for its educational system in September 2000. Notice how the two frameworks compare based on what people identify as most significant in their particular cultures:

North American Composite	*Northern Territory, Australia*
Personal Potential and Wellness	Personal Potential and Growth
Learning Challenges and Resources	Personal Well-Being and Fulfillment
Life and Resource Management	Life and Resource Management
Close and Significant Relationships	Close and Important Relationships
Meaningful and Fulfilling Pursuits	Family, Culture, and Identities
Physical and Cultural Environments	Cultural and Global Environments
Group and Community Memberships	Group and Community Involvement
Work and Productive Endeavors	Work and Productive Behaviors

When we address this first question with our constituents, we'll want them to come up with a similar kind of framework, based on what's really important to them about life and living. It will help if we use the specific words in these two frameworks as examples that simply orient, but not determine, their thinking.

Chapter 2 addresses this second strategic question as well, by providing an extremely condensed version of our book *The Future Is Now* (Schwahn and Spady 2000). We should make all kinds of resources like this book available to our constituents as they grapple with this second question because this whole process needs to be as research/insight-based as possible and we don't want them pulling answers out of thin air. Notice that the words in this question are intended to generate a range of perspectives on what people think their youngsters will face in light of this broad array of evidence. For example, the words *challenges* and *conditions* are intended to be neutral, *problems* is intended to be negative, and *opportunities* is meant to be positive. So the question implies that the future isn't all doom and gloom, but it will demand a lot from us in each domain of living.

As we help our people address this second question, we'll be wise to break them into domain-specific study groups so they can really focus on the things that are likely to matter in each domain. This will make their responses more focused and concrete, and that's what we'll need to work with at later stages of the design. And please remember that our biggest challenge is to keep the discussions and the responses/descriptions focused on *what our youngsters will face*, not on what they *need* or *need to be like*. It's very easy to jump to those kinds of conclusions in addressing this questions, but we mustn't let it happen. At this stage of the process the focus must remain on the future, not the kids. We'll turn to them soon enough.

We seek two products from this stage of the process. The first is a domains of living framework. The second is a comprehensive list of future condition statements, organized by domain if that helps. Together these two products give us key components of the rationale we need for deriving our framework of life performance essentials.

Preparing to Derive Our Life Performance Essentials

With a clear picture in hand of the domains of living and future conditions that our learners inevitably face as young adults, we're ready to tackle the most important aspect of this third Strategic Design step: systematically deriving our framework of life performance essentials. This is a challenging process, and it requires that we take several key things into account before formally starting on the design itself.

First, our experience with this process over the past decade indicates that we have two broad choices in how to proceed. One is to derive a particular kind of life performance essential for each specific domain of living identified. For example, we just noted two different domain frameworks with eight elements each. This first alternative would treat each domain as its own self-contained arena of living with its own unique set of future conditions requiring its own specific set of life performance essentials. Consequently, this design approach would create a direct match between a specific domain and its performance essentials.

The other approach is to generate a potentially more comprehensive set of essentials that operate across multiple domains. The logic underlying this alternative is that life is a seamless web of these domains with overlaps and connections everywhere. Therefore, being an effective communicator, for example, is essential to one's success in virtually every domain, not just one. This approach, therefore, would create a framework of essentials that are assumed to apply across the domains. Excellent frameworks have resulted using both approaches, but we have found the latter approach to be both easier to develop and generally more valuable to its users.

Second, from the origination of this process in 1990 to the present, we have defined life performance essentials in role performance, top-of-the-mountain terms. This means using what we've called "role performer labels" such as the twenty that constitute the Life Performance Wheel described in chapter 2, figure 2.3. These labels—for example, *leaders* and *organizers*—imply that there's a real person there carrying out a complex configuration of skills and tasks, who's doing it across a range of performance contexts, while dealing with a wide range of content, and facing all kinds of challenges and contingencies in the process. It is precisely the richness, complexity, and versatility of these role performer labels that gives this approach its unique power and appeal. But since so many different kinds of skills and abilities are implied by a single label, deciding on the best, strongest, or most appropriate label is a genuinely awesome responsibility requiring both scientific precision and artistic sensitivity. The best advice is to keep a thick thesaurus close at hand at all times.

Over time, however, groups have had to decide whether to define their essentials around single role performer labels or related pairs, as in the wheel. More recently most groups have preferred pairs, but we'll show both kinds of examples shortly.

Third, from the very outset, this process has used descriptive adjectives along with the role performer labels to define LPEs. Why? Because these adjectives convey an enormous amount about the qualities of the performer and performance being sought. For example, being a courageous leader is very different from being a leader with no other defining attributes. And it's a lot different than being a friendly one—or an analytical one, or a shrewd one. So we quickly learned that these adjectives had an enormous influence on the qualitative attributes that we wanted the role performers to possess and demonstrate.

At first we simply used single adjectives because that's what emerged in the very first role performance framework ever developed (see Spady 1994). But over time we found singles to be too constraining, so we began to use pairs with great success. But please never use more than two. Otherwise you'll find that they stack up like a laundry list and they lose their rhetorical and operational power. We'll see examples of both single and double qualitative attributes later in the chapter. But in each case we took extreme care in selecting them, simply because their defining power and implications go so deep.

Fourth, while exploring the link between the Life Performance Wheel and the concept of professionalism in 1998, we came across a missing piece in the overall design process: the guiding ethos that we want our learners to use in their life performances. Consequently, recent designs have included this third element as well, using the ten principles of professionalism described in chapter 8 and the ten core values described in chapter 9 as their grounding points. Here too we must be careful to select these ethos elements with great care because their defining power and implications are also very strong.

Integrating the Defining Elements into a Framework

To see how this all comes together into a coherent framework, let's use the 1998 Total Professionals model as our example. To facilitate this explanation, we'll show the Life Performance Wheel from chapter 2 again here as figure 10.3.

Note that the wheel consists of ten pairs of role performer labels and that there also happen to be ten core values and ten principles of professionalism. We wondered whether this was just a coincidence, or if these elements could be brought together into a framework that had real power and integrity. We agreed to link one value and one principle from each framework to its most appropriate role performer pair to see if there was a genuine match. In order to bring all the necessary pieces together, we only needed to develop and apply ten definitive/relevant pairs of qualitative attributes that gave an appropriate character to each distinctive role performance.

Here's the resulting set of defining elements for you to study as an example of what you might create in your local setting. Whether they constitute Total Professionals or not, this is an impressive framework of real-world capabilities:

- An inquisitive, self-directed searcher and learner, guided by an ethos of reflection and inquiry, who:
- A diligent, high-quality producer and conributor, guided by an ethos of productivity and contribution, who:

The Life Performance Wheel

Figure 10.3

- A creative, knowledgeable innovator and designer, guided by an ethos of risk-taking and future-focusing, who:
- An imaginative, insightful problem framer and solver, guided by an ethos of openness and clarity, who:
- An adept, consistent implementer and performer, guided by an ethos of excellence and accountability, who:
- An open, receptive listener and communicator, guided by an ethos of honesty and connection, who:
- An energetic, resilient leader and organizer, guided by an ethos of courage and inclusiveness, who:
- An astute, trustworthy mediator and negotiator, guided by an ethos of integrity and win-win, who:
- An enthusiastic, patient coach and facilitator, guided by an ethos of teamwork and alignment, who:
- An empathetic, steadfast advocate and supporter, guided by an ethos of commitment and improvement, who:

Quite apart from how useful you find this Total Professional framework, there are three particular things to note here that will help in your own design process. First, the pairs of qualitative attributes add enormous specificity and character to the nature of the performances we're expecting. "Energetic, resilient" and "enthusiastic, patient," for example, really send a distinctive message about the qualities of the leader/organizer and coach/facilitator we're seeking to develop. So select these attributes with as much care as you do the role performer labels.

Second, the same can be said about the guiding ethos elements in each item. They, too, strongly influence the overall character of what the learner will demonstrate, so choose and match them with great care as well.

The third point involves the word *who*, which appears at the end of each item, followed by a colon. This indicates that something is to follow, and that something is the set of performance statements that we'll eventually need to develop which must *perfectly embody* the words in the framework stems. We call these statements essential performance components (EPCs). Defining them is the technically most demanding aspect of this design process, so we're going to defer addressing them until we can review some additional examples.

In the meantime, however, remember that framework elements like the ten above are like the chassis of a car. They provide a basic structure that enables the car to be built, but they're not the final product, the functioning car itself. Our "car"—the life performance essentials—will function once we've defined our EPCs. Meanwhile, we need to stay focused on designing the soundest and most responsive chassis possible.

Keys to Deriving Our Defining Elements

Before proceeding, let's quickly review figure 10.1. It says that we're going to directly use three of the weight-bearing walls from the foundation we built in chapter 9 to develop our framework of life performance essentials. They are our paradigm perspectives, our research realities, and our guiding ethos. We now know that those LPEs are actually made up of three different elements: role performer labels, qualitative attributes, and guiding ethos elements. We also know now that three of our research reality elements from chapter 2 have a direct bearing on this process: the domains of living, future conditions, and human learning (the performance mountain). We can also safely assume that a fourth, human potential, will directly contribute as well.

While this may seem like trying to keep a dozen balls in the air at the same time, the pattern of connections that we need to work with is much simpler, as is shown in figure 10.4. The key to following this diagram correctly is to stay focused on the three defining elements of our life performance essentials and take them one at a time, starting with the role performer labels on the left. If we do, then the first guiding question we need to ask is,

> Given what we know about human potential, human learning, and the domains of living our learners face, what kinds of role performers do we want them to be after finishing school?

We'll need to have these three bodies of evidence in front of us to address the question, of course, but we've got the wheel and its Total Professional elements to work with as starting points for answering it. There are other frameworks to consider as well, and we'll review some of them shortly.

Key Factors in Deriving Life Performance Essentials

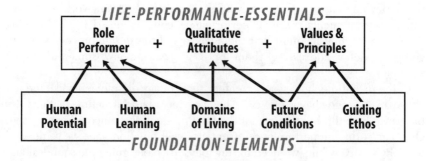

Figure 10.4

Moving to the right in figure 10.4, our second guiding question is,

> Given the domains of living and future conditions our learners face and the potential they possess as individuals, what qualitative attributes will they need in order to lead successful and fulfilling lives?

To address this question, we'll need our domains of living, our future conditions statements, and our newly derived framework of role performer labels in front of us. In effect, we're asking, If this is what they'll be facing, and this is what they can bring to the table, what are they going to have to be like in order to cope or thrive? In choosing powerful and appropriate qualitative attributes, opt, if possible, for adjectives that respond to several future conditions at the same time, simply because every word needs to carry enormous weight in a tightly defined framework like this.

Moving to the right side of the diagram, we can see that our potential third guiding question almost answers itself because the values and principles that we developed earlier for our guiding ethos will clearly help us answer the following guiding question:

> Given these future conditions and our TLC's guiding ethos, what values and principles do we want to guide our learners as they carry out their lives?

Our challenge will be to decide which of the many available alternatives best fits particular future conditions and role performances.

So, using figure 10.4 as a guide, and dealing with each component in its proper turn, allows us to start with a strong foundation for our Strategic Design and systematically derive from its elements a powerful framework of life performance essentials similar to the ten elements that constitute the Total Professional model.

TOTAL LEARNING PERFORMANCE EXAMPLES

We devoted chapter 3 to explaining that the Total Learning for Total Living framework lies at the heart of a new-paradigm approach to education. We are now ready to revisit that argument by showing how this compelling five-component model underlies a powerful life performance essentials framework. To understand the utility of this model, let's look at figure 10.5 and revisit what we called the essence of Total Learning.

Figure 10.5 quickly helps us recall the five types of Total Learning—conscious, creative, collaborative, competent, and constructive—and the essence of each.

The Essence of Total Learning

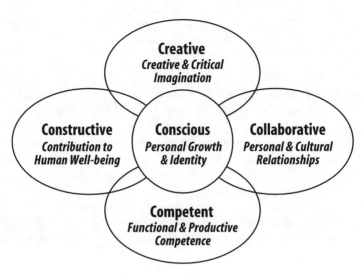

Figure 10.5

Now let's shift our perspective just slightly and think of each of these components in role performer terms. At their core, what kinds of role performers would constitute a total performer—someone equipped to thrive in each of the model's five domains of living by embodying the essence of each kind of learning? Here's what we produced by addressing that question:

- Conscious performers are open, growing *learners*, guided by an ethos of purpose and integrity.
- Creative performers are imaginative, undaunted *innovators*, guided by an ethos of future-focusing and risk-taking.
- Collaborative performers are honest, affirming *partners*, guided by an ethos of collegiality and teamwork.
- Competent performers are reliable, exemplary *producers*, guided by an ethos of excellence and improvement.
- Constructive performers are caring, committed *contributors*, guided by an ethos of win-win and accountability.

The diagram portraying these results is shown in figure 10.6, and it can be super-imposed directly atop the pattern in figure 10.5. What this is saying in the larger sense is that Total Learning generates Total Learners, and Total Learners are ultimately Total Performers who live "totally." The connection looks like this:

Total Performers

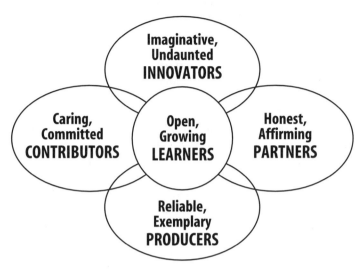

Figure 10.6

- Performers who are open, growing learners, guided by an ethos of purpose and integrity, will inevitably live consciously.
- Performers who are imaginative, undaunted innovators, guided by an ethos of future-focusing and risk-taking, will inevitably live creatively.
- Performers who are honest, affirming partners, guided by an ethos of collegiality and teamwork, will inevitably live collaboratively.
- Performers who are reliable, exemplary producers, guided by an ethos of excellence and improvement, will inevitably live competently.
- Performers who are caring, committed contributors, guided by an ethos of win-win and accountability, will inevitably live constructively.

Let's stop and reflect on the power of this framework. It's saying that five key qualities are fundamental to humans living fulfilling lives, and these qualities could be realized if we all left education as open, growing learners; imaginative, undaunted innovators; honest, affirming partners; reliable, exemplary producers; and caring, committed contributors. After all the courses are over, the books are read, the assignments are turned in, and the evaluations made, these five life performance abilities are what really matter to all of us in the long run—five key domains of living requiring five key kinds of role performers developed through five key kinds of learning. It's compelling, it's not magic, and it sure beats test scores and GPAs as a vision of learning essentials.

Moreover, from a life performance perspective, we can take this model even further by mapping out the set of role performance abilities that directly support the five key patterns just identified. By doing so we are dramatically expanding the range of abilities we can address and develop through this kind of life performance design process. Just consider these possibilities:

- Open, growing *learners* result from people being courageous *seekers*, perceptive *observers*, reflective *assessors*, and insightful *assimilators*. So in developing conscious performers, we should directly foster these supporting abilities as well.
- Imaginative, undaunted *innovators* result from people being expansive *visualizers*, self-directed *explorers*, probing *questioners*, and energetic *catalysts*. So in developing creative performers, we should directly foster these supporting abilities as well.
- Honest, affirming *partners* result from people being trustworthy *friends*, responsive *communicators*, respectful *mediators*, and inspiring *mentors*. So in developing collaborative performers, we should directly foster these supporting abilities as well.
- Reliable, exemplary *producers* result from people being enlightened *planners*, resourceful *mobilizers*, thorough *organizers*, and adept *implementors*. So in developing competent performers, we should directly foster these supporting abilities as well.
- Caring, committed *contributors* result from people being principled *advocates*, versatile *facilitators*, conscientious *stewards*, and steadfast *supporters*. So in developing constructive performers, we should directly foster these supporting abilities as well.

Clearly, then, this Total Learning/Total Performer model holds great promise as a tool for helping us generate the life performance essentials of our TLC.

An Australian Example

Developments in Australia clearly reveal that the model has proven useful there as well. In September 2000 the curriculum design team from the country's Northern Territory Department of Education redesigned its entire Essential Learnings framework around this model. With some slight wording changes, they developed for review and public comment the following broad categories, plus (1) detailed essential performance components statements that they identify as their "criteria for essential learning outcomes"; (2) a clear set of "growth point indicators" of these essential learnings for students of different ages—elements that we refer to as "supporting competences"; and (3) and sample teaching strategies for each set of growth point indicators. Their broad categories include:

- The *inner* (conscious) learner—"Who am I and where am I going?"A thinker and learner who:
- The *creative* learner—"What are life's possibilities?"A searcher and innovator who:
- The *collaborative* learner—"How do I connect and work with others?"A communicator and team member who:
- The *constructive* (competent) learner—"How can I use my skills and knowledge?" A producer and implementer who:
- The *contributing* (constructive) learner—"How can I make a useful difference?" An advocate and participant who:

To keep things as simple as possible for their constituents, the team imbedded the substance of their qualitative attributes and guiding ethos elements directly into their essential performance component statements and then further down into their growth point indicators. Their clear intent is to equip all their learners with the abilities to be Total Performers in life as well as in school.

A South African Example

With the change of government in the Republic of South Africa in 1995 came a parallel change in the direction of its education system. Operating under the banner of "Outcome-Based Education," South Africa's curriculum efforts have been focused on the accomplishment of twelve things called "critical outcomes," five of which have direct parallels to the five components of our Total Learning model.

With assistance from the Delta Foundation in Port Elizabeth, a small team of program developers began to explore the potential of designing an entirely new approach to education, using a strengthened version of five particular critical outcomes as its foundation. These five outcomes addressed life role performances that would be required of South African adults in the modern global economy. To fit the South African context, they were named Personal, Entrepreneurial, Peer, Career, and Citizen life role performers. In substance and character they directly parallel our Conscious, Creative, Collaborative, Competent, and Constructive performers, respectively.

The particular value of this concluding example is that it lets us see how a role performance framework can be fully developed and expressed using a set of definitive essential performance components (EPCs) for each kind of role performer in the model. As we noted briefly earlier, these EPCs are the proof of the pudding—how we'd know a particular kind of role performer if we saw one. They are our equivalent of the functioning automobile, not just its chassis; and they're the "real" life performance essentials we're seeking to develop.

So, with some minor adaptations to fit our context, imagine the South Africans saying that they seek to develop:

1. Capable personal life-role performers (*conscious learners*) who consistently operate as conscientious, self-directed life managers guided by an ethos of reflection and improvement, and who
   - insightfully assess their unique personal qualities and explain how strengthening them will open doors to continued learning and life success
   - perceptively identify the ways they learn best and consistently employ them as tools for ongoing growth and improvement
   - consistently probe new information, ideas, and experiences for their deeper meaning and connection to their desired quality of life
   - regularly initiate and sustain endeavors that strengthen their skills, health, quality of life, and opportunities for advancement
   - consistently manage their time to allow for regular periods of study, exercise, and self-improvement in their daily lives
   - sensibly select and consume foods and nutrients that contribute to their long-term health and well-being
   - consistently make prudent financial planning and personal expenditure decisions
2. Capable entrepreneurial life-role performers (*creative learners*) who consistently operate as resourceful, future-focused opportunity creators guided by an ethos of initiative and innovation, and who
   - independently collect, analyze, organize, and critically evaluate emerging trends and possibilities in various fields for their entrepreneurial potential
   - routinely look beyond conventional approaches and understandings to reveal the unexplored potential in all life situations
   - purposefully locate and assess information on current and emerging work and income-generating opportunities and create innovative ways to capitalize on them
   - continuously assess existing business practices and propose innovative ways to expand and improve them
   - adeptly use any available resources to legitimately generate personal and community income
3. Capable peer life-role performers (*collaborative learners*) who consistently operate as forthright, collaborative team members guided by an ethos of honesty and reliability, and who
   - actively develop joint projects with their peers in which plans and responsibilities are clearly defined, equitably shared, and reliably carried out by all members
   - adeptly apply leadership skills and knowledge of effective teamwork to accomplish team goals

- consistently fulfill commitments, without excuses, and support others in doing the same
- actively listen to the intent and spirit of others' words and consistently offer them constructive feedback and suggestions when appropriate
- skillfully use a variety of means and strategies to communicate clearly in all situations
- consciously take into account the interests and viewpoints of all parties in openly airing disagreements, and consistently work to resolve them ethically and equitably

4. Capable career life-role performers (*competent learners*) who consistently operate as adept, productive career performers guided by an ethos of diligence and quality, and who
   - consistently set high performance goals for themselves and work until they are accomplished
   - independently research the challenges that career professionals face in their fields and the standards they must maintain to be successful
   - consistently use these professional standards and the most advanced methods in their fields to assess and complete their work
   - gather and effectively utilize the people, resources, and technologies need for accomplishing projects successfully within agreed-upon time and resource constraints
   - periodically update a portfolio of their strongest personal aptitudes, technical skills, and accomplishments and present it to potential employers for evaluation

5. Capable citizen life-role performers (*constructive learners*) who consistently operate as active, responsible community contributors guided by an ethos of caring and commitment, and who
   - sensitively address the country's problems by respecting and advocating the democratic rights of all
   - consistently stand firm in the face of challenges and pressures in advocating causes affecting the common good
   - freely devote their time, talents, and knowledge to improving the environment and the health and well-being of others
   - actively work with others in their community to maintain or improve the quality of understanding and living in the world around them
   - persistently seek and employ ways to address and solve problems affecting the well-being of their local communities and global environment

Let's acknowledge what an enormous paradigm shift from educentric content and skills this framework represents, but how much more relevant, real, and significant it is to learners who view life, rather than education, as the real definer of who they are and what they can experience and contribute.

PLANNING OUR CLIMB

Congratulations! We've reached the peak of the performance mountain described in figure 10.2. In reviewing this South African life role performance framework, we've taken several daring steps toward defining learning essentials in genuine life performance terms. Those steps have taken us from bottom of the mountain thinking about curriculum skills and classroom assignments to top of the mountain realities that reveal what real people do to keep their lives, careers, relationships, and communities functioning effectively.

Since Warren Bennis has advised us to plan our climb from the peak back, we now sense what the peak looks like: the South African framework developed around the five components of our Total Learning for Total Living model. This is what real *life-role* performance entails when based on four of our grounding foundation elements: domains of living, future conditions, life performance, and guiding ethos.

The results of this kind of rigorous strategic design may represent too bold a step for some of our constituents to take away from the safety net of educentric thinking and practice. If that's the case and the altitude's too high, we've got three other alternatives to offer that will allow us to climb to the level of the mountain just below the peak itself. They are the Life Performance Wheel/Total Professionalism framework, our extended Total Performer framework, and the Australian Essential Learnings framework. All three clearly represent this complex role performances category very well.

The foregoing has given us the tools to reach this very high sector of the mountain if we want to lead our constituents here. Hopefully it's because, as figure 10.1 reminds us, whatever we create as our life performance essentials will end up serving as our Total Learning Community's functional purpose as well—its reason for being—the main motivator for people coming to work in the morning. As leaders it's our responsibility to make that purpose as inspiring, future-focused, enlightened, empowering, and realistic as we can. Anything less will leave us vulnerable to the educentric inertia that eventually pulls everything down the mountain into the ravine of the three Rs: regulation, routine, and ritual.

11

STEP 4: ENSURING EMPOWERING LEARNING EXPERIENCES

Once they leave our TLC, our learners are going to have to be self-starters, lifelong learners, and competent performers in a world of continuous discovery and constant change. If they've become dependent on teachers for direction and evaluation, they'll be sunk.

We've arrived at the major moment of truth in designing our Total Learning Community. This is where the culture of Total Professionalism created in Step 1, the foundation of insight and inquiry constructed in Step 2, and the framework of life performance essentials derived in Step 3 all get directly translated into the kind of learning system that embodies and supports our TLC's ultimate purpose. That's a lot to account for as we take Step 4: ensuring that all our learners continuously receive the kinds of learning experiences that will equip and empower them for a successful, fulfilling future.

To stay on track, we'll need to create a formal decision screen—a set of criteria through which all of our decisions and actions must pass before being endorsed and implemented. We'll need to use the screen to ensure that this new instructional system is fully aligned and consistent with seven key things:

- The twelve visionary goals of TLCs that are laid out at the beginning of chapter 7.
- The essence of the Total Learning for Total Living model described in chapters 3 and 10.
- The essential performance components of our life performance essentials as we developed them in Step 3, chapter 10.

- The new research realities described in chapter 2 and utilized in chapters 9 and 10.
- Criteria for operating outside the seven constraining, educentric boxes described in chapter 6.
- A repertory of new-paradigm operating possibilities such as those listed and summarized early in chapter 9.
- The principles and strategies required for creating and sustaining a culture of Total Professionalism described in chapter 8.

Again, this may seem like an awful lot to handle and integrate at once, but we'll find as we did in chapter 10 that taking things one small step at a time will allow all of these elements to come together compatibly. The good news is that the foregoing chapters have given us a powerful set of resources, frameworks, and strategies with which to work.

DEVELOPING AN OPERATING MODEL

Creating and implementing a powerful and empowering learning system will first require us to understand and frame the key elements that actually constitute such as system. While this could take a book in itself, we'll focus on a model that covers the most ground with the fewest individual components. And to be sure we stay on course, we'll relate each of its components back to the elements in our decision screen as we describe them.

Let's step back for a second and think about what goes into a learning system of any kind. Then we'll give those elements the qualitative attributes that will give them the character suitable for an empowering, future-focused TLC. Four things immediately jump out for consideration, and some others fall right in behind them.

First, a system needs to be guided by a set of *intended learning results*. It needs to know what it's trying to accomplish before it can design or implement anything that we'd ultimately consider "appropriate."

Second, a system needs *curriculum substance*. There has to be something tangible for the learners to grapple with and learn. It will need clear criteria for what that content should be.

Third, a system needs *people* and *processes*. There must be human beings there guiding and facilitating processes that directly support and facilitate the accomplishment of the intended learning results.

Fourth, a system needs *tools* and *technologies* that directly support the intended learning. Whether it's books, materials, paper and pencils, computers, Internet access, videotapes, or machinery, appropriate resources are needed.

But there's more, and it's imbedded in what we've called the system's "structure." Two of those things are *opportunity* and *qssistance*. It's about getting the learning experiences and help you need as a learner when you need them from the best people and resources available.

We also need *access* and *advancement*. It's about how long, how often, and when essential learning experiences are available to learners before they're expected to be "finished" with something and "move on."

A seventh component relates to the "reality" of learning situations. It's about *context challenges*, the situations, settings, and circumstances in which learning occurs and is formally demonstrated and credentialed.

Now if we took these seven components, either translated them into our terminology or gave them the qualities that best embody a new paradigm TLC, and put them into a diagram, the system we're creating would resemble the "flower" diagram in figure 11.1. At its core would be our Life Performance Essentials because they are the operational heart and soul of the system. Surrounding and directly supporting them are the system's Future-Focused Curriculum Content, Empowering People and Processes, Advanced Tools and Technologies, Continuous

The Key Components of an Empowering Instructional System

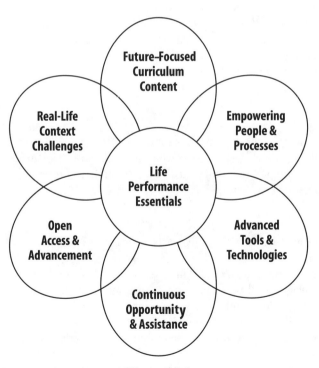

Figure 11.1

Opportunity and Assistance, Open Access and Advancement, and Real-Life Context Challenges. These seven components allow everything this book advocates to come together in a coherent, cohesive system. Now our job is to apply the elements in the decision screen to the design of each of these components and get this system functioning as an inspiring constellation of empowering learning experiences for all our learners.

DESIGNING OUR EMPOWERING LEARNING EXPERIENCES

There's only one place to start as we take this next major step in our Strategic Design Process: with our framework of life performance essentials which we've just called the heart and soul of this model.

Implementing Our Life Performance Essentials

We've suggested since chapter 3 that at least the implied, if not formal, purpose of our TLC is to foster learning that encourages and engenders conscious, creative, collaborative, competent, and constructive living among all members and constituents. To do any less is to deny the new research realities described in chapters 2 and 9, the principles of Total Professionalism explained in chapter 8, and our deeper nature as enlightened human beings.

So let's bring what we've called the essence of total learning (figure 10.5) front and center one more time and unequivocally state,

If our TLC's learning experiences do not positively, consistently, and continuously foster each learner's personal growth and identity, creative and critical imagination, personal and cultural relationships, functional and productive competence, and contribution to human well-being, we cannot legitimately call them *empowering*.

Note: Because we view these five criteria as keys to people living lives of joy, meaning, accomplishment, and fulfillment, we're willing to make them the centerpiece of our operating model. This means that as we conduct this step of our Strategic Design, we'll be committed to infusing these five clear, compelling, and overriding criteria into every learning experience that we provide—no holds barred, no excuses, and no whining!

This is a huge step forward because embracing and endorsing these five criteria means that we've given our TLC an explicit definition of what the term *empowering* will mean. It's the qualities that foster these five criteria in all learners!

In addition, we have also simultaneously made Total Learning for Total Living the purpose and spirit of our operating model and established the five criteria against which all six of the other components in our TLC's instructional system will be assessed. To be absolutely explicit, this means that all of the other six components in figure 11.1 need to be designed to facilitate and support every learner's

- personal growth and identity, given that s/he comes to us with at least twenty-five identifiable "intelligences" and a unique personality that deserve encouragement, exploration, development, and validation
- creative and critical imagination, given that s/he comes to us with an innate curiosity and desire to explore and create that deserve encouragement, exploration, development, and validation
- personal and cultural relationships, given that s/he comes to us with an innate desire for authentic interpersonal connection and belonging that deserve encouragement, guidance, development, and validation
- functional and productive competence, given that s/he comes to us with multiple performance-related intelligences and interests that deserve encouragement, exploration, development, and validation
- contribution to human well-being, given that s/he comes to us with an innate caring about others and capacity for good that deserve encouragement, guidance, development, and validation

Notice the words that appear again and again in these statements: encouragement, exploration, guidance, development, and validation. They're the keys to an empowering approach to successful learning. They give learners a sense of being wanted, important, capable, and supported. That's what empowerment is about, and it must pervade everything we do. So put those five words on posters and hang them everywhere in your TLC. Next to each of them in a different color hang posters that say Identity, Imagination, Relationships, Competence, and Well-Being. And next to those, hang ones that say Total Learning for Total Living. Openly celebrate your TLC's essence and celebrate its commitment to empowerment!

But in doing so, remember that there's another aspect to this stage of the process that must also be explicitly addressed: *Essence* needs to be backed up with tangible *life performance*. Total Learning is manifested through Total Performance, and we devoted chapter 10 to exploring how we might define it in insightful and compelling ways. The frameworks that localities develop will inevitably vary, but the basic structure of their respective life performance essentials models should, as we suggested, be defined around role performer labels, qualitative attributes, and guiding ethos elements. Fully developed frameworks will also have sets of essential performance component statements for each key element (as in the South Africa example in chapter 10), giving them far more specificity that we'll be able to illustrate here.

For illustrative purposes, let's again consider the Total Performers model described in chapter 10 (figure 10.6) precisely because it is fully aligned with the five essences just described. How will we know that these essences are being embodied in our instructional system? Because each will be reflected in the observable performance of our learners. What should we look for? The key elements of the Total Performers framework—evidence that each individual is

- an open, growing *learner*, guided by an ethos of purpose and integrity
- an imaginative, undaunted *innovator*, guided by an ethos of future-focusing and risk-taking
- an honest, affirming *partner*, guided by an ethos of collegiality and team-work
- a reliable, exemplary *producer*, guided by an ethos of excellence and im-provement
- a caring, committed *contributor*, guided by an ethos of win-win and ac-countability

And to generate these kinds of results we explicitly

- encourage all learners to explore "who they really are" by assessing, using, and acknowledging their many unique qualities and abilities; guide them in developing each area of potential to the fullest; and validate and rein-force their desire to learn and grow
- encourage all learners to explore the endless possibilities that exist in all areas of learning and living; guide them in using and developing their imaginations to the fullest; and validate and reinforce their unique ways of expressing their originality and ideas
- encourage all learners to explore the qualities and dynamics that make suc-cessful relationships possible; guide them in using and developing these at-tributes as they relate to others; and validate and reinforce their ability to re-late congenially and collaboratively with a diversity of other people
- encourage all learners to explore the many kinds of productive compe-tence required in life and careers; guide them in developing and using abilities that open promising doors of opportunity; and validate and rein-force the productive abilities they develop
- encourage all learners to explore the many avenues open to them for en-hancing human well-being and contributing to the greater good; guide them in developing opportunities to benefit others; and validate and rein-force the satisfaction they experience from the contributions they make

In sum, then, it's clear that a framework of life performance essentials can very productively encourage and reinforce our most enlightened thinking about empowerment and establish genuinely empowering learning experiences for all our learners. Now we'll strengthen that linkage strengthened even more.

Implementing Future-Focused Curriculum Content

Although life performance essentials are fundamentally about the kinds of competence and character we want our learners to be able to carry with them into their personal, family, community, and career lives, we should be the first to make clear to our constituents that "you can't be competent at nothing!" In order to be competent, we need content, substance, concepts, ideas, and issues to assimilate, grapple with, and apply. Competence doesn't exist in a vacuum.

The best way of addressing this reality is to combine content and competence, rather than approaching them as entirely separate entities. To build this connection, let's turn directly to the curriculum design models described in figure 11.2. The diagram in the figure has the appearance of being a matrix because it has a vertical and a horizontal axis, but it's not a "pure" matrix.

The vertical axis represents the "competence base" of a curriculum design—that is, what the curriculum's designers take to be the form of competence that its most important learning results should take. If we look closely at the words on this axis, we'll see that they closely resemble the six forms of competence

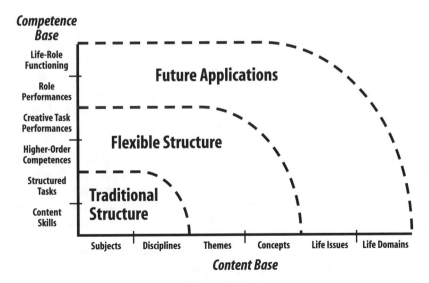

Figure 11.2

described in the performance mountain we examined in chapter 10 (figure 10.2). As we think back on the mountain, we'll recall that the higher we climbed, the more macro, comprehensive, complex, and significant the nature of the desired/expected performances were. The same holds for this diagram. So let's note that the life performance essentials we developed in chapter 10 fall above the second dotted line into the top sector of this diagram called Future Applications. By contrast, the competences required in Standards-Based Reforms fall mainly in the bottom Traditional Structure sector.

The horizontal axis of figure 11.2 operates differently, however. It reflects the "content base" of a curriculum, but the categories do not represent a continuum from low to high as they do on the vertical axis. This dimension of the diagram shows three very different patterns for defining, organizing, and teaching content.

The Traditional Structure approach organizes content around the disciplines and subjects described in chapter 6. This type of content matches up with the more narrowly defined, specific kinds of competence we find at the bottom of the performance mountain. However, in 1996 through 1998 Helen Burz and Kit Marshall developed a series of four handbooks subtitled *From Knowing to Showing* that assist teachers in moving traditional subject-matter content up the vertical axis of this design framework by linking it to more authentic/complex kinds of performances.

The Flexible Structure model organizes content around major concepts and themes that cut across the traditional disciplinary boundaries. That's why this middle sector approach is widely regarded as "interdisciplinary."

We, however, are opting for the third approach: content that is grounded in the domains of living and the issues, challenges, and future conditions that inherently accompany those domains. Our decision to work with content in this "transdisciplinary," Future Applications way is based on three things.

First, content framed this way is more realistic, relevant, comprehensible, and meaningful to learners. It's about what they observe and understand about life as they encounter it. No translation into abstract categories is needed. Second, it is tremendously more motivating and engaging to learners, which Edward Clark's *Designing and Implementing an Integrated Curriculum* (1997) clearly demonstrates. Third, as we can see in figure 11.2, it forms a natural match with the kind of Future Applications performance abilities our TLC is committed to developing. We want our learners to grapple with "life-based" content precisely because we want them to develop life performance abilities— each facilitates and reinforces the other. And yes, as we'll see later in the chapter, this implies that they'll also engage a lot in real-life performance settings and contexts.

Using the now familiar domains of Total Living as our content base, let's briefly explore how we might develop this kind of curriculum structure. We'll select "conscious living" as our example, both because it's the heart of the model, and because its content may not be initially obvious.

If we consider conscious living in its broadest sense, it's about how we human beings function as enormously complex physiological, psychological, and spiritual living organisms (see Kessler 2000). It's about our having at least two dozen different "intelligences" or arenas of potential growth, development, and expertise—not a handful, or even just one. It's about every factor that leads to sound health, growth, and happiness, and all the stressors and factors that impede and undermine them—and why. It's about how our physical body is intimately connected to what we call our mind, and how that interaction shapes how and why we function as we do. (For insightful and compelling documentation of this point, see Candace Pert's 1997 book, *Molecules of Emotion.*) And it's about how the brain itself develops and functions; what affects our attitudes, personalities, and motivations; and the many different ways people learn and grow.

But most of all, it's about what makes us conscious, aware, attentive, mindful, and capable of discovering, nurturing, and expressing our true inner selves. To study humans as fully conscious beings is, in effect, a declaration that Total Learning Communities are committed to *Total* Learning, not just abstract academic learning, and that we as unique creatures with enormous untapped potential deserve first and foremost to learn about ourselves. When you stop and think about it, conscious living represents an intriguing and invaluable lifetime of study for all of us. We just need the impetus, opportunity, encouragement, and support for doing so.

And what significant issues, challenges, and conditions would inform this study? Life is full of them. What causes stress? What causes emotional pain? What environmental factors affect our physical well-being? The list could go on for pages. So we don't lack content, issues, or topics that would motivate intense personal interest in conscious living. All we lack is the experience of putting it together in such a totally integrated form.

Let's also acknowledge at this point that we could do the same with creative living—*openly exploring and expressing life's boundless possibilities*—which opens the door to learning virtually anything and everything in the universe; collaborative living—*deeply connecting with others to share common experiences*—which invites learning about what makes human relationships of all kinds work; competent living—*directly crafting skills and possibilities into positive results*—the gateway to learning about how virtually everything in the world works; and constructive living—*fully sharing my best to enhance the greater good*—our invitation to learning how to make a difference in the world. All we need to begin developing these designs is to immerse ourselves in the substance and essence of each domain, to reflect on what makes it such an essential aspect of living totally, and to ask what one would want to know to function optimally in it. Valuable answers will come pouring out in droves.

Employing Empowering People and Processes

This third component of our empowering instructional system gets to the heart of what we all know as "teachers" and "teaching." We've judiciously avoided using these terms in the last several chapters because they both carry an enormous amount of old-paradigm baggage that we don't want to bring into this design process. We're designing a learning community, not a "school"; and as we've seen again and again since chapter 7, learning communities require different thinking, different substance, different processes, and different structures from conventional schools.

So let's acknowledge right up front that this component is about engaging people from a diversity of backgrounds to participate in our TLC, either full or part time, people who can directly help develop our children into Total Learners with the life performance essentials to succeed in today's complex world. Some of them will have the credentials and backgrounds of traditional teachers, but many will bring with them other kinds of experience and expertise that most teachers simply don't have.

Regardless of formalities, however, there should be three overriding criteria for selecting the people who work with us. First, they must clearly demonstrate an *empowering* style of interacting; and that, as we saw earlier, means encouraging, exploring, guiding, developing, and validating as they work with people of any age or status. Some would call it a "positive" approach, others a "supportive" one, and yet others a "personal" one. All three work. Second, they must have something important to share—knowledge and/or skills—that will significantly expand the conscious, creative, collaborative, competent, and/or constructive abilities of those they influence. Third, they will need to be Total Learners and Total Performers themselves—learners, innovators, partners, producers, and contributors—with all the qualitative attributes and ethos elements that accompany those role performer labels.

Given that we'll be able to recruit and engage empowering people, what kind of guidance can we give them regarding an instructional approach that genuinely facilitates the kind of life performance essentials that we seek? Fortunately such a model exists. It's called the Action Learning Model (ALM), and it's shown in figure 11.3. The model's original design was developed and applied with great success in the mid-1990s by Helen Burz and Alan Rowe, outstanding instructional leaders from Michigan and Iowa, respectively. It was revised into its present form in 1999 in collaboration with myself. If employed with teams of learners working together on given projects, the ALM has the power to directly address and develop virtually all of the abilities in the Life Perfor-

The Action Learning Model

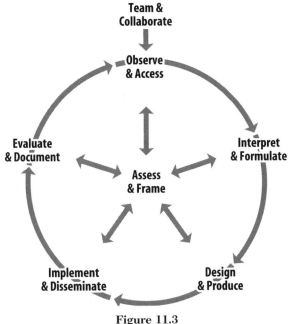

Figure 11.3

mance Wheel (figure 10.3) or the fully expanded Total Performer framework as described in figure 10.6.

In fact, the ALM operates on the assumption that children inherently want to and can readily perform as open, growing learners; imaginative, undaunted innovators; honest, affirming partners; reliable, exemplary producers; and caring, committed contributors. We just need to create the empowering learning experiences that allow those qualities and abilities to surface; and that's exactly what the ALM does by encouraging and allowing learners to be responsible for the quality of their own learning, improvement, and growth.

There are five keys to the model's power and success. First, learners are encouraged to survey their world and pick an issue or need that, if addressed, would directly benefit a definable group of people in their school or community. This is known as identifying both an *authentic issue* and an *authentic audience* that will be directly affected by having the issue addressed. This corresponds to the Observe component in figure 11.3.

Second, they are responsible for seriously investigating that issue, accessing the information and resources needed for doing something about it, thoroughly interpreting and analyzing the meaning and implications of that information, and eventually formulating their new understandings into a plan for addressing their authentic issue. This corresponds to the Access, Interpret, and Formulate components in the diagram.

Third, they are responsible for bringing their plan to fruition, which means formally designing a project, product, or process that explicitly addresses the issue; actually developing that product; and then directly applying it with the authentic audience they identified. This corresponds to the Design, Produce, Implement, and Disseminate components in the diagram.

Fourth, they are responsible for formally evaluating the quality and impact of what they produced, for documenting those results, and for diagnosing how their effort could or should be improved to be even more effective. They do this by having the authentic audience (i.e., recipients) of their effort give them formal feedback on its utility and effectiveness. This corresponds to the Evaluate and Document components in the diagram, and it potentially leads to a continuation and upgrading of the project based on the evaluation results and new under-standings developed throughout this learning/performance cycle.

Fifth, the key to the success of this entire model is what lies at the center of the diagram, what we call "Assess and Frame." The double-headed arrows throughout the diagram are meant to indicate that at every small and large step in this cycle there is a dynamic process of assessing, comparing, testing things out, expanding options, seeing new possibilities, and charting mid-course cor-rections going on, in which the learner is continuously developing new insights, meanings, understandings, alternatives, and opportunities for improvement. This can happen only when learners are continuously guided in developing their own criteria for what constitutes adequate, successful, or quality under-standings and results and learn to self-assess based on these continuously ma-turing criteria.

This latter point, then, speaks to the Action Learning Model's ultimate pur-pose and intent: to develop self-directed, self-governing, and self-assessing Total Learners and Performers (see figure 11.4). Why? Simply because once they leave our TLC, our learners are going to have to be self-starters, lifelong learners, and competent performers in a world of continuous discovery and constant change. If they've become dependent on teachers for direction and evaluation, they'll be sunk. And if they have to run to their local community col-lege to take a course every time they encounter a new challenge in their lives, they'll become paralyzed and never leave the false security of "school."

As you think about the applicability of the ALM in your local learning com-munity, keep the following three things in mind. First, when learners engage in this learning and performance cycle as *teams* instead of just as individuals, it re-quires of them all ten of the interpersonal role performer abilities that appear in the top half of the Life Performance Wheel. Hence, we get a double-whammy benefit from a single process. Second, the model is as applicable for

Keys to Personal Empowerment

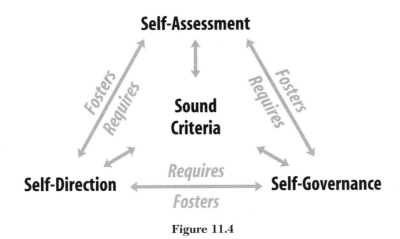

Figure 11.4

young children as it is for older ones. Young children carry it out at a level of complexity and sophistication that their maturity allows, and older ones at theirs. Third, the model is wholly consistent with the Encourage/ Explore/ Guide/Develop/Validate components of our empowerment approach to instruction. It simply gives us a focused, systematic, and compelling way for consistently applying those five components.

We would be remiss, however, if we failed to mention another promising body of work that attempts to honor the learner as a unique individual by developing classroom strategies that link Harvey Silver and Richard Strong's "learning styles" model with Howard Gardner's multiple-intelligences framework. The result is a 2000 publication by Silver, Strong, and Matthew Perini called *So Each May Learn* that gives teachers a host of how-to strategies for working with learners who fall into the learning/performance patterns they call Mastery, Understanding, Self-Expressive, and Interpersonal.

Implementing Advanced Tools and Technologies

Given the dynamic and challenging doors to learning and performance that have been opened so far in this chapter, it may be either anticlimactic or self-evident for us to now address the tools and technologies that can contribute directly to our empowering learning experiences. But before rushing in to declaring computers and Internet access to being the obvious silver bullet solutions here, let's stop and briefly examine this issue more critically.

The most central issue and criterion in this matter is whether any given instructional tool, resource, or technology directly supports our framework of life performance essentials. To make the point, let's consider whether any given textbook could directly enhance a learner's personal growth and identity, creative and critical imagination, personal and cultural relationships, functional and productive competence, contribution to human well-being. Our honest answer would have to be that very special content and exercises would have to be designed into the book for it to genuinely enhance any of these five essences of our Total Learning framework. Otherwise, we're left with the realization that, as instructional tools, almost all books will seriously miss the target of our learning essentials. Fair enough.

But, would we be willing to say the same thing about the Internet? If you're hesitating, it's probably because the Internet is something you access through a computer, and computers carry with them the aura of being the versatile learning tool of both today and the future. Well our answer needs to be, Yes and no. Let's stay focused on the specific issue of the Internet. With a few exceptions, the Internet is little more than the planet's thickest, fastest reference book. That is, if the Internet is mainly about accessing content, then the good news is that it lets anyone access anything from anywhere at anytime in pursuit of any content goal that they may have. But the bad news is that content is simply content no matter what its source. It is not competence or the ability to do complex things. Competence development is going to require more—namely, tools and technologies that go beyond accessing content to actually enhancing life performance abilities.

So let's look at computers loaded with advanced software for designing and creating products of various kinds as a different technology from machines that simply help us access content. With that distinction in mind, let's revisit the essences of Total Learning and Living. Can "smart" computers help enhance:

- personal growth and identity? Only in a very limited way.
- creative and critical imagination? Yes, in many different ways, but not fully.
- personal and cultural relationships? They can help us communicate better technically, but there's no human relationship there. They're no substitute for human beings.
- functional and productive competence? Clearly they can with regard to technological things like computers themselves. But there are many other arenas of competence and performance where they're of little or no help.
- contribution to human well-being? They can help generate products or services that might help some aspects of the greater human good, but again they're no substitute for human contact and intervention.

So where does this leave us? Smarter and wiser than many others who are indiscriminately sprinkling computers over the top of everything willy nilly, assuming that they are indeed a bullet coated with something special that will address human needs with a technological tool. We clearly see the difference, and that lets us design what's required for fundamentally different kinds of learning situations and essentials. And in the end, we won't be standing there wondering, "Who was that masked man, anyway?"

Providing Continuous Opportunity and Assistance

. These final three components of our empowering instructional system all relate to the formal structure of our TLC. And as soon as we say *structure* we are dealing with the seven major boxes described in chapter 6 that constrain educational thinking and practice. While we haven't called direct attention to these boxes in this chapter until now, we have actually been addressing and transcending them as we've put each component of our new model in place.

First, in our commitment to generate an empowering instructional system that totally aligns with and supports our life performance essentials, we've broken out of the Control Box, the Curriculum Box, the Standards Box, the Testing Box, and the Achievement Box. We've both taken control of the design and implementation process ourselves and given a great deal of influence over our ultimate results to our learners and those who assist them.

Second, our decision to create a Future Applications curriculum (figure 11.2) grounded on our life performance essentials and the substance in our domains of living has further liberated us from the serious constraints of the Curriculum, Standards, Testing, and Achievement Boxes. We've completely transcended all of the educentric thinking and practice related to those constraining boxes as we've designed our empowering learning experiences.

But now we face the Grade-Level Box head-on, along with its assumptions of assembly-line standardization and of teachers in self-contained classrooms teaching a prescribed curriculum for a given amount of time at uniform pace and schedule in the same way for children of a given age. It is this constellation of grade-level factors that so profoundly governs the conditions of opportunity and eligibility in schools and the resulting pattern of instructional assistance to learners. Clearly, our challenge in TLCs is going to be to dramatically expand these traditionally limited opportunity/assistance conditions.

If, as we noted in chapter 6, opportunity, eligibility, or assistance is the result of when we *let* and when we *make* learners address given segments in our curriculum, then we're obligated to dramatically transform the conditions governing these windows of opportunity and help. The key to this transformation lies in replacing the system-centered words "we let and make" with the learner-responsive words "learners need and want." This allows learners to get help when they can best take advantage of it, and, as Stephen Rubin and his colleagues discovered more than twenty years ago, it leads to exceptional learning results (see Rubin and Spady 1984; Rubin 1994). Why? Primarily because the focus, quality, and timeliness of instructional time are enhanced dramatically.

But the power of the model that Rubin and his colleagues developed was based on one key factor that remains central in the structuring and operation of our TLCs: The entire staff of their school, including instructional aides and other support personnel, operated as a *totally cohesive and coordinated instructional team*. No one "owned" a particular group of learners, segment of the overall curriculum, or set of books. Learners were flexibly grouped across classrooms and grade levels for short periods of time based on their personal learning levels and needs, and staff were flexibly deployed during segments of each day to work with these unique learner groups, using whatever tools, resources, materials, and technologies would work best for each group. These assignments were made by matching the needs of particular learning groups with the unique expertise of given instructors and aides, which meant that instructors were often teaching outside their "normal" grade level.

As a high school principal in Kansas City, Missouri, stated in 1990: "The issues of opportunity to learn and succeed in our school are clear. On what calendar date is it appropriate to tell learners that we'll no longer be able to help them learn, improve, and get credit for anything essential in our curriculum? That's easy: *Graduation night!*"

Guaranteeing Open Access and Advancement

Another aspect of the system-centered "when we let and make" dilemma is the traditional structuring of the curriculum into year-long segments called either grade levels or courses. In this overwhelmingly prevalent model, the conditions of learner opportunity and eligibility are determined by two major factors. One is what are called "prerequisites," and the other "promotion."

Prerequisites means that students must take and pass specific segments or courses in the curriculum in order to acquire access to others. Often these chains of eligibility are tied to program differences called "tracks." In effect, if you start in one track, you're locked into it for the rest of your career because the segments in your track only "qualify" you for the later curriculum segments in your track, no matter how well you might do in those segments. Promotion, then, is your actual advancement to the next curriculum segment. But since promotion is tied to these year-long curriculum "events"—segments or courses—you're really only allowed to move forward once a year. If you don't advance then, you just have to wait another whole year to do so.

The Rubin model dispensed with both "program prerequisites" and "curriculum promotion" because both were determined to be artificial, unfair, arbitrary, and extremely wasteful of both instructional time and talent. They were replaced by the notion of "continuous progress learning," which meant that students could advance to next steps or levels of curriculum challenge whenever they could demonstrate that they were ready to handle that higher level of work. Using our terminology, they had open access to any aspect of the cur-

riculum they could successfully handle, and their advancement in those respective areas was not tied to any arbitrary calendar date.

Now for this whole concept to make any sense operationally, a learning community would have to have a curriculum structure and learning standards that
encouraged and embodied continuous development and growth—which is exactly what ours does. By focusing on life performance/Total Performer abilities
that evolve in different ways and rates for different learners, we can simply
focus on moving our learners continuously forward in each of these domains of
development as they prove themselves ready for a next level of challenge.

But when, for example, will they study algebra? Answer: When they've got
the *cognitive*—not *program*—prerequisites to tackle it successfully. Some of
Rubin's sixth graders were learning algebra, and a few managed to finish successfully by June. Others didn't begin until March because that's when they
were ready to begin. They started in March? Yes, because modules dealing with
basic algebraic concepts were made available in March to those ready to address them then. That's what open access and advancement means.

Well, when will learners in our TLCs take American history? They won't
"take" it, they'll "learn" it—every day, every year—because you can't grapple
with the domains of living and the conditions and challenges they embody, or
contribute to human well-being, or conduct community improvement projects,
without examining the origins and causes of those conditions and the cultural
and political structures that maintain them.

The only thing to add here is that we've used the word "guaranteeing" to define our approach to this component, and that may seem, well . . . too daring to
some people. If that's true, then so be it, because the reality facing us is that a
TLC either guarantees, embodies, and implements an open access and advancement structure of learning opportunity and eligibility, or it becomes vulnerable to
falling back into all of the old constraining time-based boxes of educentric schooling. We've come way too far in our thinking and design work to succumb to those
regressive possibilities, and furthermore, let's again acknowledge that it would
run counter to everything in our TLC's foundation of insight and inquiry.

Providing Real-Life Context Challenges

This final component of our empowering instructional system is a natural extension of its life performance essentials and future-focused curriculum content components. If we want our learners to grasp and be able to use content
organized around real life, then what better place is there to encounter and
deal with the deeper meaning, implications, and applications of this content
than in real life itself? And the same holds for our life performance essentials.
If we want our learners to perform successfully in life, then let's have them
practice performing successfully in life. To illustrate this notion, let's look at two
familiar examples: pilots and skiers.

To be a successful pilot you need to master three critical elements of successful performance: content, competence, and context. Content is extremely important because there are so many critical things about airplanes, aerodynamics, navigation, weather, ground and flight control procedures, and so on. that you have to know or you simply can't fly a plane at all, let alone safely. That's why student pilots have to pass written tests before they ever get into an airplane to fly. But passing the written test doesn't make you a pilot. You have to be able to fly the plane, and that requires competence. Coordinating all the movements of pedals, the control column, trim tab and flap controls, and many other things all determine whether you can actually fly competently.

But those two factors combined aren't enough. Pilots have to be able to take off, fly, and land under all kinds of conditions. Those conditions are what we mean by "performance contexts." They can range from ideal—a calm, clear day with a runway at sea level—to dangerous—a windy, cloudy, stormy night with a runway at 8,000 feet near mountains. The real test of pilots' expertise is their ability to get that plane down safely every time under either of these sets of conditions. And what determines that? Their mastery of *context*. They've practiced and practiced taking off and landing under these various context conditions until they know exactly what to do when, first in a simulator, then live. What does this mean for us? Simply, that no one is competent in a vacuum. You're only competent when you can adeptly execute your skills in the context you face. So the more context experience you have, the better your chances of success.

With this in mind, think about skiers. In general, you can correlate skiing competence with the degree of slope of the hill. Some people can ski fluidly on 10- degree slopes or less, and that's it. Any steeper and they crash. Others can handle 20-degree slopes before they hit their context limit. Still others can ski fluidly on 30-degree slopes, while truly advanced skiers can handle 40 degrees. The ones in Warren Miller movies can actually do 50 degrees and even beyond in "extreme" situations. So what does it mean that someone can "ski fluidly"? Obviously the answer cannot be separated from the context in which the skiing occurs. Again, context defines competence! But the paradox in skiing is this: If skiers used their 50-degree technique on a 10-degree slope, they'd probably fall down. But if they used 10-degree technique on a 50-degree slope, *they'd die*!

So to make the case for our TLC, the more authentic context experiences we can give our learners, the more they can develop and refine their abilities in the very kinds of situations and settings where they will ultimately pay off. This, of course, means that we'll have to expand our designs and practices to include settings that lie beyond the walls of classrooms and school buildings. And that, in turn, will mean developing strong connections with businesses, agencies, and organizations in our communities willing to devote time to encouraging, exploring with, guiding, developing, and validating our learners.

When that happens, we'll truly have empowering learning experiences to offer our learners in what will be a genuine Total Learning *Community*.

12

STEP 5: MOBILIZING RESOURCES TO SUPPORT LEARNING

Our Total Learning Communities will stand as exciting models for others to emulate, realizing at last that they and their colleagues and learners can step beyond counterfeit reforms to an educational future abundant with conscious, creative, collaborative, competent, and constructive learning and living.

Here we stand at the culminating point of our Strategic Design Process, having addressed and designed component after component of our Total Learning Community. What awaits us during this fifth and final step of the process are the elements of what many would consider our empowering instructional system's infrastructure—the basic resources and processes that enable us to function effectively as we pursue our ultimate learning purpose.

As we noted at the end of chapter 7, this infrastructure consists of five distinct elements: extensive constituent involvement, qualified personnel, material resources, open communication, and data-driven decisions. As their names imply, two of them pertain to how we recruit, involve, deploy, and utilize people; one relates to the tangible resources we marshal to carry out our work; and two of them involve organizational processes that affect our ability to function effectively. As we'll soon see, by having already established a culture of Total Professionalism, a foundation of insight and inquiry, life performance learning essentials, and a framework of empowering learning experiences, we've already laid much of the necessary groundwork for getting these supporting resources and processes into place.

It may seem unnecessary to say so this late into our process, but we've been holding ourselves to extremely high standards of consistency and alignment. Up to this point each and every component that we've designed has totally matched and directly supported the substance and character of every other component in our TLC. This remarkable consistency and synchronicity creates a multiplier effect of purpose, intention, motivation, and contribution among the people involved. Therefore, it's critical in this final step that we remain as consistent and focused as we have been because, if they're defined right, these five infrastructure resources are the glue that will keep our TLC functioning beautifully. We'll address the people resources first because nothing is more essential to the success of a Total Learning Community than to have committed Total Learners as constituents and employees.

EXTENSIVELY INVOLVING OUR CONSTITUENTS

No One of Us Is as Powerful as All of Us

Extensively involving our constituents in every aspect of our TLC's design and implementation is desirable from every vantage point that we can take. It is politically wise, strategically smart, morally sound, and operationally critical. The fundamental grounding of all four of these criteria goes back to the pillars of change described in the first half of chapter 7.

There we discovered that change efforts are virtually doomed unless Total Leaders can work with their people to establish and sustain five major conditions: purpose, vision, ownership, capacity, and support. When starting from scratch to design an organization as we've done, leaders quickly discover that, in the absence of these five respective pillars, their potential constituents and members lack

- a compelling reason to create a TLC in today's uncertain world
- a clear picture of the ideal they're seeking to create
- the deep commitment to take the daring steps necessary for putting something fundamentally new and better into place
- the tangible ability to soundly design and implement the ideal they seek to create
- the day-to-day opportunity or assistance needed to sustain the implementation of this new design

A Paradigm of Attraction and Creation

But our Strategic Design is not a conventional "change effort" in which leaders have to drag their people kicking and screaming *away* from something to which they've become endeared. Inevitably those typical situations contain within them strong elements of *threat*—that people will lose a whole host of real and symbolic benefits that they've gained by having the organization they've had. People's internal *resistance* to change is why *change* is so difficult; and it's one of the key reasons iceberg schools never change—their members and constituents don't want them to.

But we're dealing with a different issue here. We're at Step 5 of a paradigm shift—and act of *creating something new*—not an act of asking unwilling iceberg schools to change and intrusive counterfeit reforms to disappear. The simple choice is whether we want to invest our time and energy in *creating what we want*, or *changing what we don't want*. "The Path of Least Resistance," as Robert Fritz (1989) calls it, is to go where our energy will yield the best results. The magnitude of the institutional, cultural, and political inertia we'd have to overcome to change iceberg schools and counterfeit reforms lies somewhere between staggering and overwhelming. But creating a Total Learning Community from scratch with willing constituents and participants would take only a minuscule fraction of that same energy.

So let's acknowledge that we're on the positive path of creating something that we and people like us want because we've seen the futility of what's described in chapters 4, 5, and 6. From that perspective, our Strategic Design is akin to the Declaration of Independence, except that we're in the twenty-first century and we're already free—free of the psychological necessity of implementing icebergs, boxes, educentric standards, and counterfeit reforms. We've discovered and embraced a new set of research realities and possibilities for learning and living that are incredibly more enlightened, empowering, and compelling than anything the old paradigm has to offer. And we've decided to integrate them into an entity that we can genuinely embrace—an entity whose essence and character are fully reflected in the design we've been creating since chapter 7.

But to do that creating, we need all the empathetic, sympathetic, enlightened, imaginative, and courageous insight, participation, resources, talent, support, and help we can get because no *one of us* is as powerful as *all of us*! Clearly, those parents, educators, business leaders, and other community members who join us in this groundbreaking Strategic Design effort will want a *stake* in establishing the new purpose, creating the new vision, building heartfelt ownership for the new endeavor, applying their capacities and talents, and offering support in establishing and sustaining this new entity. And for a hundred good reasons, they deserve and should have that stake in our future.

This is why we as leaders need to make every effort to invite the ideas, active participation, and contributions of everyone that expresses a sincere interest in any step, standard, or component of our Strategic Design. And once the design is in place, we really need them to assist us in making it happen—the actual operations of a learner-empowering Total Learning Community.

Three Key Roles

There are three key roles that our diverse constituents can and should actively play in advancing the creation and implementation of our TLC. While it isn't necessary for people to have to play all three roles in order to bolster our efforts, the three naturally come together. To do one of them creates the impetus for doing the others as well.

The first role is *architect,* someone who will participate actively with us in all the steps in our Strategic Design and have direct input into how each standard and component of our TLC is designed. Our constituents bring with them a wealth of ideas, experiences, and expertise that will inevitably contribute to the complex mosaic we're constructing. So we should seek and welcome their participation in all of these design steps.

In saying this, however, there is a stipulation here that we must consider to protect the integrity of our process. The reason is that our design is both systemic—everything connects with and affects everything else—and systematic. *Systematic* means that we carefully mapped out the logical sequence of Steps 1 through 5 because, if they are to have design integrity, the later steps are dependent on the prior steps. This goes back to that very basic cause-and-effect, ends-and-means, and dog-and-tail issue that we've been discussing since chapter 1.

So, when people enter this process after it's been under way for a while, it's very easy for things to go personally or collectively sideways or in circles for a while. The main difficulty is that new people have not had the same experience in building a common frame of reference for what is now occurring as have those who've been involved from the beginning. Their assumptions, points of view, and priorities may not match those that you and other participants have painstakingly developed by wrestling with prior issues and reaching common understandings and agreements about them.

Consequently, we've got to develop an increasingly lengthy orientation program for newcomers to our process that (1) engages them fully in whatever has transpired in the process prior to their entrance and (2) secures their agreement and endorsement of its fundamentals. No matter how badly we might want someone's immediate input, if we don't insist on these two conditions, we'll run the serious risk of continuing misunderstandings bogging the whole process down. Yes, every step in the process should invite divergent thinking and open exploration of all possible options when it is being addressed, but once we've gotten closure on the best way to frame that particular step—at least in the first phases of our work—we need to hold firm on what we've decided as we proceed to address subsequent steps.

The second key role is *ambassador.* Ambassadors represent, speak for, advocate, and symbolize the organization or institution they represent; but their job also includes smoothing out the rough political roads and removing obstacles to progress that their entity might encounter. Anyone who has been heavily involved in our efforts and earned our "authentic architect merit badge" will have a strong grasp of what we're about and strong ownership for it. This certainly qualifies them to be ambassadors to the larger community on our behalf, and in all such matters, the more oars we have in the water pulling in the same direction, the easier it will be to gain acceptance of our design and implementation efforts.

Two criteria will be critical to their and our success in this ambassadorial role. The first is their grasp of our work and ability to describe it succinctly, accurately, and persuasively. The more central their role as an architect, the more likely it is that they'll be able to meet this criterion. The second is their personal credibility and influence within the constituency they represent. Since we'll need support from every possible sector of our communities, we'll be well advised to deliberately recruit people from the widest possible range of constituents to participate with us as both architects and ambassadors.

With this diversity of participants is bound to come differences of perspective. This can be positive if orchestrated masterfully—or a disaster if allowed to fragment the larger design group. This is precisely why we chose "Establishing a Culture of Total Professionalism" as the first formal step in our process. Without a set of operating principles and agreement about a way of operating, we might never be able to come to agreement about what we're creating or why. So we'll be smart to keep chapter 8 or its equivalent handy as a reference guide to the principled way we've agreed to operate.

The third key constituent role is what we call a *supporter*—someone who strengthens the functioning and effectiveness of how our TLC actually operates. Supporters contribute their time, talent, ideas, and other resources to improving the ongoing instructional and administrative functions of the organization. Some supplement the efforts of regular staff by sharing their considerable expertise directly with learners of all ages through teaching, tutoring, advising, mentoring, and facilitating applied projects. Others directly assist staff in organizing and implementing whatever kinds of functions and support activities that may arise. Still others may make facilities or other tangible resources available for projects and activities—whatever helps most.

Regardless of what form these contributions may take, our TLC will gain enormously from each and every one of them. And without an active cadre of TLC supporters, we'll be hard pressed to accomplish our goals.

ATTRACTING AND USING QUALIFIED PERSONNEL

Qualities as Our Most Valuable Resources

Despite all the advances in technology, media, and software in the past decade, education remains a "people business" simply because technologies can only partially assist us in developing the kinds of life performance essentials we want for the learners in our TLC. In fact, when we really focus on the deeper essence and qualities of our Total Learning for Total Living model, there's no question that the quality and qualities of the people who work with our learners are absolutely central to the integrity and success of our TLC.

So the questions that surface immediately are, What do we mean by "qualified"? And, qualified to do what? Based on some points we began to develop in chapter 11, there are clear answers to both questions.

For starters, let's acknowledge both the positives and negatives of formal credentials. Yes, we want to hire people who are "well educated." Does that mean they should have at least a bachelor's degree? If they don't, we'll be vulnerable to all kinds of suspicion and criticism, so the answer is a "qualified" yes. But let's acknowledge right now that we may make some exceptions, largely because we'll be seeking kinds of expertise that don't always require or translate into formal university credentials. And let's also acknowledge that the more education and professional training our people have, the better, as long as they also possess a range of other top priority criteria. Recall from chapter 5 that what's in a person's "performance portfolio" is going to be a lot more important to us than what's on their transcript. So with these considerations as a backdrop, what really qualifies a person to be on our instructional staff?

First, they must possess and be able to consistently demonstrate at very high levels the things were asking them to teach and model for our learners. The absolutely most important of those expected outcomes—in whatever framework we've defined them—is our life performance essentials. Must applicants, for example, have all the competences in the Life Performance Wheel? Perhaps not all of them, but if they're missing any, we've got to be sure that several other people on our staff have them, and in spades. Otherwise, we'd be vulnerable and not operating from integrity as Total Professionals.

Must they, then, also clearly demonstrate the essence of each domain in the Total Learner framework? On that, a definite yes, because it's hard to conceive of anyone either fitting in or contributing to our TLC with weaknesses in one or more of those five domains. This is a huge point, so let's let it sink in a moment. By answering this question with a yes, we're upholding the very essence of what our TLC is and exists to accomplish: a place that embraces Total Learning for Total Living. Therefore, any and all applicants must show us that they are conscious, creative, collaborative, competent, and constructive in the ways that we have defined those qualities.

We know who we are, and we don't need to compromise it right off the bat by hiring people who are something else. Applicants need to show us that they belong in a place like ours, and we need to show them what that represents. We're seeking a perfect match, but not everyone is. This applies to the roles played by our constituents as well as potential staff.

Second, we've devoted attention throughout the book to the importance of human potential. And we even took some time in chapter 3 to identify and categorize twenty-five different kinds of intelligence, aptitudes, and potential that reside within us. No, we're not going to say that all our applicants have to be high on all twenty-five or we won't consider them, but we will put three clear expectations on the table for both our applicants and ourselves. The first is that applicants assess themselves on some comprehensive framework of potentials and give us clear evidence of their strengths in at least half of them. The second is that they explain how they would assess learners on this same large set. And the third is to show how they would work with learners whose profiles were like theirs, and how they would work with learners with divergent profiles from theirs.

This would give us an even better sense of who they are as people and performers, and it would also indicate the range of their instructional skills. We're not expecting totally versatile people in every case, but we need to know that we're not loading the staff too heavily along one given profile of attributes.

Third, we'll need to ask them for clear evidence that they can competently facilitate learning on our life performance essentials. This is a giant step beyond "living" and demonstrating those essentials; it's about teaching and strengthening them in others. So as we observe applicants working with a group of learners, we'll want to keep front and center the encourage, explore, guide, develop, and validate components of the empowerment approach to instruction we described in chapter 11. By having them conduct either real or simulated instructional experiences, we'll discover a lot about their capacities to relate to and inspire learners in our priority areas of life performance learning.

Fourth, we mustn't forget that we're hiring people who will be our peers and colleagues, as well as teachers, tutors, mentors, models, advisers, and facilitators for our learners. More than anything, this means we need people who will fully embrace the principles and other processes that define and guide our culture of Total Professionalism. This, like the other three key criteria, should be made an explicit expectation for every applicant. Chapter 8 lays it out in detail for both them and us. We need to communicate as authentically and persuasively as we can that a TLC is *not* a conventional school; it is a *community* of enlightened human beings where everyone learns, everyone grows, everyone shares, and everyone teaches—children and adults alike, and staff and constituents alike.

If, all other things being equal, they want to formally endorse and fully embrace our guiding ethos and culture of professionalism, then they'll be welcomed with enthusiasm. But if they can't make this commitment, then working with us would be a mistake. Again, we're looking for direct alignment between who they are and who we are. Without that alignment of qualities and essence, paper credentials offer us very little of deeper value.

Before leaving this critically important component, let's remind ourselves that in an "everyone teaches everyone" environment, one of these combinations of persons is that children teach children. This, of course, doesn't mean continuously, but it does mean that having learners regularly share their new insights and skills with other children is an enormous validator of who they are, what they can do, and what they represent. If "qualified" means "capable of meeting the preceding four criteria," then we should look for opportunities to both cultivate and utilize these qualities in our learners whenever we can—keeping in mind that sometimes the best way to learn something is to teach it.

MARSHALING APPROPRIATE MATERIAL RESOURCES

Working Smarter with Better Tools

To address this key infrastructure element, we simply need to continue focusing on the driving component of our Strategic Design: our life performance essentials. With no extras, bells, or whistles, the key challenge for us here is to identify those resources that directly support the development of these complex competences. Here again, we need to step away from conventional expectations and practices and really come to grips with the best way to spend our money, allocate our human resources, and utilize the resources that are available.

Before looking at specifics, let's look at a major present-day paradox. There is a mounting frustration across the land about the high school. Various critics recommend that it be profoundly changed, linked far more closely to the real world, shortened to two years. The disconnect between school curriculum and real life that we described in the first half of the book is turning learners off by the droves. And what are many communities doing about it? Spending multi-millions of dollars upgrading their high school's physical plant and infrastructure. Millions and millions that could be invested differently. What will they have when they finish? A spiffy, high-tech iceberg with droves of kids who still lose by being there.

Since we don't have millions and millions to spend, we're going to have to think more carefully about our resources. And we'll start at the heart of this paradox. In chapter 2 we grounded our thinking on five research realities. One was domains of living and another future conditions. Both are about the real-world context our learners face, and both became key definers and organizers of the empowering curriculum design we explored in chapter 11. If you recall, the chapter ended with major implications: No one is competent in a vacuum. You're only competent when you can adeptly execute your skills in the context you face. The more context experience you have, the better your chances of success.

External Performance Contexts

Given that there is merit in these two observations, what do they imply about mobilizing and utilizing resources? First, we need to invest far more than conventional schools do in cultivating significant relationships with every organization we can in our communities because these organizations need to become sites for a variety of short- and longer-term learning experiences and internships for our learners. Second, we need to invest in a person or persons who can manage all of the logistics surrounding these relationships and the movement of learners in and out of these settings. Third, we need to bring people from these organizations into our learning centers to orient our learners to what they'll encounter once they're out there and to work with our staff on developing needed prerequisites.

If we use our imaginations, we'll be able to think of many other possibilities for strengthening these connections and assuring that our learners experience a variety of realities that await them once they finish their formal education. But it doesn't take great imagination to figure out whether we should invest heavily in our own facilities or invest in giving our learners experiences in other better-equipped facilities and settings that provide more realistic challenges.

Internal Allocations

But what kinds of investments should we make at our end? After all, we'll still have to handle the lion's share of the learning experiences. To see how this might unfold, let's return to two key points made in chapter 11 about implementing advanced tools and technologies—then add a twist.

First, in terms of addressing the requirements of our life performance essentials, not all technologies are created equal. Offering Internet access or providing drill-and-kill exercises on math skills is not the same as generating original multimedia products and so forth. In addition, there are many other kinds of tools and resources needed for developing certain competences that are not electronic and sophisticated at all. Second, our model requires many kinds of human contact, interaction, and intervention that no computer or machine can provide. The implication here so far is that we'll have to invest as least as wisely in technology as we do in screening applicants who want to join our TLC.

But here's the twist. Why invest in humans to do things that computers or other technologies can handle at least as well, if not better? That is, why invest in humans to carry out routine content transmission and skill-building activities when well-designed machines can do it, too, liberating the humans to address the many intra- and interpersonal aspects of our model that only people can. If this sounds like we're arguing in circles, we're not. We're simply dividing up the responsibility load into three segments.

The first is to invest in technologies that are very learner-responsive and allow individual attention on building basic skills of various kinds, for example, developing language and math skills or acquiring information. The second is to have humans attend to the many conscious, creative, collaborative, competent, and constructive elements of our Total Learning model that tools and technologies simply can't address. The third is to also invest in more sophisticated technologies that facilitate the more technically related creative and competence dimensions of our model, which only advanced technologies can.

If we could orchestrate these three factors properly, we'd have an aligned distribution of resources that genuinely matches and supports the diverse aspects of our learning model, enabling us to use the specific resource that is truly best for the learning result we're trying to achieve.

MODELING OPEN COMMUNICATION

Shared Information as Power

In an era called the Information Age, we've all learned how vital timely and accurate information is to the way virtually all modern organizations operate. There are two key reasons for this. One is technical, and the other psychological.

Technical Power

The technical side of this issue emanates directly from the maxim Knowledge is Power. From this technical perspective, the statement means that knowledge is the source of expertise, is the bedrock of competence, directly facilitates effective performance, is the gateway to new understandings and progress, and so on. The essence of this set of messages is absolutely vital to our Strategic Design Process since a major part of its bedrock are the five things we've called the new research realities. These new knowledge bases underlie virtually everything we've developed in this book. Without them we would remain stuck in the iceberg thinking of 1893, 1983, and the decades since, and we'd have a much weaker foundation of insight and inquiry than we now enjoy.

So from this perspective, it's been imperative that we share and model every bit of insight and every framework that we develop because they have greatly strengthened the capacities of our participants and significantly expanded our support base. Because of this knowledge development and sharing, our people now understand things about education differently, have new tools for addressing issues, and see possibilities that simply hadn't occurred to them before. In addition, shared knowledge has enabled us to develop more solid rationales for what we've done, to ask more informed and insightful questions, and to design a far more enlightened and empowering model of learning than we would have otherwise done.

To date, then, the benefits of openly communicating, discussing, and refining everything we've done in our design effort have been positive and apparent. It's almost as if there's a multiplier effect operating: the more our people know and understand about the components of this process, and the more of them that know them, the more we can collectively get accomplished. That revelation needs to be gold-plated and framed on everyone's desk, dresser top, or refrigerator door, especially since we've declared ourselves to be a *learning* community. When in doubt, remember: It's hard to learn if you don't have new knowledge to work with.

Psychological Power

The psychological side of this issue emanates directly from the same maxim: Knowledge is Power—except that it reflects multiple paradigms and has multiple meanings. The positive interpretation parallels the technical interpretation above. We can rephrase it as Knowledge is Empowering. The more knowledge I have as an individual, the more capable I am of thinking, making decisions, and acting under my own power—that is, operating without having to be dependent on the intentions or actions of others. From the perspective of our Total Learning for Total Living model, the more knowledge, understanding, competence, and ability to be self-governing and self-directed one has, the better.

However, it is the potentially darker side of this psychological maxim that we've got to monitor and address if our TLCs are to avoid what happens to the cultures of so many organizations. In this negative case, the maxim means, "Knowledge gives me power over others." Its corollary is "If I want power, I've got to hoard the knowledge I have."

In an instant, we have shifted paradigms from shared knowledge being a *multiplier* of both organizational and individual power/empowerment, to shared knowledge being a *threat* to individual power. And when that happens, organizational power/empowerment be damned! It's a shift from the paradigm that Tom Peters and Robert Waterman were endorsing in *In Search of Excellence* to the hierarchical and controlling bureaucratic paradigm they were criticizing. We've all seen and lived with both kinds of examples, and we know their effects.

Preventing the Downward Spiral

Therefore, as we proceed with the implementation of our TLC, we must constantly guard against this all-too-prevalent syndrome of scarcity and protectionist thinking because it eventually breeds a climate of negativism and cynicism and a self-destructive culture of deceit and manipulation. Once this downward spiral of morale and psychological isolation sets in, organizations have an extremely difficult time reversing it. That's why prevention is your greatest asset, and there are three ways to infuse it.

One is for every person with any leadership role or responsibility of any kind to totally model everything we know about sound, open communication. This means openly and receptively listening to any communication that comes our way and forthrightly, openly, and clearly sharing any and all information that directly or indirectly affects someone's role or status in the organization. In short, we won't have open communication and information sharing unless we openly model it in spades each and every day ourselves. Think of this as a case where "talking our walk" is at least as important as "walking our talk."

Our second key prevention tool is our TLC's culture and guiding ethos. We need to keep reminding our colleagues that we've established and collectively endorsed a set of values, principles, expectations, and indicators of what constitutes Total Professionalism—and connection, clarity, inclusiveness, win-win, honesty, openness, courage, integrity, and teamwork top the list. Anything less than full endorsement and adherence to these ethos elements will erode their meaning, integrity, and impact. And once our ethos is diminished, our culture suffers; and once our culture is weakened, our effectiveness and success are dragged downhill along with it. Once that happens, blame and finger-pointing begin, and soon people go into a protectionist retreat, with barricades up, transmitters off, and letters to the director complaining about inhumane working conditions and low morale.

The third way of preventing this downward spiral is to "catch people being good," that is, to openly compliment them when they exemplify something we say we stand for, whether it's one of the ethos elements or executing a task in an exemplary way. The five elements in our empowering instructional strategies—encourage, explore, guide, develop, and validate—pertain to our leadership as well. These spontaneous pats on the back to colleagues, constituents, and learners serve as encouragement, guidance, and validation all rolled into one. That's a lot of benefit for one quick but sincere "I really appreciate what you did there!" or "Way to go!" or "Attaboy!" This is clearly a case of authentic positive reinforcement reaping enormous benefits.

MAKING DATA-DRIVEN DECISIONS

Using Best Knowledge, Not Precedent

Unless they're random and whimsical, almost all organizational decisions are based on data or information of some kind. If that's so, then advocating data-driven decisions may sound a bit like predicting that the sun will rise at dawn. Obviously there's more to it than this, because the kind of data we're referring to are absolutely essential to the functioning of a learning community.

To explain one key aspect of this final resource element more thoroughly, we'll pull together key concepts from chapters 1, 4, 6, 9, and 11 that all relate to how we can structure an instructional system. We discovered early in the book that structures—consistent patterns of organizational decision making and action—can be based on, or defined around, ends or means. We clearly showed in chapter 4 how thoroughly defined around means iceberg schools are, and without question one of the most powerful means-based definers in education is *time*.

Time-Based Decisions

The clock, schedule, and calendar are literally definers and structurers of the system and also serve as major decision points. When a particular block of time ends, it's like saying, "Well, we've just run out of time, so . . . ." And what almost always follows the "so" is "it's over" or "we're finished" or "you're done" or "it's time to move on to something else." These typical and "understandable" responses are reflected in two of the items we identified at the end of chapter 4 as constituting what we called the CBO Syndrome: Calendar-Based Opportunities and Convenience-Based Operations.

When combined, these two CBOs encourage educators to take a very matter-of-fact attitude about student performance at the end of specified time blocks. The decisions of declaring opportunity to be over, of giving permanent grades, and of moving on are based on time data, not on learner data. And this is why reformers fought so hard during the late 1970s and 1980s to shift the focus of decision making from *time* to *learning results* (see Spady 1994). Our argument was, use student performance data, not the schedule or calendar, to determine whether a student is "done" and, therefore, requires no more help!

From this firm stance about focusing on learning results came the notion of data-driven decisions. And it's precisely this notion that supports the continuous opportunity and assistance, and open access and advancement, components of our TLC's empowering instructional system and accounts for the exceptional effectiveness of the Stephen Rubin model described at the end of chapter 11. Rubin's colleagues couldn't have accomplished the extremely accurate placement of students into targeted, short-term learning groups without precise information on learner performance being available on a daily basis to faculty and an instructional coordinator. And they managed this in an era that predated sophisticated computer data-management systems.

Finally, given our strong emphasis on developing self-assessing, self-directed, self-governing learners, here's a provocative way we could apply this notion in our TLC: Make our learners responsible for generating the data or evidence that allows them to advance to a more challenging level of learning. How would we do that? By having them establish and maintain a personal performance portfolio that they would continuously update with examples of their best and most advanced work. When they feel their evidence is sufficiently strong to present to a committee of assessors—including staff, peers, and parents—they can make their case for advancement, using all the criteria that we taught them and reinforced as they carried out the Action Learning Model described in chapter 11. Both we and our learners would gain enormously from this strategy, for their paradigm will have shifted from "teacher-dependent students" to an "articulate advocate" for their own education and future opportunities.

EXPANDING AND SUSTAINING ENLIGHTENED PRACTICE

From chapter 1 onward, we've been making the case for TLCs being knowledge-driven learning organizations—entities capable of altering their direction, priorities, and operations based on what both external and internal research indicated about optimal practice. Now we can see that this final element—data-driven decisions—has actually been the mechanism we've used to carry out this entire Strategic Design Process. It has enabled us to use the new-paradigm perspectives in chapter 1 and the knowledge and insights in the five new research realities of chapter 2 to address and design all five standards that define an enlightened and empowering Total Learning Community.

Now that these five significant steps have been taken, it becomes our continuing responsibility as leaders to regularly monitor these five research bases for new discoveries and insights, and continuously incorporate these new findings into the substance and ongoing operation of our culture of Total Professionalism, foundation of insight and inquiry, life performance essentials, empowering learning experiences, and resources that support learning and organizational improvement.

If we do this, our Total Learning Communities will stand as exciting models for others to emulate, realizing at last that they and their colleagues and learners can step *beyond counterfeit reforms* to an educational future abundant with conscious, creative, collaborative, competent, and constructive learning and living.

EPILOGUE

THE CULMINATING STEP:
FORGING AN AUTHENTIC FUTURE FOR ALL LEARNERS

As we saw in chapter 5, there are two major paradigms of achievement. One is *cumulative*—where we add up and average everything that's been done up to a certain point. The other is *culminating*, which, we discovered, is about ultimate results—what learners can do at or after the "end."

Well, we're exactly at that culminating point in this book, and goodness knows that we've explored and learned a lot together. Now it's time to assess the giant "So what?" of the understandings we've developed. From my perspective, this comes down to one key issue: Are we prepared and willing to forge a strong and authentic educational future for all our learners?

If you personally aren't, then I can only hope that this book has provided you with some genuine insight into the nature of learning systems that will have meaning for you in your personal and professional lives. Hopefully, it will have at least broadened your perspectives about the educational options open to us as a country and civilization—options for creating learning systems that genuinely support and enhance the potential for growth and contribution that resides in all human beings.

If you are personally willing to take this next step toward creation and change, then I'd like to offer you my personal bedrock criteria for proceeding. Two of them are quite familiar; the third adds a couple of key points to the Strategic Design Process we've been exploring since chapter 7. The first familiar one is that forging an authentic future for all learners is going to require that we individually and collectively operate as fully functioning Total Learners, Total Performers, Total Leaders, and Total Professionals. The second is that people will resonate with our discussion about "boxes." The new one is that any change process is inevitably going to go through five stages which, if led by a conscious, creative, collaborative, competent, and constructive Total Leader, will become a *continuous cycle* of learning, change, improvement, and implementation. Let's look at these three criteria one at a time, then pull them together.

EMBODYING AND IMPLEMENTING THE "TOTAL" APPROACH

Regardless of how it's framed or presented, the challenge and the opportunity of creating the kind of Total Learning Community described in this book is going to require the best of what we as human beings can bring to the occasion. Whether we see ourselves as learners, participants, performers, leaders, and/or professionals, we'll have to ourselves embody the very things we offered as ideals for our learners in chapter 10. With only a slight shift of phrasing in what we called Total Performers, we'll each need to be prepared to lead and participate in this endeavor as:

- open, growing *learners*, guided by an ethos of purpose and integrity, who are committed to participating consciously in this challenging endeavor
- imaginative, undaunted *innovators,* guided by an ethos of future-focusing and risk-taking, who are committed to participating creatively in this challenging endeavor
- honest, affirming *partners*, guided by an ethos of collegiality and teamwork, who are committed to participating collaboratively in this challenging endeavor
- reliable, exemplary *producers*, guided by an ethos of excellence and improvement, who are committed to participating competently in this challenging endeavor
- caring, committed *contributors*, guided by an ethos of win-win and accountability, who are committed to participating constructively in this challenging endeavor

There are two overriding reasons for bringing this framework into play here. First, as we saw in chapter 7, the design and implementation of a Total Learning Community will require all the skills and orientations of Total Leaders so that the five pillars of change—purpose, vision, ownership, capacity, and support—can be established. Total Leaders need to embody and exercise the abilities, qualities, and ethos that enable these five conditions to be established. If we look closely, those essential attributes directly parallel the five characteristics of Total Performers we've just presented.

For example, *authentic* leaders need to be open, growing learners guided by an ethos of purpose and integrity; *visionary* leaders need to be imaginative, undaunted innovators guided by an ethos of future-focusing and risk-taking;

cultural leaders need to be honest, affirming partners guided by an ethos of collegiality and teamwork; *quality* leaders need to be reliable, exemplary producers guided by an ethos of excellence and improvement; and *service* leaders need to be caring, committed contributors guided by an ethos of win-win and accountability. So to be Total Leaders, we'll need to be Total Performers; and to be Total Performers, we'll need to be Total Learners.

Second, unlike some of the architects and advocates of the Standards-Based Reform movement, we cannot ask our learners to demonstrate things that we ourselves cannot carry out and model. If we want them to be Total Learners, Performers, and Leaders because that's what life's challenges require of people, then what bigger and better challenge could we face than asking them to join us in implementing a learning system that (1) transcends the entrenched institutionalized, legalized, and internalized features of the existing system and (2) explicitly includes many key things which that system and its reforms all but ignore—namely, what we know about human potential, human learning, domains of living, future conditions, and life performance? When we face up to this challenge, engage them in it, and explain to them every step of the way what it requires of all of us, we can make each of these five Total Learner/Performer/Leader domains real, relevant, and compelling to them, to ourselves, and to our various constituent groups.

This, in turn, will require that we openly advocate, acknowledge, and affirm whenever possible the things we described in chapters 3 and 10 as the essence of Total Learning: personal growth and identity, creative and critical imagination, personal and cultural relationships, functional and productive competence, and contribution to human well-being. These five things become the glue that holds everything in our model together: our life performance essentials, our guiding ethos, and the resources that make our implementation possible. Without consistent attention to and support for these five qualities, we're not likely to establish the purpose, vision, ownership, capacity, and support needed to design and sustain a Total Learning Community of any integrity or durability, no matter how sound our technical design.

GETTING BEYOND THE BOXES

The second key criterion for forging an authentic future for all learners is to use our Total Learner, Leader, and Performer abilities to help our colleagues and constituents get beyond the boxes that so severely constrain educational thinking and practice. Our biggest advantage here is that people resist doing things that don't make sense to them, and we've got some powerful tools to use to create the "dissonance" needed to "unfreeze" their thinking about learning and learning systems.

I'm proposing a strategy that accompanies the first of the weight-bearing walls described in chapter 9: paradigm perspectives. The strategy is to get our constituents to recognize how poorly the existing boxes that define schooling—the iceberg categories in chapter 4, the numbers and report card boxes in chapter 5, and the reform boxes in chapter 6—actually match the research realities described in chapter 2 and developed more fully in chapters 10 and 11. We need to introduce compelling real-life examples about these new realities and repeatedly compare them with the artificial, limiting features of what are in the educentric boxes. The overriding questions we'll be posing and inviting them to address are:

- If this is what reality is all about, why continue doing things that don't match it or get us there?
- Don't our learners deserve something more realistic, relevant, and challenging than this?

From my experience, the most effective place to begin is with the fifth of the new research realities—life performance—then work back down the list from there. Get people to look at the Life Performance Wheel (figure 2.3) and relate its various elements to things they do in their personal, family, career, and community lives. Using this strategy, we're connecting people with the visible and tangible things in their lives that directly affect their success and sense of efficacy and worthiness. Nothing is more compelling than that.

Then ask them to relate those role performance abilities to each of the boxes that now define schooling and reform. Is this performance ability, or the wheel as a whole, supported by the Curriculum Box? No. Is this performance ability, or the wheel as a whole, supported by the Standards Box? No. Is this performance ability, or the wheel as a whole, supported by the Grade Level Box? No. And on and on you can go down the list of performance abilities and the list of boxes: testing, achievement, accountability, and finally back up to control.

What you're doing is creating enormous dissonance between what exists and what they feel should exist, and out of that frustration you will have established a need and desire for something different. But don't stop with life performance. There will also be enormous dissonance surrounding future conditions, domains of living, human learning, and human potential; and these other four deserve as much as attention as life performance—primarily because we must ultimately bring the issue down to the individual human being. We want people to recognize that major arenas of human potential are being ignored in our boxed-in approach to academic content, and we want them to see that significant alternatives to that narrow, sterile approach exist. And when addressing this fifth reality, don't forget to use the expanded framework outlined in the final part of chapter 3. It will really expand people's perspectives of what's possible.

ADDRESSING THE STAGES OF CHANGE

A few years ago I developed a series of implementation guides for school districts that went into considerable detail on how to lead and implement a productive change process (see Spady 1998a, 1998b, 1998c). These documents drew on a lot of the classic approaches to organizational change, the work that Chuck Schwahn and I had summarized in *Total Leaders*, and the work we had done internationally with Strategic Design. In the second of those documents, called *Action Steps for Leading and Implementing Productive Change*, I identified three different kinds of action steps that organizations must take to make productive change happen: detailed steps for initiating change, implementing change, and extending change.

The *initiating change* action steps are structured around the "why drives what drives how" approach to all our work. Consequently, there are action steps for addressing an organization's rationale for change (why), the substance of change (what), and the strategies of change (how). We're clearly at that initiating stage in this book right now.

The *implementing change* action steps are structured around the five pillars of change described earlier. There are detailed steps for defining purpose, framing vision, establishing ownership, building capacity, and providing support for each of the major operational components of an organization.

What I'd like to emphasize here, however, are the major steps related to *extending change*. This means keeping the change alive, moving, expanding, and growing. What do organizations need to do to sustain what they've initiated and implemented? If they don't do these things, their initial impetus for change will inevitably erode away.

Let me suggest that extending change involves the same critical kinds of steps that initiating and implementing change require, except that they occur after the initial implementation has taken place. So let's assume for the moment that we have gone through all five major steps in our Strategic Design Process and established the initial form of our TLC. What happens next? If we truly establish a culture of Total Professionalism, lay a foundation of insight and inquiry, and mobilize resources to support learning, we'll have suggestions for what to do to improve what we're already doing coming at us every day. That means we'll be dealing with the issue of *changing our change effort*—going into a process that the followers of W. Edwards Deming and Peter Senge call "continuous improvement."

In a nutshell, continuous improvement means continuously examining what we're doing and taking steps to make it better. It means *continuous change*, and continuous change means that at some level or other, things will be in a constant state of flux. Given those realities, my *Action Steps* suggests that any leadership team must be prepared to address four key things on a continuous basis: (1) managing dissonance; (2) clarifying possibilities; (3) formulating new prototypes; and (4) implementing new prototypes. In view of what we discussed in the previous section, this means that the initial dissonance that we create to get people off of their old, educentric dead center will persist as we continue to question whether our newly implemented approach is really the best way to do things. New research, our own performance results, and changes in the real world may all dictate that we'll need to change what we've already changed.

Consequently, we'll need to psychologically prepare our people for this inevitability, because to change is to learn is to grow is to expand one's perspectives and capabilities is to change is to . . . . This is exactly what is meant by the saying, Change is a process, not an event. We'll succeed at continuous change/improvement if we have process steps in place for managing the dissonance that will always be present, clarifying possibilities for new actions by using insightful frameworks and criteria, formulating new prototypes that colleagues will be free to try out and assess, and implementing the most promising of those new prototypes on a wider scale in our TLC.

Yes, this will take exceptional people to accomplish, but it's what a Total Learning Community represents. Total Learners everywhere. Total Performers everywhere. Total Leaders everywhere. Total Professionals everywhere. All assisting each other to be the most enlightened, very best human beings they can be.

Is this too much to ask of ourselves? Not when you consider the dead-end street education is on and the consequences our children, our nation, and our world will pay if we remain there. For me the dissonance is too great and the realities and alternatives too appealing to remain stuck in such profoundly limiting boxes of our own making. History is being shaped every day by people like us who step up and step forward. Often they're surprised by how many others have been waiting for someone else to assure them that that first step is possible. That's the essence of going *beyond counterfeit reforms*.

INVITATIONS TO ACT

Accepting the Invitation to Change Education:
From Reading to Communicating to Acting

by Arnold F. Fege

The timing of *Beyond Counterfeit Reforms* is profound. It sets into motion the next stage of action in improving learning opportunities for our children and moves us beyond the tired old strategies of the past.

In response to national concerns that our education system was not changing fast enough to meet the demands of the new knowledge society, it is understandable that our policy makers responded with what seemed like a cultural consensus around educational change. In launching "new" reforms, they reached back to what they thought we'd all feel most comfortable with: having schools do the same things they've always done, but harder, with more vigor, and with mandates that required every school district to standardize these familiar but ineffective strategies from the past.

But cracks are beginning to appear in the armor of the Standards-Based Reform (SBR) movement. In virtually every state in which these "reforms" exist, parents have mounted efforts against high-stakes testing; teachers are beginning to seriously question the narrowing of the curriculum caused by irrelevant standards; local school districts are protesting the negative impact of top-down, compliance-driven regulations; civil rights organizations are questioning the fairness of using a single test as the sole measure of academic performance; and local school boards are seeing that they have become nothing more than regulatory shills for their state's education bureaucracy. All these constituencies are anxious to move beyond counterfeit reforms.

In addition, the promises of policy makers to focus attention and leadership on children in the most difficult schools have, for the most part, turned into hollow promises and headaches. The concept of having high academic expectations for *all* of our children is as salient as ever as a legitimate policy and educational goal for the nation. But, as we are discovering, the problem is that the current SBR movement emphasizes standardized state-controlled requirements that take major education decisions out of the hands of parents, teachers, and community leaders (i.e., the public). This, in turn, almost silences the voices of grassroots community activists and shuts most citizens out of the decision-making process.

CHOOSING WHAT COMES NEXT

So if we assume that this counterproductive SBR movement will begin to crumble under the weight of opposition, inertia, and diminishing support, what comes next? Do we go back to "schooling" the way it was before the reforms started, or do we have a plan in place that states what we are actually *for*?

Happily, *Beyond Counterfeit Reforms* steps into that potential vacuum. It is the quintessential, enlightened next step for any community desiring to forge new-paradigm changes in their schools. Bill Spady reframes the problem in terms of not just what should be done to improve learning but also what should be done to fundamentally change education—an issue we've been avoiding for several decades. The "counterfeit reforms" he debunks include both the top-down, high-stakes, compliance-driven SBR movement and other simplistic gimmicks such as vouchers and privatization, which offer iceberg education with new labels but no operational change at all.

Spady clears the air, so to speak, and moves the national conversation beyond the polarization of polemics. He challenges us to recreate institutions of learning based on purpose, rather than form—on what our students will be facing when they leave school, rather than on what their SAT score will likely be. Beginning in chapter 1 he gives a clear indication that if we gave learning the "power change" it deserves, education would look much different than it currently does. This fear of real change may be why some absorb themselves in tinkering with improvement, rather than addressing the deeper implications of Spady's message and meeting the millennial learning needs of our students and nation head on.

Five Steps to Change

Every informed American understands the gravity of the problems we face today. Yet the problems themselves are not as perplexing as the questions they raise concerning our capacity to gather our forces and act on a capacity commonly and much too vaguely described as political will.
—John Gardner, founder and former president, Common Cause

Challenging an existing public education system is one thing; changing it is quite another matter. In old-style parental involvement paradigms, parents and the community are relegated to the status of being the "external audiences," as many school districts define them. This often keeps education systems mired in old political and philosophical mindsets, protects the status quo, and prevents new and exciting ideas about learning opportunities from surfacing.

I have always believed that parental and community involvement was essential in melting Spady's iceberg and evoking educational change; and I have openly supported cries for greater parental and community involvement in education decision making. Often these cries were a challenge to the status quo. When they were, they were frequently ignored by embattled educators and policy makers who rode out the waves of protest to live yet another day. No matter how well-intentioned these parents and community activists for public education were, they were frequently dismissed because they lacked content, explicit alternatives, or foci. Moreover, they were often trumped by special-interest groups that pushed superficial, quick-fix solutions to complex educational problems.

They were also resisted by an educational establishment hanging on to its iceberg of inertia and by a community that was more interested in debating the advisability of its proposed football stadium than in building modern schools or in creating new educational designs. This is not to diminish the significance of parent and community activists, but to suggest that in any effort to push for twenty-first-century education—as Spady does in chapters 7 through 12—we also need to move toward a twenty-first-century model of community involvement that builds on, but goes way beyond, the community and parent involvement models of the past (see chapters 8 and 12 particularly). In this new model, the community builds new frameworks, forums, strategies, and decision-making vehicles that allow it to assume and take greater responsibility for high achievement and new-paradigm model schools.

From my recent work with school districts and the Public Education Network in the United States, with UNESCO, with the Catholic Relief Services of Eastern Europe, and with other community-based organizations intent on developing

new theories of communityaction and accountability for schools, I offer five lessons that, while still tentative, can take current community involvement models
to the next level. Each of these has a "beyond" that we must progress to.

First, using Spady's Strategic Design Process as a vehicle, we must progress
beyond the old special-interest politics to forge large-vision education outcomes that we can all agree on. If we are going to make significant improvements, we must first stop beating up on ourselves. The thirty-second sound
bites of personal venting and blaming featured on the evening news must give
way to meaningful community discussions about school change. And the old
personal baggage that we bring into the conversation needs to give way to principled ways of listening to and communicating with each other—as Spady
clearly outlines in chapter 8. This will help raise trust levels, diffuse anger, and
enhance the understanding of where each of us is coming from.

As a result, school politics based on special interests' needs, which often pits
the community against itself, must give way to collaborative politics where the
interests are less important than the agreed-upon purposes. Fundamentally, the
new involvement is a working-through process of connecting with issues of mutual concern and grappling with them until there is some closure.

Second, we need to progress beyond where parents and community are defined
as the "external audience" to one where they are equal partners in school decision
making and in judging the efficacy of the system in meeting its declared purposes.
This requires school districts to share more of their power with parents and the
community, and it promotes the change in decision-making culture that Spady addresses in chapters 8, 9, and 12. For the most part, traditional parental involvement has been reduced to fundraising, volunteerism, and serving on school advi-
sory councils, while issues such as influencing how schools and classrooms are run,
choosing curriculum, selecting teachers, and defining the responsibilities of professional educators have been off-limits to them.

While education may not improve by redistributing power alone, it is essential that we address issues of *who* should participate in the decisions vital to
parental and community welfare. We simply must find a way for schools to be
more responsive to the needs of their citizens. Many educators do not fully understand that the knowledge explosion and the easy access to it by almost anyone, which Spady describes in chapters 1 and 11, have shifted the balance of
power from school officials to the public itself. The educational community
must understand that it no longer has a monopoly on learning and that the
schools do not "belong" to educators.

Third, we must progress beyond being afraid of discussing "hot-button issues" to engaging the community in both learning and "unlearning" from each
other. As Spady rightly points out in chapter 12, the challenge of change is so
complex, so filled with booby traps, and so full of dilemmas that no one set of
individuals has all the answers. Instead, successful change demands the ideas of
the community all come together and assist each other in developing new pos-

sibilities. As a school community, we must begin to ask a series of questions to bring to an explicit level our implicit assumptions about the structure of schools and the changes that need to be included in new-paradigm plans. This is a risky challenge for both community members and educators because it calls into question the beliefs and rules that we have used to govern much of our lives.

Fourth, we must progress beyond the concept of parent involvement as a means of fundraising to one where the community is responsible for holding the schools and itself accountable for quality education. This implies that parents and the community, using a process such as Spady outlines here, should reach conclusions about what schools are or should be. This is not a punitive function where the community punishes the school for low performance, but a civic function where the community itself takes the direct responsibility for assuring a quality education, not only for individual children but for all children in the school district.

Here the community would become a "purpose agent" to determine, on the basis of data and other information, how the school district is doing in relation to the purposes agreed to by the community. Moreover, in this kind of model the community actually develops a "contract" with the district and assumes the responsibility for providing the necessary leadership, resources, and follow-through of effort in return for sustaining change initiatives.

Fifth, we need to progress beyond parents to including the entire community in the engagement process. This is not to offend parents, who have an important role to play in encouraging change in their school districts, but they only constitute one of the stakeholders. Business-, faith-, and community-based organizations, senior citizens, students, policy makers at all levels, civil rights organizations and civic associations should all be engaged in the change effort and be held accountable for quality education in their locality. This expands the issue of change from the school or school district level all the way out to the larger community. Approximately 25 percent of the adults in any community have school-aged children, which means that there are many people not involved directly in the educational process unless they are deliberately included in engagement activities.

From this perspective, the great strength of *Beyond Counterfeit Reforms* is that it identifies *real* choices about *real* designs about *real* outcomes and allows us as a citizenry to make up our minds about the direction *our* education system should be pursuing. It also recognizes that there is a vast difference between changing our schools and dismantling them and is dead serious about predicting that if real change does not occur, then dismantlement will gain momentum—fueled by dissatisfied parents, an impatient business community, public education cynics, and opportunists—and privatization of public education will ensue. It brilliantly explains that if we want educational experiences that will prepare our children for the real twenty-first century, we can't continue to employ nineteenth-century thinking and strategies to get us there.

There will be no more important civic and educational work over the next decade than pursuing this book's five steps for creating Total Learning Communities. How can we resist Bill Spady's invitation to be part of forging an authentic future for all learners? It's either that or the prospect of more iceberg education for millions more children who deserve something far better from us and from the schools they now attend.

❊   ❊   ❊

Translating Compelling Insight into Local Action Plans
by Ursula M. Ahern

Beyond Counterfeit Reforms represents a remarkable parallel to my lifelong experience with formal education—as a student, as a parent, and now as a school board member. Its disarming insights, enlightening frameworks, probing questions, and penetrating analysis strip away everything about education that is all "appearance" but not the real thing. What we've all taken for granted over the years as learning, achievement, and success is now exposed for what it is: deceptive and appealing labels and symbols about authentic learning that are reinforced by reforms that will only give us more of the same.

DISCOVERING THE REALITY OF "SCHOOL"

As a student, I always loved school—or so I thought. In elementary school I was always looking for ways to make subject matter fun and do projects in a slightly different way. Whether it was getting a group together to knit a full-sized flag for the bulletin board in fifth grade or drawing the map of the world on a piece of wood and using my brother's wood-burning kit to outline all the countries in seventh grade, there was always a new twist and a way to make it challenging. In high school those opportunities came in the form of extracurricular activities—so many wonderful opportunities for fun and for learning!

When our first child started school it was only natural that I looked forward to all the fun that he would have. He was inquisitive, eager to learn, and loved being around people. He did very well. Two years later our second son entered school. He too did very well. Our third son entered school and also did very well. They all did very well, but *they enjoyed their time in school very little*!

I did supportive parent things: volunteered in their classrooms, helped with field trips, and worked with them on their homework. From private schools to home school co-ops to public schools, all these schooling settings seemed very similar to what I had loved. So why didn't my children find the same enjoyment in them? Had school changed that much since I had been there? I turned to their teachers for answers during parent-teacher conferences, and the comments were always the same: "You should be so proud of your children; they are doing so well!"

Was I proud? Yes. Were they doing well? Extremely, by the school's conventional standards! But inside I was incredibly sad because they found no joy in school. I began to ask more probing questions during conferences—the kinds this book asks in chapters 5 and 6: What is an "A" really worth? What does it really measure? What can you tell me about my child's strengths and weaknesses? How do they learn? What can you show me that tells me they are learning things of lasting value?

Yes, they had good teachers, dedicated teachers, kind teachers, but for the most part—since my children were "successful"—these teachers couldn't understand what more I could want! Didn't their grades show that they were learning what the school considered essential? After reading chapters 4, 5, and 6, I now understand the source of my frustration. These teachers were totally absorbed in what Dr. Spady calls "educentrism." They couldn't see beyond the boxes in which their roles and work were defined and constrained.

So I began to look seriously at my own educational experience. What had I loved about school? I loved the learning and the opportunities to interact with people and to create connections for knowledge and the activities that I could be involved in. And then it hit me—when did *most* of that occur? *Outside of the boxes* of my 8-to-2 school day! And what did my children enjoy? The time *outside of the boxes* of their 8-to-2 school days! Yes, they were learning, but their learning time and their school time didn't overlap 100 percent! The overlap was hit and miss—some days in the single digits and on other days at the 50-percent mark.

One more factor hit me. My boys were all identified for their schools' "gifted programs" and spent time in math and literature every day with other similarly "gifted" students. This, it turned out, was both the best and the worst thing to happen to them. It was the *best* because they were being challenged. And it was the *worst* because they saw in stark contrast how little effort they needed to expend in their regular classes and how infrequently they were challenged outside of that time. These gifted classes were a bright spot that made the rest seem that much darker, in part because the teachers in those classes understood that the grades were not *the* measure of their learning. They challenged them to think, to give their best, and not to settle for the minimum effort! Now I wish they had had Spady's Life Performance Wheel and Action Learning Model to work with as well!

I continued to volunteer in a variety of other capacities—including three years tutoring in special education classrooms at a variety of grade levels—eventually spending time with other parents of those students. I was astonished to hear the same questions from them and the parents of children in "regular" classes that I had been asking: How do I know my child is learning? How do I know my child is being challenged? How do we make this time called "school" more stimulating and filled with learning for all? The parents of *all* children felt that their children needed more challenging opportunities for learning, and they knew that grades and standardized test scores were inadequate answers to those questions.

It was this desire to impact *all* students that led me to run for a seat on our local board of education three years ago. It is the board that determines policies, allocates resources, calls on the community for input, and actively supports the district's definition of learning and achievement. It has been an incredible three years. With a superintendent who strongly shares the perspectives in this book, we have had conversations that have gone to the very core of "Why do we do this thing we call school?" We have asked ourselves why we open the doors every day, what we believe about learners and learning, what we believe about staff development, and who we believe are the learners in our district in addition to our students.

THE CHALLENGE OF MOVING BEYOND COUNTERFEIT REFORMS

Now our district is looking to take the five strategic steps to "forging an authentic future for all learners"—The Strategic Design Process described in chapters 7 through 12. We know we're a very good district by conventional "educentric" standards, but we know that those standards can't measure up to the five research realities described in chapters 2, 9, and 10. If we do absolutely nothing different, there will be many really good things happening for students in our district, but it's highly unlikely that we'll be content with random acts of improvement, with rearranging the boxes that define iceberg schooling, or with scores and numbers as definers of who and what we are. We know that this means starting with a blank sheet—a clean slate—and coming together with our community to answer the strategic questions posed in chapters 8 through 12, and more—with our best hopes and dreams for creating a Total Learning Community.

After totally absorbing myself in this book for over a month, I'm convinced that those of us who care about learners, learning, education, and the future should do everything we can to get it in the hands of every parent, board member, educator, and community leader we know. Will it resonate as deeply with all of them as it has with us? Probably not—largely because some of them will not be willing to be challenged by its unique and penetrating perspective about educational structures and practices that have become so familiar and comfortable over the generations. They may see it as too challenging, too different, too idealistic, too demanding, or too open-ended.

But if you're like me, those are the very things that make *Beyond Counterfeit Reforms* powerful and compelling. It challenges us to think beyond any education book we can remember, it forces us to put our deepest beliefs and convictions on the table, it compels us to go back to the drawing board to develop a truly reality-based approach to learning in today's world of continuous discovery, and it gives us the latitude to create what will genuinely work for our communities without being excessively prescriptive.

This is not the kind of book that sits well on a shelf! Its framework and concepts cry out to be discussed, investigated, and wrestled with. Each of our communities needs to start the dialogue, invest the time, and take the steps outlined in the second half of the book. There is no "one size fits all" answer or "silver bullet" here that will magically transform our schools, but that is one of the most delightful and irritating things about it.

Beyond Counterfeit Reforms truly takes us to a new place in educational policy and practice. It provokes our thinking without telling us what to think or thinking for us, and it quickly convinces us that if we really want change— change that is lasting, substantial, and effective—it has to begin internally, with how we think and the questions we're willing to ask. There's no one "out there" that can make it happen for us; and there's also no one out there that can stop us from doing the absolute best for our learners—*if* we really want to invest the time and energy.

Our process of designing and implementing a Total Learning Community needs to clearly model what it will be. We need to provide every participant in our process—parents, community members, principals, teachers, lunchroom helpers, superintendents, board members—with genuine opportunities to learn and grow because we will, indeed, be creating a culture of Total Professionalism. We can't impart something we can't live, we can't teach something we don't know, and we can't expect something we cannot model. That's why we need to clearly identify our paradigms and choose the principles we want to guide us. And it's also why we can't afford to leave *anyone* behind in this process because, if we do, we'll inevitably do the same with our students.

Is *Beyond Counterfeit Reforms* idealistic? Yes! Is it challenging? Very! Is is necessary? Absolutely! There's no way of *forging an authentic future for all learners* unless we do.

BIBLIOGRAPHY

Armstrong, T. 1997. *Seven Kinds of Smart: Identifying and Developing Your Many Intelligences.* New York: Penguin Books.

Armstrong, T. 1998. *Awakening Genius in the Classroom.* Alexandria, Va.: Association for Supervision and Curriculum Development.

Barker, J. 1988. *Discovering the Future: The Business of Paradigms.* St. Paul, Minn.: ILI Press.

Bennis, W. 1989. *On Becoming a Leader.* Reading, Mass.: Addison Wesley.

Burz, H. L., and K. Marshall. 1996. *Performance-Based Curriculum for Mathematics: From Knowing to Showing.* Thousand Oaks, Calif.: Corwin Press.

Burz, H. L., and K. Marshall. 1997a. *Performance-Based Curriculum for Language Arts: From Knowing to Showing.* Thousand Oaks, Calif.: Corwin Press.

Burz, H. L., and K. Marshall. 1997b. *Performance-Based Curriculum for Science: From Knowing to Showing.* Thousand Oaks, Calif.: Corwin Press.

Burz, H. L., and K. Marshall. 1998. *Performance-Based Curriculum for Social Studies: From Knowing to Showing.* Thousand Oaks, Calif.: Corwin Press.

Callahan, R. 1964. *Education and the Cult of Efficiency.* Chicago: University of Chicago Press.

Clark, E. T., Jr. 1997. *Designing and Implementing an Integrated Curriculum: A Student-Centered Approach.* Brandon, Vt.: Holistic Education Press.

Cooper, R., and A. Sawaf. 1996. *Executive EQ.* New York: Grosset/Putman.

Covey, S. R. 1989. *The Seven Habits of Highly Successful People.* New York: Simon & Schuster.

Deming, W. E. 1986. *Out of the Crisis.* Cambridge: Massachusetts Institute of Technology.

Fritz, R. 1989. *The Path of Least Resistance: Learning to Become the Creative Force in Your Own Life.* New York: Fawcett Columbine.

Gardner, H. 1983. *Frames of Mind: The Theory of Multiple Intelligences.* New York: Basic Books.

Goleman, D. 1998. *Working with Emotional Intelligence.* New York: Bantam Books.

Kehoe, J. 1997. *Mind Power: Techniques to Harness the Astounding Powers of Thought.* Vancouver, B.C.: Zoetic.

Kessler, R. 2000. *The Soul of Education: Helping Students Find Connection, Compassion, and Character at School.* Alexandria, Va.: Association for Supervision and Curriculum Development.

Kohn, A. 1993. *Punished by Rewards: The Trouble with Gold Stars, Incentive Plans, A's, Praise, and Other Bribes.* Boston: Houghton Mifflin.

Kohn, A. 2000. *The Case against Standardized Testing: Raising the Scores, Ruining the Schools.* Portsmouth, N.H.: Heinemann.

Kotulak, R. 1996. *Inside the Brain: Revolutionary Discoveries of How the Mind Works.* Kansas City, Mo.: Andrews and McMeel.

Maslow, A. H. 1954. *Motivation and Personality.* New York: Harper & Row.

National Commission on Excellence in Education. (1983). *A Nation at Risk.* Washington, D.C.: U.S. Department of Education.

Ohanian, S. 1999. *One Size Fits Few: The Folly of Educational Standards.* Portsmouth, N.H.: Heinemann.

Perelman, L. J. 1992. *School's Out: Hyperlearning, the New Technology, and the End of Education.* New York: Avon Books.

Pert, C. B. 1997. *Molecules of Emotion: Why You Feel the Way You Feel.* New York: Scribner.

Peters, T., and R. Waterman. 1982. *In Search of Excellence.* New York: Harper & Row.

Popham, W. J. 2000. "The Mismeasurement of Educational Quality." *the School Administrator* 57, no. 11: 12–15.

Rubin, S. E. 1994. *Public Schools Should Learn to Ski: A Systems Approach to Education.* Milwaukee: ASQC Quality Press.

Rubin, S. E., and W. G. Spady. 1984. "Achieving Excellence through Outcome-Based Instructional Delivery." *Educational Leadership* 41: 37–44.

Sacks, P. 1999. *Standardized Minds: The High Price of America's Testing Culture and What We Can Do to Change It.* Cambridge, Mass.: Perseus Books.

Sacks, P. 2000. "Predictable Losers in Testing Schemes." *School Administrator* 57, no. 11: 6–9.

Schwahn, C. J., and W. G. Spady. 1998. *Total Leaders: Applying the Best Future-Focused Change Strategies to Education.* Arlington, Va.: American Association of School Administrators.

Schwahn, C. J., and W. G. Spady. 2000. *The Future Is Now: The Shifts and Trends That Are Redefining Organizations and Life in the New Millennium.* Dillon, Colo.: ChangeLeaders.

Senge, P. 1990. *The Fifth Discipline.* New York: Doubleday.

Silver, H. S., R. W. Strong, and M. J. Perini. 2000. *So Each May Learn: Integrating Learning Styles and Multiple Intelligences.* Alexandria, Va.: Association for Supervision and Curriculum Development.

Sizer, T. R. 1983. "High School Reform: The Need for Engineering." *Kappan* 64: 679–683.

Spady, W. 1994. *Outcome-Based Education: Critical Issues and Answers.* Arlington, Va.: American Association of School Administrators.

Spady, W. 1998a. *A Strategic Process for Developing Future-Focused Student Learning Outcomes.* Dillon, Colo.: ChangeLeaders.

Spady, W. 1998b. *Action Steps for Leading and Implementing Productive Change.* Dillon, Colo.: ChangeLeaders.

Spady, W. 1998c. *Guidelines for Leading and Implementing Productive Change.* Dillon, Colo.: ChangeLeaders.

Spady, W. 1998d. *Paradigm Lost: Reclaiming America's Educational Future*. Arlington, Va.: American Association of School Administrators.

Spady, W. 1998e. "Transcending Educentric Achievement through Strategic Design." *On the Horizon* 6, no. 3: 1–8.

Spady, W., and G. Marx. 1984. *Excellence in Education: Making It Happen*. Arlington, Va.: American Association of School Administrators.

Spady, W. G., and C. J. Schwahn. 1999. "Keys to Professionalism." *American School Board Journal*, March: 26–30.

ABOUT THE AUTHOR

William Spady is senior partner in ChangeLeaders, an international consulting company dedicated to maximizing personal and organizational effectiveness in business and education, located in Dillon, Colorado. He is known across the globe as a cutting-edge theorist, writer, developer, and leader in new-paradigm models of learning, curriculum, instruction, assessment, and outcome-based learning systems. His pioneering work on future-focused strategic planning and alignment, leadership development, and systemic change is reflected in his three widely acclaimed books published by the American Association of School Administrators (AASA), a book on South Africa's outcome-based educational reforms, and a series of detailed handbooks on the whys, whats, and hows of leading and implementing productive change.

A native of Milwaukie, Oregon, Spady holds three degrees from the University of Chicago—in humanities, education, and sociology. He held faculty positions in the sociology of education at Harvard University and the Ontario Institute for Studies in Education, and he served as senior research sociologist at the National Institute of Education associate executive director of AASA, and director of the Far West Laboratory for Educational Research and Development. His extensive speaking and consulting career has taken him to virtually every state and Canadian province and on multiple trips to Asia, Australia, Europe, the Middle East, and South Africa. He was named a distinguished lecturer at AASA's National Conference on Education six times.

In 2000, Bill married Pamela Ballan of South Africa and added four children to his family of two adult daughters, Jill and Vanessa. He is a many-time

NASTAR gold-medal ski racer, an avid bicyclist, and thoroughly enjoys golfing, scuba diving, wind surfing, and fond memories of thirty years as a classical trumpeter. He can be reached at P.O. Box 4388, Dillon, CO 80435. His email address is billspady@aol.com.

ABOUT THE CONTRIBUTORS

Ian Jukes is writer, consultant, publisher, and speaker. As the director of the InfoSavvy Group, he works extensively with school districts, businesses, community organizations, and other institutions to help shape preferred futures. His two most recently published books are *Net.Savvy: Building Information Literacy for the Classroom*, coauthored with Anita Dosaj and Bruce Macdonald, and *Windows on the Future*, coauthored with Ted McCain.

Arnold F. Fege is the founder and president of Public Advocacy for Kids, a public interest nonprofit group, devoted to strengthening grassroots advocacy and promoting increased parental and citizen engagement on behalf of children and youth. As an activist, teacher, writer, organizer, advocate, speaker, and association leader, Fege has more than thirty years of experience in public education, children and telecommunications, and health policy, and is regularly at the forefront of issues pertaining to civil society and democratic decision making. Fege is currently focusing on models of engagement that will lead to increasing community voice and responsibility in raising student achievement, especially in low-income school districts.

Ursula M. Ahern lives in Grayslake, Illinois, with her husband and four children. She has been involved directly with students in a variety of settings—tutoring special needs and ESL students, coaching Science Olympiad and Odyssey of the Mind events, assisting in the technology lab and in the classroom. Within the school district, her committee and activities range from school improvement planning, finance, gifted, technology, testing, to PTO volunteering. The past three years she has served on the board of education and is an advocate of all children having an equal opportunity to learn something new and relevant every day.